CENtral *1179*

Back row: 'Sid' James, Brian Carthy, Jack, Jamie, 'Dappy' Dave, John Finney
Front row: John Shoan, Don Morgan, Phil Law ('Lawman'), Pete Bickerton
Taken at 7.30am outside Piccadilly Station, Manchester by Tommy 'Tombo' Gregory,
directly after a Twisted Wheel All-nighter in 1967.
(Photo courtesy of Brian Carthy)

CENtral
1179
The Story Of The Twisted Wheel Club

KEITH RYLATT & PHIL SCOTT

BEE COOL PUBLISHING (BCP) LIMITED

Published by Bee Cool Publishing (BCP) Limited
PO Box 16924, London SW18 4ZU
First published 2001
Copyright ©Keith Rylatt & Phil Scott/Bee Cool Publishing (BCP) Ltd 2001

Printed and bound in Great Britain by Butler & Tanner, Frome, Somerset

ISBN 0 9536626 3 2

"Back Street" Words and music by Charles Hatcher and B. Sharpley
©1965 Jobete Music Co Inc, USA
Reproduced by permission of Jobete Music Co Inc/EMI Music Publishing Ltd,
London WC2H 0EA

DEDICATED TO CALVIN, LEON AND LUCY

ABOUT THE AUTHORS

Keith Rylatt was born in 1950 in Rotherham.

The beat boom of the early '60s gave him a taste for pop music – the Who, Rolling Stones and Spencer Davis in particular. Live performances by the likes of Root & Jenny Jackson and the Victor Brox Blues Train at his youth club whetted his appetite for R&B.
He first encountered 'real' soul records at the Bee Gee Club and Spinning Disc in Leeds and later of course, the Twisted Wheel.

A move to Manchester College of Art at the end of the decade enabled him to attend the Wheel on a regular basis, soon acquiring a taste for 'rare soul'.
Shortly after the closure of the club, Keith left the north to become a teacher in Kent where he met up with Chris Savory and his *Hot Buttered Soul* magazine, for whom Keith interviewed such artists as the Intruders and Harold Melvin in the '70s.
Similar work for Rod Dearlove's *Midnite Express* in the '80s inspired him to launch his own fanzine *Come And Get These Memories* a few years later.

Phil Scott was born in Manchester in 1948, and grew up amongst Teds listening to American rock and roll in his aunty's coffee bar.

In his early teens, he was an avid listener to Radio Luxembourg and keen fan of early '60s beat groups, in particular, 'exponents' of R&B like the Rolling Stones, Yardbirds and Cyril Davis' All Stars whose 'Country Line Special' he first heard on, of all programmes, *Desert Island Discs*.

A chance visit in 1964, to see John Lee Hooker at the Twisted Wheel All-Nighter, Brazennose Street changed everything. He witnessed the early Mod movement, and fashions and dance styles that were a major part of it, and became a convert to the emerging sounds of young black America.

After the club's move to Whitworth Street, Phil became a regular enjoying many of the visiting American artists – with particular memories of Junior Walker, Alvin Cash, the Coasters, Marv Johnson and Ben E. King.
Phil currently lives and works in France, still collects vinyl, and attends as many soul 'dos' as he can.

CONTENTS

FOREWORD by Dave Godin

SOCIAL HISTORY IS NOTORIOUSLY DIFFICULT TO RECORD BECAUSE, BY ITS VERY NATURE, IT IS fleeting, ephemeral and experienced in many different ways, and on various levels, by different people. This is why the personal memoir is so valuable, and the more memories one can tap into, the more the actual, as opposed to the fantasised, truth will emerge. Memory plays strange tricks; events overlap, time sequences get out of kilter, and above all, the wisdom of hindsight often colours and exaggerates how it really was.

Many attempts have been made to create a 'definitive' history of Northern Soul, but, as so often happens, how it reads will all too often depend on whom you're speaking to, and where their particular Road to Damascus once led them! This book focuses on one particular and very special part of the Northern Soul panorama; a highway which many travelled to discover the exquisite and very special joys of Northern Soul, and as captured through the genuine devotion to its memory by two guys who lived the life, and walked the walk, and which is, therefore, all the more valuable and authentic because of it.

I once wrote that when I first coined the term 'Northern Soul', nobody knew what it meant. Then everybody knew what it meant, and now everybody thinks they know what it means. But what people now tend to forget, (since many spokespeople who claim to be authorities on Northern Soul weren't even actually on the scene when it first began to emerge as a definable entity, and, like so many people in so many different fields of specialist enthusiasm, tend to think the world which is now their passion was also born the very same day on which they 'discovered' it), was that in its early days the scene was fragmented, scattered, and even, tribal, in its allegiances and passions. (Much like football remains to this day!).

Records in those days were 'rare', (often because they were so expensive, and the MCPS Gestapo did all they could to stop American imports coming into Britain, and only middle-class toss-pots could buy up everything they really wanted), and, as we again now conveniently forget, the DJs themselves were often so cautiously conservative about playing anything that might dent their 'reputation' or clear the floor, new sounds were often two or three-years-old before someone had the nerve and balls to spin them, so that each location had its own repertoire of specialities and favourites. One spot might have the Sandi Sheldon classic as its number one 'exclusive', whereas thirty miles away Billy Butler ruled the roost.

By defining Northern Soul, which, prior to this, was just plain old soul music, and which was brought into usage solely because of the gulf in differing musical tastes that developed with regard to the style of Blackamerican music that was finding favour in the north of Britain and the south, I was able to give this fragmented phenomena a national identity; thanks in no small part to *Blues & Soul* magazine which gave me a forum from which to preach, and which in other supportive ways was often the sole champion of the right of northerners to make their own choices and dissent from what the mainstream establishment would have preferred them to have listened to. The world is not an extension of one's own personality, but try telling that to the insecure of heart and mind!

As a result, the Establishment didn't like Northern Soul at all to begin with, and was often overtly hostile towards it and me in particular for being its libertarian champion, sometimes even dragging in character assassination, (remember how I was once attacked simply for being a vegetarian? But then, so what? When have I ever claimed to be 'normal'?). They saw it all as a threatening phenomena that was getting way beyond their ability to control and manipulate, and this really riled them. But, by setting this into a national context rather than treat it as a merely factional and regional manifestation, I think I facilitated a sort of temporary truce breaking out between competing ego-trippers, (aka DJs), and the rank and file soul fans, who just wanted to have a good time anyway.

I have never forgiven those opportunist journalists who trekked up north to 'check out the scene'; accepted the warm welcome and hospitality extended them, and then, when safely ensconced back down in London, proceeded to pen vitriolic and patronising put-downs of it all.

The uneasy truce between locations however, was always fragile to say the least, and the road to prominence and 'fame' for DJs largely hinged not on them ever bothering to log the records they played so that the composers could at least earn their rightful mechanical reproduction dues.

Of course too, not all DJs were tarred with the same brush, and one of the sadder aspects of any musical scene is how the genuine and altruistic enthusiasts and pioneers often get shoved aside by those of a more pushy and self-serving disposition, and who were able to make a name for themselves simply because they had the longer purse strings. Such is life! (As presently organised at least..!). Love of money and power does strange things to people, and, for a while,

...; but surely it is a little unfair to penalise the pleasure and enjoyment of the majority because of the irresponsible behaviour of the few. Whereas too the majority might find it very difficult to find or create an acceptable alternative to their outing to places like The Wheel, the minority will encounter no such problems, and closing their access to all-night discotheques is hardly likely to alter any anti-social behaviour patterns they may have developed. The Wheel's reputation is highly thought of here amongst "Soul" music fans in London, and so far as they are concerned a trip to Manchester would not be complete without a visit there. Surely it is better that they spend an evening in such a place rather than sleep out rough or take their chances as to how they will pass the night. On my own visits to this particular club I have always been impressed by the manner in which the vast majority conduct themselves, and no doubt they despise the antics of the irresponsible minority with as much contempt as yourselves. I therefore hope that you will think again before terminating what for many is the highlight of their working week.

Yours sincerely,

David Godin

Extract from Dave Godin's letter to Manchester Corporation protesting about the closure of the Twisted Wheel

THE DAVE GODIN COLUMN

Land Of A Thousand Dances

BBY SOME miracle I managed to catch the train on time at Euston. Anyone who knows me will gladly confirm that I am a terror for time and usually see the tail end of the train I had planned to catch drawing away from the platform. However, with about two whole minutes to spare I made it, and before I had time to realise the reality of my long awaited situation I was travelling at great speed to the heart of the North's Soul lands; to Manchester City; home of the famed Wheel club, and meeting ground for some of this country's most ardent and dedicated Soul fans.

Believing all the propaganda that the South spreads about anywhere north of Tottenham I had taken my raincoat, and when I got into Manchester Piccadilly sure enough a fine drizzle of rain was making the roads glossy and reflecting the neon signs all about the station entrance. Luckily I had a base to go to first since some fans had very kindly offered me hospitality before going to The Wheel, and so I jumped into a cab and gave the address I had been give.

"Never heard of it" said the cab driver. As I was in a highly optimistic mood I merely smiled and said "I'm sure you'll be able to find it" and jumped in before he had time to take an easier fare from the waiting queue behind me! After a brief consultation over his inter-com we were swinging round endless corners to my destination.

Somewhere out in that black dim night gloom—in this city of what looked like perpetual night—there was an oasis known as The Wheel. It was as if all the life energy of the great city was channelled into this spot and hidden away under the ground for fear of disturbing the "respectable" citizenry, because looking out of the cab windows on this dank and murky night, Manchester looked like a ghost town. How wrong first impressions can be was to be shown by later events and happenings. Soon the cab drove up a side street and I saw a young man running down a garden path in the miserable night air stripped to the waist and waving! Being a simple-lifer I much admired such Spartan fortitude, and I thought such exuberant behaviour could only come from a raving lunatic or a Soul brother!

Part of the queue that had formed half an hour before the doors opened.

Time for one more pint before going in!

Sure enough it was the latter, and for the first time I was meeting Francisco O'Brien (or Fran Francisco as I stubbornly persist in calling him) whom I felt I had known for ages through correspondence, but it is always a great experience to finally meet some one face to face who you have up tili then only known through letters and the odd phone call.

Soon we were all in Jackie's place getting to know one another. There was Les Cokell one of the DJ's at The Wheel who I hardly recognised since in a picture I'd seen of him he had had really long hair, but had now transformed himself into a suede-head. Boly from Earby was there (whose pash is Jackie, hence her being persuaded to put up with so many of us using her place as a central gathering point), and young Tim from Skipton, and Boly's cousin Alan. We were soon talking like we'd known each other for years (a common experience amongst Soul people since we always have so much to talk about which bores the pants off your average non-Soul fan), and the time flew by.

Soon we were joined by Tommy Barclay who was in town on a special visit, and everyone was busy getting themselves together for the evening which to all intents and purposes was going to be the last all-nighter at The Wheel since it has pleased the City Fathers to put a ban on such activities.

The fellows in their mohair suits and "right on now" black gloves, and Jackie looking as splendid as Brigitte Bardot, and we somehow managed to squeeze all of us into Les' van and we were off.

Before going to The Wheel however we stopped by the pub next door where all the brothers and sisters gather for a few bevvies before going in, since The Wheel would please the strictest teetotaller in being only able to serve cokes, coffee, flings and milk. The pub was crammed to the doors, and nearly everybody seemed to be young and together. Boly, Fran and the others knew almost everyone, for there is

none of the social stand-off-ishness in the No that plagues human relationships in the Sou Soon people were coming up to me introducing themselves, and I was able to ma long-known names with newly discovered face

We decided to take a few photos there then, and of course the flash gear wouldn't wo Eventually it did however, and the delays and excited tension caused by them not working c served to break the ice more. Crazy rumc were flying round that the last all-nighter at Wheel would he honoured by a police raid, ar was told that special wire mesh pens had b constructed out the back to herd various pec into. The prospect of this imminent drama ad to the general elation that I felt, but I relieved that as events turned out it was only empty rumour. Young people have become much a target for police harrassment in Bri these days and one gets the impression that are at times returning to the dark days Victorian "morality" when all pleasure considered improper and wrong, and one s into a club to dance the night away with furtiveness that people dropped into speakea in America during prohibition. Since the po station is directly across the street from Wheel I could only hope that at least I'd not of exposure in a pen before being put into a ce few yards away!

I was reminded of how London's "Tiles" C was virtually closed because of continued po activity which entailed people undergoing indignity of a strip search for drugs, and a could hope if the worst happened was that my fronts would be as spotless as when I first them on!

Soon it was time for the pub to close, when they call "time" in Manchester they m it. Not like lax London where you can still drinks up to about fifteen minutes after official closing time, and by three minutes eleven the pub had emptied itself of brothers sisters who by this time had joined the seemir endless queue which had formed outside Wheel. The club itself is in what appears to be ex-warehouse or church mission. I like to thin the latter since it can at least be said it is carry on a tradition of spreading the faith as wel doubling as a meetinghouse for the faithful.

The Wheel itself is on two levels. When enters there is a cloakroom and drinks bar wr is always crowded, and music from down belo relayed through speakers at this level. lighting is subdued but not so dark that you c see where you are going! Naturally such scar of illumination tends to have a widen effect the pupils of the eyes. Being amongst the first I thought it would take a time for things to w up, but on going down to the lower level I surprised to see that already people swinging out and doing their thing. The walls the lower level are painted red, white and bla and the original arches which divided the vari rooms have been left in place to act both natural crush barriers, and also provide sepa

Another group which includes Zan, Janet, Jim and the lovely Miss Lesley Brown.

Francisco O'Brien (Fran Francisco) from Skipton gives his "Right on now" salute, and is joined by Alan and Boly, both from Earby.

A group of swingers and friends doing their thing and letting it all hang out.

reas for groups of friends to form their own circles of dancers. Not that there is any suggestion of clannishness or of cliques forming. Anyone is welcome to get up and join in, and soon the place was alive with sounds and movement!

All over, the Wheel motif is repeated; rows of unused bicycle wheels line the ceiling in one place, and the whole of the DJ's area is a cage built of spokes and wheel frames, and is one of the few places that is brightly lit. The light here spills out onto the floor, and the continual rhythmic movement of the dancers is only interrupted by the cheers of recognition that greet known favourites. There is no fashion as such, but naturally people tend to follow certain styles which have found favour and popularity. Never have so many Ben Shermans been gathered in one place at one time, and I noticed a style that I have not yet seen in London (but which I am sure will eventually drift down this way) in that very many young fellows wore black "right on now" racing gloves. Apart from looking cool and groovy they also serve a utilitarian purpose for the dancing there is of such a high standard that a certain degree of acrobatic skill is incorporated, and when really carried away whole rows of lithe young bodies bend over backwards and touch the floor with their hands!

The dancing is without a doubt the highest and the finest I have ever seen outside of the USA— in fact I never thought I'd live to see the day here people could so relate the rhythmic content of Soul music to bodily movement to such skilled degree in these rigid and armoured Isles! And, unbelieveable as it seems, everybody here was an expert in Soul clapping! In the right places, and with a clipped sharp quality that only adds an extra something to appreciation of Soul music. And what a selection of Sounds there were to dance to. I had taken four treasures from my own collection which I thought would go down well, and sure enough, even on first hearing the Wheelites were able to fall immediately into the rhythm and mood of them, and were moving and grooving out as if they had all week to rehearse to them.

It is an irony that groups like Pan's People, the Young Generation, and the grotesque automatons on "Top of the Pops" are employed to combine bodily movement to Soul records, and yet even the most average dancer of The Wheel would show them how it should be done. It could be that one needs a certain amount of affection for the music in order to penetrate the unique peculiarity of its rhythms, but the people at The Wheel have done this, and have done it to brilliant effect. I estimated that there were about 350 people crammed into the premises, but at no one did it seem so crowded that one couldn't move or breath properly, and with the minimum of chat Les kept the records coming one after the

other—each a Soul classic, and each loved and respected by the crowd.

Between records one would hear the occasional cry of "Right on now", or see a clenched gloved fist rise over the tops of the heads of the dancers. Every style of dress and life style was there—hair to the shoulders as well as hair like a five-o'clock shadow. Mutton chops and potential Santa Clauses (in which category I fell!), and the completely clean shaven. The tang of after-shaves and the girl's perfumes scented the hot air. The young ladies at The Wheel must be some of the most attractive in Britain—cute as buttons, and as mean as they want to be, but in the nicest possible ways. And imaginative enough to bring a change of clothes with them, so that half way through the night the young girl you were chatting with in the white suit to begin with, was now dancing the night away in an entirely different outfit! And talk! I thought I'd never stop! Everyone was so friendly and kind, and I truly felt quite humbled that so many people knew who I was, and who came up and introduced themselves and had a kind word to say about my writings. I must mention a few of them by name.

There was young Zan who really knows all about Soul, but who still retains a soft spot for the Blues and people like Bobby Bland and John Lee Hooker. He comes originally from Scotland, and has paid his dues one way or another, but explained how in some ways Soul has played such a big part in his life that it helped reform it. He is one of The Wheel's guardians (which I am told are hardly ever needed), and he will look after any strangers or new comers and see that they

A group of Soul brothers crowd together for a picture at Manchester's famed Saturday all-nighter at The Wheel.

settle in OK and no hustler who might slip in can take advantage of them. Everybody there certainly knew how to conduct themselves. There was no undercurrent of tension or aggression that one sometimes finds in London clubs, but rather a benevolent atmosphere of benign friendship and cameraderie. Everyone seems to know everyone else, and if they don't, then they don't stand on ceremony about getting to know each other, for one thing they know they all have in common is a love and dedication to Soul music, and it is this common factor that links everyone there, and makes everyone a potential friend of the other.

Some of the brothers and sisters had travelled miles to be there, and although they couldn't make it, Viv and Radio were thoughtful and kind enough to send a message to me via a friend. There was Tony from Cheltenham, and Rod (as imposing as Goliath and a DJ at other clubs in the North), and Flash who is not in the least flash, but very hip and very much into Soul.

And then there was Ivor Abadi who is the owner of The Wheel, and who couldn't have been more welcoming and friendly, and who expressed gratitude for the efforts that "Blues & Soul" has made to draw attention to The Wheel scene, and the struggle that is going on to keep it open for swingers at the weekends. And there was one record that sticks in my mind as one always will on these occasions, which was the great "Darkest Days" by Jackie Lee.

I do most sincerely hope that The Wheel is able to carry on its traditional all-night sessions, and at the time of writing the appeal to the Crown Court has yet to be heard, and so they will continue until a final ruling is given, but win or lose, The Wheel has succeeded in becoming a legend in its lifetime, and a focal point for that aware and elite minority who are not content with the lifeless pulp that constitutes the bulk of the manipulated "hit" parade, but rather use their own taste and judgement to determine what sounds best related to their own ways of looking at things. Live and let live is a rather worn out well intentioned cliché these days when life seems to be coming more and more restricted and uniform, but you would have to search a long way to find a setting where that theory was put into such real practise as Manchester's Twisted Wheel club, and I shall always remember with gratitude that I was taken to its heart, and allowed to be part of that scene even if I could only stay for such a short time.

They are my kind of people, and as I went to the station to get the train back home the faint sounds of Soul music reminded me that the Sunday afternoon session had already begun, and no matter what obstacles are placed in its way, Soul music, like life itself, goes on and on. Because each and every one of us keeps the faith—right on now!

the Northern scene eventually became regarded merely as another potential pot of gold to be plundered. But, in those far off early days there was such idealism, such genuine enthusiasm and real love in the air...and because of this, the Wheel rightly turned into legend.

Keith Rylatt and Phil Scott both know the score about the Northern Soul scene, its good points and its lows, and because of this have been able to produce a remarkable history and authentic account of one particular location that made such an inordinate contribution to its history, and in this respect they are to be congratulated and commended. This was the scene that they knew, and exactly how they knew and experienced it; a scene to which they made a contribution by their very presence, and which is rendered all the more valuable and authentic because it focuses on what they and so many others experienced.

In all matters relating to cultural history, there is nothing of greater value and dynamic than the testament of actual experience, of actually living it as opposed to dreaming it, and this book contains a wealth of insights and observations that those who shared in this history will immediately recognise as both valid and true. Keith and Phil have 'told it like it was', and, since I firmly believe there is no religion higher than truth, it is a pleasure and a joy to be invited to write this brief introduction, and to be able to commend it. And, at the same time, I sincerely congratulate the authors on their meticulous research, their dredging of the collective memory bank, and most importantly, their ability to convey the true magic that Northern Soul brought to the lives of so many people via seminal pioneer locations like the Wheel.

Whether you remember it as the Wheel, or the Twisted Wheel, or even just as 'that great place in Manchester' you once visited, or, if you never even set foot in the place, Keith and Phil's book will fascinate and absorb, for they have captured not just the spirit of the music, but the very soul of the place itself. In performing this tricky task, they themselves have surely kept the faith; both with we soul fans, and, just as importantly, with soul music itself! And without the music, how impoverished our lives would otherwise have been.

DAVE GODIN
NOVEMBER, 2000

ACKNOWLEDGEMENTS

SO MANY PEOPLE MADE THIS BOOK POSSIBLE, AND A LIST OF THESE KIND FOLK APPEARS AT THE end of the final chapter. Some have helped with just a couple of names or record titles, others have loaned valuable photographs or memorabilia, while some spent hours, if not days, digging out information – thank you!

There have also been those who truly put themselves to a great deal of trouble to make the project possible. They, like us, knew just how important it was that the Twisted Wheel story be recorded and selflessly gave invaluable assistance to make sure it happened. Thanks again!

Big Time Operators

Ivor and Phil Abadi. For their invaluable assistance throughout the project, with dates, names, and anecdotes. Ivor in particular, for information about acts at the club and 'inside stories'.

Eddie Barnett, whose knowledge and memory of teenage Manchester in the '60s is nothing short of incredible. He was one of the young Mods who went to the first Twisted Wheel as well as Whitworth Street. He bought records – one of the best R&B collections in town. He was a fashion leader – he ran Barnett Man Boutique, first for men's Mod clothes in the city. He hung-out in the right coffee bars – worked in the Mogambo – and had his hair styled at Denny's in King Street. In short, Eddie helped shape the Manchester 'in' crowd. Now, some thirty-five-years later, he can still recall the most minute detail.

Duncan Bradly, the very helpful curator of the Manchester Police Museum kindly allowed his assistant, Christine Marks, to spend hours wading through old files tracing a subject that must have occupied a lot of police time in the '60s.

Roger Eagle. Where it all began. During the four years that it has taken to produce this book, a simple but fundamental question has always remained unanswered – why Manchester? Why not Birmingham or Bristol? We hope that this book may help a little to answer that, but unquestionably, Roger was the catalyst. He was the alchemist who mixed the Abadi Brothers, the premises, the records, the artistes and the kids to create the Twisted Wheel. Although very ill during the preparation of this book, Roger always had time to help, not only us, but many others wanting to tap into his fountain of knowledge of black R&B. We hope that this book is considered a humble salute to Roger and Les Cokell, who too loved this music, and who has also sadly passed away.

In the late '60s, when the rest of humanity had moved onto musical pastures new and Soul became unfashionable, Dave Godin became its champion, articulating our love, emotion, and frustration for the music. Dave openly fought the arrogance and superficiality of both the pop press and Radio One, all in an attempt to present soul music in its rightful place – at the top.

Then in the '70s he promoted Northern Soul and defended it against its critics, this time, mostly from within the ranks of soul itself. Our belief that this book should be written, stems directly from these principals – thank you Dave.

Those of you who can remember the then radical window display in HMV, Manchester back in '71, of Ric-Tic 45s scattered alongside Frank Zappa's 'Weasel's Ripped My Flesh', must have guessed that only a true soul fan would have done it. They were dead right, Derek Howe is totally dedicated to soul music and has been since the mid-sixties. What is probably most admirable about Derek is that he has never indulged in soul politics. He has quietly and unassumingly given this project unreserved support. Sometimes tangible, such as precious photographs, but equally as important, reliable, accurate advice. Thanks Derek.

When we started delving into the murkier depths of Manchester's '60s teenage revolution, all roads seemed to lead to Chris Lee and his M.A. thesis on the subject: 'Shake, Rattle and Rain' – Popular Music Making in Manchester (1950–1995). Simmering below the surface of some of those '60s teenage meccas lay greed and sleaze. Chris graphically portrays the period and offers intelligent answers, usually based around just how innovative the kids of Manchester have always been. Especially when the over-hyped Mersey Sound dominated the '60s music press and Liverpool was seen to be the centre of the teenage world. Chris has been on the Manchester scene for a long time and can get pretty close to El Dorado when discussing the question of 'Why Manchester?' Thank you Chris for all of your selfless help.

If we tell you that even before the end of the '60s, John Marriot's 45 collection stood at 1,300 you might begin to appreciate the depth of his commitment to our music. Upon leaving school in Sheffield, John's first pay packet went on a trip to London's Ram Jam Club All-Nighter. He has pursued R&B ever since. John's knowledge of black music is pretty unparalleled, he has also seen or met countless artistes and painstakingly chronicled many details from them. He has selflessly opened these files to us to plunder at will. Thanks also to his wife Mo for the administrative help. John, you are a gentleman.

At a time when travelling from Oldham to the Wheel was a big deal and from Stoke-on-Trent outrageous, you can imagine that for Dave Meikle, to travel from Glasgow was considered interplanetary. Dave provided us with a lengthy and informative interview and gave us a glimpse at his '60s bedroom shrine to Edwin Starr. Thanks Dave.

As you will see, Brian Phillips pops up here and there in this book with some regularity. That is simply because he was part of the place. He probably had a more comprehensive connection with the club than anyone else – member, DJ, record dealer and floor sweeper, (part of the job description for all of the DJs, irrespective of your pedigree!) Brian has provided a great deal of help and advice for this book and rightfully was acknowledged by Ian Levine (Northern Soul DJ and producer of the video *The Strange World Of Northern Soul*) as being one of the founder members of the Northern Soul scene. Cheers Brian.

Not surprisingly, Brian Rae was the first person we interviewed. Brian has been on the scene for a very long time and has put a great deal of his life into the music, as a collector and DJ. He also saw it from another perspective when involved in the record production business, in short, there is little he doesn't know. It ought to be Brian writing this, not us. Thanks Brian, this is your life!

If you are lucky enough to own volume one, issue number six of *R&B Scene*, you can see, on the front cover, Brian Smith, resplendent in his cardigan, alongside Screamin' Jay Hawkins (see page 231). Since day one back in 1963, Brian made a comprehensive photographic record of life at 26 Brazennose Street. Armed with the most basic of cameras, Brian's work is both factual and beautiful. He has selflessly provided us with any print we desired, and as you will see, they capture totally the exact mood of the time. As if this wasn't enough, Brian patiently explained how the early pop scene in Manchester developed, how its blues evolved into R&B and where the Twisted Wheel fitted into all of that. He has also been interpreter for the often incomprehensible life and work of Roger Eagle. Brian was a good friend to Roger, and his photographic work certainly made *R&B Scene* what it was – a magazine some ten years ahead of its time. We are indebted to you Brian.

While on a visit to Manchester a few years back, Ken White called in at King Bee Records, Chorlton and mentioned to owner Les Hare that he had a colour Super 8 film of the Wheel. We were soon heading across desolate moor land in deepest Cornwall to Ken's place. If you think that such a film is amazing (and it is!) you ought to see Ken's scrap book of his life as part of the British R&B scene in the '60s. Ken allowed us to view some further fantastic footage and generously put all at our disposal. Thanks to you Ken.

Last, but by no means least, we would like to thank Professor Brian Ward, lecturer in American history at Newcastle-upon-Tyne and UCL Press, for permission to use material from his highly readable and informative *Just My Soul Responding* in Chapter One. Brian's work is a benchmark for future writers on the subject of post-war Rhythm & Blues to emulate.

INTRODUCTION Part One
Keith Rylatt

IN THE SPRING OF 1996, IT DAWNED ON ME THAT IT WAS EXACTLY A QUARTER OF A CENTURY since the steel exit doors in that grubby little yard behind the Twisted Wheel Club, Manchester, had slammed shut for the last time. Their closure was symbolic; the end of the '60s, the end of an era when clothes and style were as up-front as the music, the end of Rhythm & Blues, Lambrettas and Purple Hearts.

A further thought was for all of those thousands of young people who had attended the Twisted Wheel through its many phases, and what had become of them. Where were they? Probably scattered all over the globe. And what were they doing for a living? One thing was for sure, very few could deny the indelible effect the club left upon them. But probably the most worrying thought was that soon these memories would fade and the most influential black music club outside of the USA would simply be forgotten. There would be nothing to help future sociologists and pop historians; nothing to help settle arguments in retirement homes, when eighty-five-year-olds rant on into the night about what act supported Doris Troy. Nothing to let the 21st Century know where it was all at.

Sure there have been articles in fanzines giving brief, personal recollections of the club but these are so isolated, encapsulating only a brief glimpse, usually of Whitworth Street in the High Soul era. Accurate memories rarely stretch back more than about thirty years, so I would have to act there and then if the Twisted Wheel was to be placed in its rightful place in '60s pop and youth culture – at the very top.

Unbeknown to me, 900 miles away in Toulouse, France, Phil Scott, formally of Droylsden, Manchester, had also realised that time was running out and had begun a similar project.

My first action was to send a letter to the *Manchester Evening News* about the 25th anniversary of its closure and appeal for help with the project. Sadly, only two people responded, but both were to become invaluable. An ad in *Record Collector* was similarly disappointing, again attracting only two replies, but at least the field was widening, with letters coming from Cornwall and Canada. In desperation, I contacted Richard Searling of Manchester's Jazz FM radio station, who immediately gave the project the first of regular and generous plugs. These yielded instant and abundant reaction from dozens of people without whom this book would not have been possible.

On one of my many subsequent trips to Manchester, I called in at the King Bee record store in Chorlton, where owner, Les Hare, told me about Phil and his similar plans. After some enquiries, I caught up with his brother Bob eventually meeting with Phil at the 100 Club All-Nighter. I found his knowledge and enthusiasm, infectious. Things evolved and Phil and I,

The site of the original Twisted Wheel

with the invaluable assistance of scores of others, got the project united, and what was originally a pipe dream now lies in front of you. One outstanding legacy of having attended the Twisted Wheel is how everyone identifies with the place, on a very personal level, whether they attended Brazennose Street to listen to beat music or Whitworth Street as a soul fan some six or seven years later. Camaraderie is immediate, new acquaintances chat as if they are old friends. Few other experiences manage that; it is not just a love of black music and fond memories of the '60s, but even more to do with the Twisted Wheel itself.

It is vital to appreciate a few points constantly emphasised to us while researching *CENtral 1179*. Firstly, that the Twisted Wheel meant different things to different people during its eight-year life. In the early days, it promoted Manchester-based beat music, local lads, Brylcreemed hair and Burton's suits, snare drums and Fender Strats. Nothing more, nothing less and for that alone it will go down in history alongside the Cavern for playing a leading part in developing northern beat music and the careers of such acts as Wayne Fontana, the Hollies, the Dakotas, and Herman's Hermits.

Secondly, by DJ Roger Eagle bringing black Chicago to its turntables, the club then became famed for its R&B. The black wax on the decks was soon supported by British R&B bands, followed by a mixture of UK & US acts until finally it hosted 100% authentic American names.

Each of these phases was ground breaking, with only a few London clubs competing. And so the story goes on; Duke, Chess, Atlantic, Stax and Motown recordings would all be played there, and the artists would follow. DJs would change, fashions would evolve, different crowds would come and go and as transport got easier, fans would come from further and further afield.

With hindsight one can see that in its last couple of years it had begun laying the foundations for the Northern Soul scene. Fewer and fewer '60s style soul and R&B records were being released in Britain, and because the Wheel's DJs and audience were soul connoisseurs, they demanded a constant weekly injection of new American dance music, and imports were sought and played.

By this time, most other similar venues had closed or were allowing their philosophy and music policy to change with the times. In the Wheel's final six months, fifty per cent of the records spun were imports and all, by this time, were what could be called Northern Soul, and had it remained open, the club would probably have evolved along the lines of the Torch All-Nighter in Tunstall. But it obviously didn't. If anywhere did rise phoenix-like from its ashes, it was the Pendulum Soul Club under the musical direction of staunch ex-Wheelers, Dave White and Barry Tasker.

Music wasn't the only reason the club became so popular, at least during the Brazennose Street era anyway; many people went there simply to hang out and be seen, and for many, **xvii** clothes were as important as the music. The Brazennose Street Wheel was definitely more of a whole 'scene' than Whitworth Street, being the original Mod club in Manchester and for that matter, the entire north.

The Wheel was first in so many ways, without rival beyond the capital. A melting pot of image, unique music, fashion, scooters and drugs, all so tightly interwoven, that it is impossible to separate the importance of each.

I mentioned that there were two factors which folk had constantly repeated to us and needed to be aired before the story could begin. The second, was the deep and profound impact the closure of Brazennose Street had in the autumn of 1965. For some it was catastrophic. Although it wasn't closing for good – just moving across town – it might as well have been moving to the moon. Many people that we have spoken to about the first Wheel, do so with great passion and emotion, arguably more so than Whitworth Street. Many never stepped foot in the new club and of those who did, quite a few didn't make a second visit. This was all quite symbolic; the end of the Blues and heavy R&B and the birth of a new era and a new generation that wanted uptown Detroit, Philly and Chicago Soul.

Some five years later, the closure of the Whitworth Street Wheel had a similar effect upon its members. Phil and I left Manchester soon after, going very separate ways, having no particular desire to visit the Torch or Wigan Casino, but like literally thousands of others never being able to shake off the permanent effect the club and the '60s had upon us.

If however, you never visited the Wheel, but find this scenario uncannily familiar because your scene was identical, whether it be Leicester's Nite Owl, Sheffield's King Mojo, Newcastle's Club-A-Go-Go, the Sink in Liverpool, the Place at Stoke or the Scene in London, read on, as the effect that these experiences had on the youth of '60s Britain was immeasurable.

'While queuing in a fish & chip shop in Bradford, Ted Griffiths, who started one of the first small independent blues labels called Highway 51, found himself next to Champion Jack Dupree. They certainly confused the locals when they began discussing session details of the '52 New Orleans releases.'

BRIAN SMITH

INTRODUCTION Part Two
Phil Scott

FOLLOWING THIS INTRODUCTION, I HAVE INCLUDED A NUMBER OF CHAPTERS THAT AT FIRST glance may seem irrelevant to the story of the Twisted Wheel. It isn't my intention to ramble on solely to satisfy a pedantic nature, but to provide some background on the development of post-war black American music; the artists, the record companies and its slow but eventual popularity, albeit fairly underground in the UK. I've also tried to set the scene and colour of the pre-dawn of the Wheel. It's relevant for instance to mention the important role that the jukebox and the coffee bar played in providing an alternative way for teenagers to hear records. Without the jukebox's offspring – the 45rpm disc – it's difficult to imagine there ever being a youth club and music scene at all, let alone a Twisted Wheel.

By April 1964, just after one year of opening, the Twisted Wheel had become the centre for Rhythm & Blues in the UK. Two years later, it had progressed into the glorious soul era and was home to the biggest underground following for soul music in the country. A success determined by the underground musical tastes of its members.

It will be of benefit to younger readers, who never had the opportunity to go to the Wheel, before diving headlong into the history of the club, that I try to provide some background to the evolution of black music in the UK, especially within the context of the history of the Twisted Wheel. For instance, it's OK talking about records like 'What Kind Of Lady' by Dee Dee Sharp and 'Twine Time' by Alvin Cash (both hugely popular Whitworth Street Wheel records), if the reader is a Northern Soul devotee (God bless them) or avid Soul music record collector – but to newcomers to the 'scene' or readers of this book who are, for instance, maybe more interested in the beat group or early British R&B scene of the early '60s, the naming of an obscure record means nothing. Showing how these records came to be part of an underground scene and 'big sounds', will hopefully encourage the uninitiated to seek them out.

So how did the Twisted Wheel come to be the centre for black American music in England? After all, the opening of the Wheel was on the surface just the opening of yet another coffee bar, just another small business venture. Perhaps it was the arrival of Roger Eagle and his single-minded determination to play Rhythm & Blues that kick started it all off? Or perhaps fate took a hand and it just happened to be at the Twisted Wheel, and not at another club in another city, and somehow all the right pieces fell into place. Since black American music was still a relatively unknown quantity at the time, it is remarkable that a pop music policy was not adopted at the club instead. After all the beat group era and the music of the Beatles and company which was very much alive and kicking in the '60s, surely this must have looked a more commercial proposition?

Although not an expert in sociology or contemporary history, I also thought it was important to touch on one or two broader issues. For example, how much independent record companies in the USA helped black music come out of the shadows and become big business. And in contrast, how little the BBC contributed to the development of teenage music – and black music in particular – in this country, unlike the jukebox, the youth club and the coffee bar (under which

heading I include the coffee bar dance club) which did. Then there are related topics: like the hijacking of Rhythm & Blues; the invasion of rock and roll in the late '50s which spawned a thousand beat groups; the role of the 45 and birth of the modern club deejay; and the part played by UK record companies in the promotion (or lack of promotion) of black music.

We would like to dedicate the book however to the real unknowns, the kids – without whom nothing would have happened. Whether they were the 'mad' early rockers who jumped around to beat groups in the late '50s at clubs like the Bodega and the Oasis well before the Wheel opened, the beatnik crowd from the Left Wing Coffee House, the 'originals' (whoever you were) that inhabited the Brazennose Street Wheel in its early days or the first 'in' crowd – the Manchester Mods, the faces and characters who had adopted the club as their own by the spring of '64.

Last but certainly not least, a special thanks to the soul crowd of the Whitworth Street Wheel from 1965–1971, of which Keith and I were so proud to be a part of. To them and the ones who sadly never saw the '70s and who are at the great All-Nighter in the sky, this is their tribute. At the end of the day it's their story – the tale of a legendary club and underground youth scene, forerunner of the largest and longest surviving cult music scene the UK has ever known, the Northern Soul Scene, as relevant today as it was at its beginnings.

Above photograph taken at Butlins during the summer of '65.
On the left, Phil Scott, sixteen-years-old, with Alan White of Ashton-under-Lyne.
Note white waiter's jacket, Italian knitwear and US college cuts.

*'Be bebop,
This is your Jock,
Back on the scene
With a record machine
Saying 'Hoo-popsie-doo,
how do you do?'
When you up, you up,
And when you down,
you down,
And when you mess with
Jock, you upside
down...'*

New York's JOCKO HENDERSON
AKA the 'Ace from Space'

CHAPTER ONE
Background Part One – Post War USA
R&B Over The Airwaves

Rhythm & Blues had been blasting out of independent black music radio stations since the end of the Second World War.

THE INCREASING POPULARITY OF TV IN THE STATES IN THE EARLY 1950S, BEGAN TO LURE AWAY the traditional white radio audience, and radio stations found that they urgently needed to seek alternative minority markets to bolster their audiences. An awareness of the untapped black consumer market, together with the realisation that due to greater urbanisation, the black community was concentrated within a catchment area that even a small wattage station could reach, led white radio station owners to focus more on programming that would attract black consumers. The bottom line was that the black community listened more to radio than watched TV; by the mid 1950s per head of population, more whites owned televisions than blacks and more than ninety per cent of blacks owned and tuned in daily to black radio.

Black orientated radio was an important part of the creative process that enabled Rhythm & Blues to establish itself at the heart of black popular culture. It also enabled traditional racial and cultural barriers to be breached and allowed black music to become accessible to young whites at a time when, in America, racial bigotry, segregation and inequality were all too common.

In 1947, the first radio station in America to present a totally black-formatted service was WDIA in Memphis. WDIA broadcast 50,000 watts over an area which stretched as far north as Illinois and as far south as Jackson, Mississippi. The station reached an audience of over a million listeners, and in Memphis was heard in eight out of ten black homes. Local businessmen, whether black or white, didn't need much convincing to advertise on the station. The success of WDIA, known as the 'mother station of the Negroes', led the way in the nationwide expansion of black radio. Although virtually all of these were under white control[1],

by 1956 there were twenty eight stations with an all-black programming policy and another thirty six stations that broadcast over thirty hours a week, like WXLW in Jackson, KWKH Shreveport, WWRL in New York, WMRY in New Orleans and WGES in Chicago. The mighty WLAC in Nashville was another station that had switched to an 'all black' programming policy as early as 1949. With a

23

clutch of white deejays including Bill 'Hoss' Allen, John R (Richbourg) and Gene Nobles – WLAC was beamed all over the south eastern US – not only reaching a white audience but also future black stars like James Brown.

Naturally enough on most radio stations 'hep' talking black deejays were employed, usually on a brokerage system, to host the shows. Deejays would buy the air time and then solicit advertising revenue from which they would earn commission. Most young American whites probably heard R&B for the first time via black music radio stations, listening to black deejays like Spider Burke, Bill Spence, Rufus Thomas, The Midnight Gambler (Al Benson), Dr. Jive (Tommy Smalls), Nat Dee, Maurice (Hot Rod) Hulbert, Wild Bill Curtis, Eddie O'Jay and Dr. Daddy O (Vernon Winslow) to name but a few.

Independent Record Companies

In the States by the mid 1950s, scores of local black-formatted radio stations were playing hundreds of black records – some became local hits and stayed local hits, others went on to become regional hits, and occasionally regional hits that were picked up by a major label or distributor became national hits. Many small local 'mom and pop' labels failed to get a hit and went to the wall, others were swallowed up by larger companies – but sink or swim, Rhythm & Blues was fast becoming big business.

Most of the independents involved in the production of R&B records emerged during the mid 1940s, taking advantage of a niche that was created in the market when the large major record companies were forced to respond to the enforced economies of the War years. Due to a shortage of shellac – the basic raw material from which records were pressed – most of the majors stopped producing their 'ebony' and 'sepia' products and concentrated instead on the lucrative mainstream white popular music market.

Independent record companies developed and grew in parallel with the black radio stations of the late 1940s, both were inter-dependent on each other. Black radio utilised 'indie' record releases for cheap programming and received income from promoting the latest local releases – blacks tuned in to their local radio station to hear the latest hot sounds (records usually produced and released by an independent) and rushed out to buy them.

The setting up of a recording company was also an easy way for black, and for that matter white, entrepreneurs to start up their own company. $1000 was enough to hire a studio at fifty dollars an hour, book musicians, pay AFM dues, prepare a master and press up five hundred singles at eleven cents each. Most of the new owners had some connection with the music industry, whether it was record producing or artist management, running a record store or a nightclub, deejaying or an involvement in the booming jukebox industry.

Prior to setting up Specialty in 1945, Art Rupe, who later handled Little Richard, Jimmy Liggins, and for a brief spell Sam Cooke, had at one time worked for the small Atlas label in Los Angeles. Herb Abramson, who with Ahmet Ertegan formed the giant Atlantic Record Company in 1947, was a former talent scout for National Records and had previously owned the Jubilee label. Phil and Leonard Chess ran a club on Chicago's Southside before starting up Chess Records – the two brothers had

Late '50s-Detroit independent record company Fortune

recognised well before the start of the '50s, the enormous potential for black music. Another person with previous experience of the industry was Vivian Carter, who with husband Jimmy Bracken, opened Vee-Jay Records in Chicago in 1953. Well before the advent of Motown, Vee-Jay was one of the largest black independently owned labels. Typically, Vivian had been involved in the industry for years. As well as running her own record store, which gave her an invaluable insight into what was 'hot' and likely to sell, Vivian Carter had also deejayed for WGES Chicago in 1948, after winning a deejay talent contest run by top radio jock Al Benson.

By the early '50s, the seven largest independent labels were Aladdin, Atlantic, Chess, King, Modern, Savoy and Specialty, which accounted for two-thirds of best-selling black singles – some of which notched up sales of over 100,000. Atlantic, Chess, King and Imperial went on to get national distribution deals. By the end of the decade there were some 3,000 independent labels, over six hundred of which were involved in the production of Rhythm & Blues records, although relatively few were black owned. Some of the more successful labels that went on to become part of larger concerns included – Anna from Detroit, owned by Anna Gordy and Harvey Fuqua, and later to become part of the Berry Gordy empire; Dootone from Los Angeles, run by Dootsie Williams; Peacock managed by Don Robey, a Houston club owner who went on to buy Duke from Memphis deejay James Mattias; Robert West's LuPine in Detroit and the New York label Red Robin owned by Bobby Robinson.

25

The majority of independents though were local neighbourhood, small family businesses operating on a shoestring budget. 'Mom and pop' labels like New York's Celeste and Ike and Bess Besman's Apollo label, and Jack and Devora Brown's Fortune label in Detroit, which like the Apollo label and many others were operated from garages or record stores.

These independent record companies were a big influence on the emerging Rhythm & Blues scene. For the label owners it was not only important to get their record plugged on the radio, but also to get in with the jukebox operators and the free advertising that stimulated local sales. By 1953, in the USA, there were half-a-million jukeboxes which accommodated over one third of all discs produced. Naturally, the jukebox played a massive part in exposing black music to the teens of America, and was as much a part of teenage culture as the drive-in or the hot rod. The number of times a record was played on a jukebox – and jukebox sales were carefully scrutinised – gave operators a feel for potential teenage sales, and this invaluable market research was fed back to the record companies.

Some of the smaller independents were reliant on the pressing facilities made available to them by the bigger independents or plants owned by the majors. By 1954, the larger independents had sales people on the road hustling records, by fair means or foul, to get their product on the air, on the jukebox or on the retailers' racks. Three years later, releases from independent record companies accounted for seventy six per cent of the year's hit singles, and by 1958 more than ninety per cent of the one hundred and fifty five records that appeared on the national Rhythm & Blues charts later crossed over to the pop charts.

The Majors and Cross Over

Until about 1953, Rhythm & Blues was still pretty much exclusively a black music. The growth in the popularity of R&B however, is illustrated by the successful crossing over of records like Lloyd Price's 'Lawdy Miss Clawdy', The Dominoes' 'Sixty-Minute Man', Faye Adam's 'Shake A Hand', The Crows' 'Gee' and The Chords' 'Sh-Boom'. All of which crossed over from *Billboard's* national R&B charts to the mainstream white best seller list. More black crossover hits followed – Joe Turner's 'Shake, Rattle and Roll', LaVern Baker's 'Tweedle Dee' and the Spaniels' 'Goodnight Sweetheart Goodnight'.

These early black crossover hits were not at first taken seriously by the majors, who were preoccupied with producing material to satisfy the mainstream pop market and still regarded black music as inferior and of limited commercial mileage. Most majors tactfully kept R&B off their white music labels.

In a commercial compromise, they had set up 'race' labels like Columbia's OKeh and RCA's Groove – the products of which were distributed to different deejays and retailers than those handling their white recordings. The very existence of one chart for 'race' music and a different chart for white music being as sickeningly symbolic of racism as having 'blacks only' drinking fountains or segregated schools.

The practice of covering a record was nothing new, indeed there are many examples of black versions of white songs. 'Sh-Boom' by the Chords was originally the B-side of a Patti Page single; country singer Sonny Gale's 'Wheel Of Fortune' was covered by both the Cardinals and Dinah Washington; the Orioles' 'Crying In The Chapel' was a cover of a country hymn by Darrell Glenn. In the early '50s it was accepted practice to cover another artist's song, with two

or three versions recorded in a variety of styles each aimed at different regions and markets. Black artists from larger independent labels, covered records released on smaller labels. The Cadets, for example, covered local hits like Nappy Brown's 'Don't Be Angry' and the Jayhawks' 'Stranded In The Jungle'. It was purely business driven – black covers of both black and white recordings and white covers of both white and black recordings.

However, by 1955 not just songs but complete arrangements were being lifted from black originals for the white market. This artistic theft was a direct response to the success of R&B, an attempt to dilute and present an 'improved' European version that even more whites would buy. How the claim 'improved' could have been justified is impossible to imagine when you compare Bill Haley's totally de-sexualised version of 'Shake, Rattle And Roll' to Big Joe Turner's raunchy original. The best (or worst) example of how 'not to sound black' and still get a white hit must however go to Pat Boone's sad attempt to sound hip – listen to his gormless versions of Fats Domino's 'Ain't That A Shame' or Little Richard's 'Tutti Frutti'.

Media response clearly showed a racial bias. By definition, popular radio should play the most popular records in the country, whether they are white or black. The truth was that in the mid '50s the large pop radio stations in the States didn't always play the most popular black recordings if there was a white cover available. The Vee-Jay label's 'Goodnight Sweetheart Goodnight' recorded by the Spaniels was a massive R&B hit, but it was the sanitised white version by the McGuire Sisters that became the million seller. 'Earth Angel' by L.A. doo-wop group the Penguins, shared a high national chart position with the cover by the Crew-Cuts, but received fewer plays on the radio. In March 1955, Johnny Ace's posthumous hit 'Pledging My Love', positioned at number seventeen on the white best seller list and the number one R&B smash, was receiving massive airplay until the release of a cover version by Teresa Brewer guaranteed its rapid disappearance from radio play lists. Similarly, Frankie Lymon and the Teenagers' 'Why Do Fools Fall In Love?' was getting extensive airplay until receiving the kiss of death with the arrival of two white versions, one by the Diamonds and the other by Gale Storm.

Ray Charles first scored a US Top Ten R&B hit as early as 1951. Fellow Atlantic Records' recording artiste Ruth Brown, a major black recording star of the early '50s, had also been topping the R&B charts with records like 'Teardrops From My Eyes'. But it was Ray Charles' Atlantic monster 'I've Got A Woman' that really opened everything up – it reached number two on the nationwide charts and was a massive biracial hit. A reworked song from gospel origins, white kids who would never buy 'church' rushed out in their thousands to buy 'I've Got A Woman' – they loved it.

By the end of 1954, profits generated by R&B records and tours amounted to $25 million. The increase in record sales doubled R&B's market share – from five to ten per cent of the total industry gross. By late 1955, rock and roll as performed by black artists and an increasing number of white ones, had emerged as a definite musical style. Just one year later, *Billboard* reported that twenty five of the one hundred and twenty five mainstream pop chart entries had been black Rhythm & Blues/rock and roll records and that many others were either white covers of black songs or white 'black stylised' records. The success of an increasing number of white performers, in the main from south of the Mason-Dixon Line, was a by-product of the rising popularity of Rhythm & Blues.

Hep Cats and Hipsters

Black radio burst through cultural boundaries – it could be heard in both black and white neighbourhoods...a black/white cross cultural collision.

As stated earlier, not all the R&B deejays were black. In 1950, Dewey Phillips, a white ex-serviceman at station WHBQ Memphis, was hugely popular with both black and white listeners. It was probably the 'black sounding' Dewey Phillips and his play list of blues and early raunchy R&B on his 'Red Hot And Blue Show' that influenced locally a whole new generation of young southern white Americans.

Another white deejay, Alan Freed, worked at the high wattage middle-of-the-road radio station WJW in Cleveland. In the early 1950s Freed began spinning black records at the bequest of local record retailer Leo Mintz – and the response was incredible. Freed's 'Moondog Show' was bombarded with requests from white teenagers for more of the same. Freed knew he was onto a good thing and went 'all black' overnight. In an attempt to sound 'hip', Freed mimicked the jive talk and hep phrases used by lesser known local black deejays and laid claim to coining the phrase 'rock and roll', a colloquialism for sexual intercourse that had been used by blacks since the early 1920s. The Alan Freed Show was beamed all over Cleveland, and electric blues, doo-wop, Rhythm & Blues and particularly black harmony groups, were heard for the first time en masse by a white audience. The majority of Freed's listeners were encouraged to believe that the 'rock and roll' they were hearing was new. Freed attempted to blanch black music and disguise its identity and ethnic origins. For the white teenage consumers of America, the music of Fats Domino, Little Richard, Chuck and Bo, the Robins and a host of black harmony groups was sold as 'non ghetto music', and therefore more acceptable.

Labelling R&B as rock and roll, was in truth an attempt to detach Rhythm & Blues from an uncomfortable psychological association within white culture: the mythical threat of black sexuality. To market rock and roll as 'non threatening' and not too 'black' may have made perfect commercial sense at the time, but it didn't fool the majority of white teenage Americans.

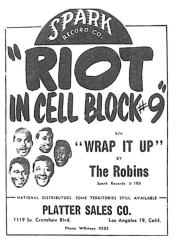

To them the allure of black music was all part of the attraction – the hip and forbidden world of black American culture.

In reality, rock and roll was fake goods – a white American, tailored music that black America had for years been calling Rhythm & Blues. Rock and roll owed its origins to black dance music laid down in the late '40s by bandleaders like Louis Jordan, who had played shuffle boogie rhythms to 'jump the blues'.

Rhythm & Blues was good time dance music, made to entertain the large number of blacks that had migrated north during the First and Second World Wars, to find work and populate the big industrial cities such as Detroit, Chicago and

Los Angeles. It was also modern day black city music with roots going back to the cotton fields, slickly interpreted by a new breed of black performers like Big Joe Turner, Roy Brown, Amos Milburn, Fats Domino, Wynonie Harris, T-Bone Walker and Ruth Brown. If anything the early success in copying black music, enjoyed by Bill Haley and a little later Elvis Presley (whose records were bought by blacks), helped increase the popularity of the authentic product. As Big Joe Turner said at the time: 'They pepped it up – after that we was in'.

In January 1956, as Hank Ballard's widely banned 'Work With Me Annie' sat at the top of the R&B charts, Elvis Presley was scoring his first national pop hit with 'Heartbreak Hotel'. He would have eleven more hits, five of them number ones before the end of the year. But strangely, it wasn't until the success of 'I've Gotta Woman' by Ray Charles that the major record companies finally sat up and took notice. The popularity and commercial potential for R&B and the enormous following and sales of Elvis Presley records, heralded the start of a new era – young white American consumers turning to black originated music for entertainment.

In the paranoid 'reds-under-the-bed' days of the Cold War, the black rock and roll of Chuck Berry and Little Richard and the white rock and roll of Presley were both savagely attacked as being part of an alien conspiracy to corrupt the hearts and souls of white American youth.

Surprisingly, in the still segregated southern states, a following for Rhythm & Blues by white American teenagers was not uncommon. Eavesdropping to black radio and playing R&B on the jukebox was an important part of a youth culture that had developed since the start of the

'50s. In 1954, the young Elvis Presley, a frequent visitor to the black sin strip on Beale Street in Memphis, was acting and dressing, like many of his peers, in the style of a black hipster. To get the right look he bought Mr. B low collared shirts, worn with attitude, collars turned up, and cool gabardine slacks from Lansky Brothers – a store where black hipsters got 'laid out'.

A more perfect example of cross-cultural influence would be hard to find – Presley wearing Royal Crown Pomade hair grease, and sporting a rockabilly/pompadour hairstyle, thus mirroring the black 'process' of having hair straightened.

Presley, like other whites his age, was no stranger to Rhythm & Blues. Beale Street, awash with clubs, juke-joints and bars, at all hours of night and day, was the focal point for black music in Memphis. Presley regularly hung out outside of Sam Phillips' Sun record company and was eventually

signed up. Sam Phillips always maintained that if he could find a white boy who could sing like a Negro, he'd make a fortune. Presley could bridge the gap, sing a black song without losing its vitality – he was the answer to Sam Phillip's prayers.

Phillips had already cut discs by Howlin' Wolf, Little Milton and Ike Turner and was regularly leasing material to majors like Modern and Chess. From a business point of view, he handled Presley superbly. It's no coincidence that Presley's early recordings had originally been recorded by established black vocalists – Roy Brown's 'Good Rockin' Tonight', Arthur 'Big Boy' Crudup's 'That's Alright Mama', and before he moved to Don Robey's Duke label, fellow Sun recording artist Junior Parker's 'Mystery Train'. These were the sort of artists that Presley admired and had been listening to for years on the Dewey Phillips show on WHBQ.[2] Guided by black songwriter Otis Blackwell (composer of 'All Shook Up', 'Don't Be Cruel', 'Fever' and 'Great Balls of Fire'), Presley imitated the voices of black singers he had heard, and copied the swaggering sexuality of local performers – he not only dressed and sang black but his highly charged sexual gesturing during stage performances mirrored that of black R&B stars.

Presley's first five releases on Sun had an R&B cover on one side and a country or rockabilly number on the other. For example, Crudup's 'That's Alright Mama' was coupled with bluegrass singer Bill Monroe's 'Blue Moon Of Kentucky'. It was a brilliant marketing move by Sam Phillips, catering for both the black and white record buying public. Later at RCA, Presley still showed a penchant for recording good R&B, covering amongst others the Drifters' 'Money Honey' and Lowell Fulsom's 'Reconsider Baby'. Whenever fellow RCA recording artist, black vocalist Roy Hamilton was due to record, Elvis would arrive hours before and position himself in the control booth.

Although the filming of Presley in the mid '50s was limited to his upper body to avoid showing his on stage 'pelvic gyrations', nobody thought there was anything too unnatural or disturbing about the way Presley's legion of female fans shrieked and swooned during his stage act. Females watching a black R&B performer on stage though would never dare show the same emotion. Not that any black male performers with any sense, when performing in front of a biracial crowd, would have dared to encourage any response from white females.

Jackie Wilson worked his black female army of fans to such a state of hysteria, that they would try and drag him from the stage, screaming 'Fill My Alley-O, Jackie'. But black performers were generally cool to the fact that to 'cross the line' and aim songs of passion, or display any lustful gestures in the direction of white females was guaranteed to cause a riot.

I'm Not A Juvenile Delinquent

Strangely enough, south of the Mason-Dixon Line, where white supremacy ruled, it was reasonably safe for white teenagers to indulge in black music, for deejays like Dewey Phillips to play black records and artists such as Presley to pretend to be black. In fact the future generation of white rock and roll performers were in the main all 'good old boys' from the southern states. Within reason it was OK for white teenagers to jump Jim Crow's cultural divide, but for blacks any such move was virtual suicide.

The commercial success of Rhythm & Blues, its illegitimate love child, rock and roll, and the popularity of black music with white American teenagers became the focal point for many pressure groups and religious organisations. Insiders in the predominately white music industry gladly welcomed the increased sales of 45s that R&B brought, but still regarded the whole notion of the success of black American music as a fad. One *Variety* editorial maintained that R&B was 'All right in the right place' – the right place presumably being back in the ghetto; the forbidden world that was probably half the attraction for rebellious white teenage Americans in the first place. *Billboard* tactfully reminded recording companies and radio stations of their moral obligation to promote what they considered decent material. The MC of the popular US television programme *Jukebox Jury* (a programme format adopted by the BBC in the late '50s), in a state of paranoia, proclaimed that all R&B records were 'as dirty and as bad for kids as

NOTICE!

STOP

Help Save The Youth of America
DON'T BUY NEGRO RECORDS

(If you don't want to serve negroes in your place of business, then do not have negro records on your juke box or listen to negro records on the radio.)

The screaming, idiotic words, and savage music of these records are undermining the morals of our white youth in America.

Call the advertisers of the radio stations that play this type of music and complain to them!

Don't Let Your Children Buy, or Listen
To These Negro Records

dope' whilst *Look* magazine warned that Presley was a 'disturbing kind of idol'.

The white status quo was under siege. The softer and non-threatening music of artists like the Platters and Sam Cooke gained more airtime at the cost of sexually tinged black hits like 'Honey Love' and 'Such A Night' by the Drifters which were dropped from playlists. The obsession with the evils of R&B and rock and roll, and in particular its exposure to white teenage Americans, led to the banning of black inspired records on many radio stations. Some of the older white radio jocks revelled in the protest and the prospect of pleasing their listeners. 'Rock and roll has got to go' became their rallying cry, and this was usually followed by the sound of black records being smashed live on air.

The anxiety over a white youth culture centred around rock and roll was rooted in an ingrained fear most southern white Americans felt – the prospect of genuine social, economic and political equality for blacks. There were fears that this would spark off a black uprising.

Rock and roll was blamed for destroying American family values and sending a generation of teenage Americans into hopeless moral decline. Rock and roll and R&B were blamed for everything; the 'attitude' teenagers had against parents and authority, crazy fashions, unwanted pregnancies, and the rise in street gangs and violence. The association of rock and roll with juvenile delinquency and promiscuity was forged in the public's mind by the playing of Bill Haley's 'Rock Around The Clock' as part of the soundtrack of *Blackboard Jungle* in 1955 – a teenage rallying cry about razor toting high school delinquents in skintight jeans. It caused riots **31** on both sides of the Atlantic – cinema seats continued to get slashed during showings of the film over a year later.

Bill Haley sounded OK (to some) but appeared middle-aged on camera. With his kiss curl and check jacket he looked square – visually he just didn't have what it took to be a teenage idol, or the sex appeal to compete with the person who followed him, Elvis Presley.

A Change Is Gonna Come

In 1955, the United States Supreme Court declared that segregated schools were inherently unequal. The Supreme Court called for segregation to be abolished as soon as possible. In late '55 and early '56, blacks took up the initiative and attempted, through mass non-violent protest, to desegregate schools and buses, swimming pools and beaches. It was the start of the year-long Montgomery Bus Boycott and the rise in prominence of black leaders like Martin Luther King. Against this backdrop of mounting political tension and racial unrest, white protest groups stepped up their actions against black performing artists, fearing that the support for black music by white youths was actually assisting the cause of integration. Statements issued by the executive secretary of the Alabama White Citizens Council typified the hysteria over black music: 'The obscenity and vulgarity of rock and roll is obviously a means that white men and his children can be driven to the level of the nigger. We've got a twenty-man committee to do away with this vulgar, animalistic nigger rock and roll bop. If we choose to call rock and roll communist ideology, I think we've hit it firmly on the head.'

In May 1956 at the Municipal Auditorium in Birmingham, Alabama, white protest groups picketed a whites-only concert featuring the Platters, LaVern Baker, Bo Diddley, Clyde McPhatter and Bill Haley. Banners on display protested 'Jungle Music Promotes Integration', 'Bebop Promotes Communism', and 'Churches – Speak Out Against Anti-Christ Forces'. A month earlier at the same theatre an attempt was made to storm the stage and assault, of all people, Nat King Cole who was performing to a whites-only audience.

On 4th May, there was serious racial conflict at the American Legion Auditorium in Virginia at a biracial revue featuring the Cadillacs, Ruth Brown, Little Richard and Fats Domino. Segregation at the theatre gave the balcony to whites and the floor below in front of the stage to blacks. Over 2,000 whites attended on the night and to avoid the crush on the balcony they moved to the black area. During the concert the sight of whites dancing and having a good time with their black brothers and sisters infuriated the whites on the balcony, who began hurling whiskey bottles down on the crowd below. The concert was halted and the police intervened, breaking up the fighting which spilled out onto the streets.

The hysteria over rock and roll continued throughout 1956. As more and more whites bought Rhythm & Blues records, black records began to get better chart positions than white records. Frightened of offending white protest groups, or being seen to pander to black tastes, the music industry banned black music from playlists and withdrew rock and roll from many jukeboxes nationwide. At the centre of the storm were Elvis Presley and Alan Freed. In August in Jacksonville, Judge Marion Gooding waited in the wings of the State National Theatre ready to serve an arrest warrant on Presley if there was any 'vulgar performance'.

There were many clashes at Fats Domino's multiracial concerts, and he regularly had to dive under his piano to avoid missiles. Performers like Chuck Berry, Bo Diddley and Ike & Tina Turner, who regularly played white college campuses did so with care. Touring black acts found that not only was it risky to perform for white audiences, but it was also impossible to get served at roadside restaurants. Black artists cancelled the southern leg of national tours for fear of the lynch mob and the racial bigotry.

Bobby Bland, Little Junior Parker, B.B. King and the Heartbeats, whilst part of a black revue about to play to an all-white audience in Chattanooga, faced a noose drawn on the dance floor. Larry Williams was arrested at a mixed audience show in the Municipal Auditorium in Norfolk, Virginia for daring to take off his shirt, diving off the stage and crossing the 'race line' to dance with his white fans.

But one of the most violent rock and roll disturbances happened at an Alan Freed Show at the Boston Arena in May 1958, when a young sailor was viciously stabbed and fourteen others were beaten up and robbed by a gang of 'satin jacketed' youths. In Boston there had always been an intense hostility to rock and roll and naturally enough Freed instantly got the blame for inciting the riot. All future concerts were cancelled, Freed lost his job at WINS New York and after a trial that dragged on for eighteen months, Freed although found not guilty, was staring bankruptcy in the face.[3]

'When the **espresso** craze arrived, a lot of the old ice cream parlours converted to coffee bars.'

BRIAN SMITH

CHAPTER TWO
Background Part Two
Meanwhile In England 1955–59

AN ENTHUSIASM WHICH SPRANG UP DURING WARTIME BRITAIN FOR THE BLACK AMERICAN JAZZ of the '20s led to the 'revivalist' jazz movement. By 1948, revivalist jazz was not only being played in the jazz clubs of the capital, but had also reached the provincial outposts of Britain. In 1952, Humphrey Littleton and a number of other jazz musicians broke away from the revivalist school and focused on the original exponents of New Orleans traditional jazz. And for the rest of the 1950s trad enjoyed tremendous popularity.

Two distinct jazz scenes had evolved by 1954 in London's West End. Down at the 100 Club on Oxford Street, working class youths and battle-dressed art students jived away the night to the trad of Humphrey Littleton, whilst at the Club 11, in nearby Carnaby Street, lounge-suited modern jazzers tapped their feet to the Dankworth Seven.

Don't You Rock Me Daddy O

Compared to teenage white Americans, who had by then become a considerable social problem, kids in England were a pretty tame bunch. Although, this would swiftly change with the commercial introduction of the jukebox and subsequent invasion of Elvis Presley and rock and roll, which sparked a teenage revolution. Prior to the screening of films like *Blackboard Jungle* and *Rebel Without A Cause*, teenagers, their fashions, and the whole 'identity' thing were clearly without direction.

At Art School and college bops throughout the country, students in baggy jumpers and sandals happily raved the night away to local trad outfits. The British hit parade had little to offer younger listeners. Although there were decent records beginning to be released from Decca's London label, airtime exposure on the BBC was insignificant. For the average British teenager, a musical fad called skiffle, which appeared just before the wholesale exposure of rock and roll was where it was at.

The sudden overnight popularity of skiffle was mainly due to the efforts of one man, Tony Donegan, who adopted the first name of his hero, the New Orleans blues musician Lonnie Johnson. In 1955, the BBC transmitted a live trad concert from the Festival Hall in London, and during the concert Donegan, together with established jazz musicians Chris Barber and Ken Colyer, performed a re-worked uptempo skiffle version of an old black work song by Huddie 'Leadbelly' Leadbetter entitled 'Rock Island Line'. After repeated plays by the BBC, the often requested recording was released by Decca and 'Rock Island Line' stayed in the hit parade for half of 1956. Donegan was snapped up by Pye-Nixa and consistently hit the charts during the next six years.

Jukebox

Despite being invented by Englishman Charles Randal in 1888, the coin-operated phonograph machine was ignored in the UK, crossed the Atlantic where it became the jukebox – a multi-million dollar industry and an institution as American as mom's apple-pie. Yet in the UK it was the opposite. Before the start of World War Two, the number of jukeboxes in the UK numbered only a couple of hundred; it was of curiosity value only, a novelty item often found on fairgrounds. Unlike in the States, the commercial potential of the jukebox was not even a consideration. Many jukeboxes, imported during the war years to satisfy GIs stationed at American bases in the UK, surfaced in English cafés after the war. The early post-war years saw Britain in a period of austerity; most everyday necessities were rationed and the importing of luxury goods, including jukeboxes was on hold. The importing and subsequent distribution of jukeboxes solely for the UK market didn't really get under way until the mid 1950s, around about the same time as the arrival of rock and roll. Teenagers, rock and roll and the jukebox – now that was a commercial proposition.

This Magic Moment

Not all teenagers were as stereotypical in their musical tastes. In 1955, a young Dave Godin, innocently enjoying an ice cream in the Silver Lounge Ice Cream Parlour in London's Bexleyheath, heard a record that would change his life.

Dave Godin instantly became a devotee of black American Rhythm & Blues. In future years he would go on to help Berry Gordy's Tamla and Motown labels establish a foothold in Britain, form the Tamla-Motown Appreciation Society, open the first specialist soul music shop in the country and launch the pioneering Soul City and Deep Soul record labels with friends David Nathan and Robert Blackmore. Dave Godin also became a staunch supporter and campaigner for the Anti-Apartheid and Black Civil Rights' movements, having a special window display at the Soul City Record shop dedicated to Martin Luther King the day after he was tragically assassinated. One of the most significant soul music supporters and the black American music guru for a whole generation of *Blues & Soul* readers.

In the same year in a small cafe in Oxford, another atypical young teenager called Roger Eagle, was busy putting threepenny bits into a jukebox to hear records like the Rays' 'Daddy Cool'. The US Cameo 45 was on the jukebox simply because the cafe was close to a US airforce base. Eagle was about to embark on a similar musical journey. His destiny would lead him north to Manchester where he too would become a pioneer for black music and play a major

'I heard a record on the jukebox I'd never heard before, it sent goose bumps down my back. I asked one of the guys who had just helped to install the jukebox who the artist was and he told me it was a Rhythm & Blues record by Ruth Brown called 'Mama He Treats Your Daughter Mean'. I can only describe it as one of those rare 'magical moments' that a person experiences every once in awhile, a bit like falling in love. That moment truly affected the rest of my life.'
Dave Godin, 1998

part in the promotion and development of the early British Rhythm & Blues and soul club scene.

Coffee Bars & Jukeboxes

There was no overnight rush by cafés and pubs to get jukeboxes installed, but the prospect of attracting teenage trade and money hadn't gone unnoticed. As well as installing chrome monsters like

The Merry Chest Café on the old A2 in Kent, where in the late '50s, Dave Godin would listen to London-Atlantic R&B favourites on the jukebox

the Seeburg Trashcan and the AMI Continental, a number of entrepreneurial café owners also completely refitted their premises. At places like the Belle Reve – probably one of the first coffee bars in London – dull, greasy fixtures and fittings were ripped out to be replaced with bright, colourful modern interiors and sparkling chrome Gaggia espresso coffee machines. Cafés had got hip to the modern teenager, wise to their money, and became coffee bars – the perfect haunt for the first modern generation – the first post war generation with money to spend. The highly stylised and flashy '50s jukebox, like the fins of American cars, may have reflected the optimism of new age America, but their arrival in England was met with a furore of disapproval and opposition. Local town and village authorities either refused to grant music licences or compromised and imposed a 'no dancing' restriction on premises with jukeboxes. Nervous café owners welcomed the influx of teenage trade that the jukebox brought in, but hypocritically banned 'hand clapping' and the 'stomping of feet', worried that local councils would come down hard on them. Residents in towns and villages throughout the country organised petitions and wrote furious letters of complaint; 'Disreputable elements and jukeboxes are invading our village' wrote a newspaper reader in Glossop, while in Sheffield a very disgruntled lady, complaining about the shocking disturbance coming from the nearby El Mambo, declared: 'The beat from the jukebox is shaking my head'.

Teenagers ignored the adult disapproval, they loved the jukebox and they loved the independence rock and roll gave them. Prior to the jukebox's arrival, the only way kids could get to hear recorded music was to suffer their parents' selection of 78s or tune in to the BBC's Light Programme, which typically churned out a carefully controlled, conservative repertoire of family music – music hardly likely to fan the flames of rebellious youth. For jukebox distributors the only consideration given to determine which records were stacked on the jukebox was simply how many times the record would be played.

Although the majority of kids at the time were relatively harmless and quite happy digging trad and skiffle, after the showing of *Rebel Without A Cause* in 1955 things were never quite the same. Released a year before *Rock Around The Clock*, for lots of teenagers struggling with an identity crisis the film was a big culture shock and massive youth hit – the first film UK teenagers had ever seen that identified with teenage consciousness.

Around the same time, a handful of working class, street-wise teenagers, hanging around the cafés of the East End of London, took to wearing the Edwardian style suit or 'Teddy suit,' which had been introduced by tailors just after the war. Originally intended for smart, young city gents, these prototype Teddy Boys radically altered the styling of the suit. The velvet- **37** collared jackets were worn long and the trousers were narrowed to drainpipes. A few of them even sported outrageous 'Apache' style haircuts, shaven head with a flat strip of hair running front to rear down the centre of the head. These original hard-core Teddy Boys were generally bad news, and confrontation with parents and authority was inevitable. One year after the arrival of Presley, the 'pompadour' hairstyle had become standard and the association of the Teddy Boy and rock and roll was complete

The Establishment was not so enthusiastic about the changing times. Cafés and coffee bars were seen as a breeding ground for the estranged youth of the country and rock and roll threatened to corrupt the minds and bodies of the young. Newspapers fumbled for the right words, earnestly proclaiming that 'Teddy Boys are going on a downhill path to an undesirable spot'. Of course, British teenagers didn't see it that way, in the past they had been repressed with limited options, and now they had suddenly come of age. As had happened in the States, disturbances broke out during the showing of *Blackboard Jungle* and Teddy Boys, by now greater in number, were involved. The banning by local authorities of jiving in the aisles during the showing of *Rock Around The Clock* in 1956, led to the copycat slashing of cinema seats. The inevitable national press coverage only helped increase public outrage and glamourise the Teddy Boy image to teenagers. In 1957 there were ugly scenes at a Bill Haley concert in the capital; the stage was invaded, Haley and Co. had to run off, fighting broke out and the show was abandoned.

The Teddy Boys were pilloried by the press and there was public hysteria over the 'Teenagers from Hell'. In towns and cities throughout the country, youth clubs and church hall 50-50 dances were invaded and smashed up by Brylcreamed hordes. There were disturbances involving the police at Brighton and Southend, and on a more worrying note, white teenagers were involved in the Notting Hill race riots of August 1958. Sure enough rock and roll got the blame – the root cause of juvenile delinquency.

The introduction of jukeboxes coincided perfectly with the invasion of Elvis Presley and his white rock and roll classmates. Presley was the catalyst, and within weeks rock and roll was all the rage in every city in the country; post-war working class British teenagers had been waiting in the wings, waiting for a role model, impatient for change and a chance to rebel. In 1956 alone, Presley had six best sellers in the UK, his first 'Heartbreak Hotel' stayed in the UK hit parade for four months. As Presley hysteria took hold, the writing was on the wall, and teenage interest in skiffle and trad began to fade. Due to the government's easing of hire purchase conditions the new rock and rolling 'wannabees' were now in a position to dump their improvised skiffle instruments to buy electric guitars on the 'never never'. Although Donegan and skiffle had shown British teenagers that it was possible for kids to make music, it was rock and roll that provided the new found inspiration – the dawn of the British beat music scene.

As the end of military conscription came in sight, in church halls and youth clubs up and down the country, teenagers formed themselves into rock and roll bands. Old skiffle numbers like 'Rock Island Line' and 'Cumberland Gap' were forgotten and the repertoire of Presley and Little Richard were quickly memorised. Coffee bars like Soho's 2Is on Old Compton Street, became a mecca for scores of rock and roll hopefuls.

Attracted by the prospect of creating a home grown Presley or Buddy Holly, show biz agents like Larry Parnes descended on the coffee bars eager to sign up young hopefuls. British rock and roll artists attempted to mimic and capture the 'pepped up' rock and roll of Presley but failed. Instead of becoming mirror image equivalents of their American cousins, most ended up making safe and diluted pop records. Instead of accommodating their real audience, the kids, they became part of the jaded UK variety circuit, MOR polished pop artists with mother and daughter appeal – the very thing kids were trying to escape from.

Early Underground

'Only those precious few who heard the ultra rare London EP 'R&B With Bo Diddley' (issued as a single seven years later by Pye in July '63) can fully appreciate the cosmic culture shock it caused in 1956.'
Dave Godin

For a handful of people however, the white rock and roll of Elvis Presley and company was seen as fraudulent. In London, and most major cities, there was a small following, for black rock and roll/Rhythm & Blues. Black American music in the UK at the time, unless it was jazz, blues or gospel was regarded as 'low life'. That being so, black American records were being released by Decca's London-American label and could be found on jukeboxes in cafés and pubs in white working class areas of London and at truck stops like the Merry Chest and Ace Café on the main arterial roads leading from it.

In Manchester it was a similar story, there were a minority of individuals who were into black rock and roll/Rhythm & Blues. The earliest recorded example of the sale of black American records in Manchester, was from a record shop on Tib Street in the city centre, called Dobb's Records. In the late '50s, Ted Griffiths and Bob Groom, who went on to edit *Blues World* in the '60s, regularly used to go down into the cellar underneath Jim Dobb's record shop. They would walk over a carpet of broken 78s and sift through thousands of US imported records, on such labels as Red Robin, Aristocrat, Chess, King and Crown. Legend has it that Ted actually went into Dobb's as early as 1955 after completing his National Service and bought UK-Vogue 78s by Muddy Waters for five shillings each, a considerable sum at the time.

The arrival of West Indian immigrants to industrial cities like Manchester in the mid 1950s was another factor that helped popularise and support black music at the time.

Teenagers would jive to either black or white rock and roll; after all a jive record was a jive record and all they wanted was a good time, simple as that. Not that the average teenager on the dance floor had any say or for that matter any real knowledge of what was being played anyway. That there were more white American rock and roll records played than black is sadly also true – the exposure and promotion of black dance records to the masses was non-existent. Black Rhythm & Blues records of the mid 1950s (as with soul music in the '60s) had to rely on promotion from within, and any expansion in the popularity of black dance music in the UK would as always, be determined by the kids who loved and danced to it.

The misuse of drugs, apart from booze, cigarettes and the occasional reefer was minimal. Amphetamines could be bought over the counter at chemists and regarded at the time as no more than a keep-you-awake stimulant similar to coffee. Although they were openly available, surprisingly enough, amphetamines were not generally abused by teenagers. The average kid at the time had little knowledge of the effect of stimulants, and there was no real teenage all-night **39** scene. Dave Godin recalls getting smartly dressed up on a Saturday night for trips to a club in Soho called the Granada which unusually for the time, played Blues/Rhythm & Blues records. Unfairly, the Granada was wrongly portrayed in the *News Of The World* as an 'evil drug den'. Perhaps the real issue was the press getting at what the kids were digging – music that was altogether different – black music.

The Granada used to close at 2.00am and teenagers waited around all-night tea stalls until the first train home. Eventually the Lyceum, a large dancehall of the day on the Strand, started putting on Sunday afternoon record hops. It was black American rock and roll all the way – LaVern Baker, Ruth Brown, Big Joe Turner and the like, and probably the first regular Rhythm & Blues session in the UK. As for black music being a threat to teenage morality, nothing could be further from the truth. No alcohol, no drugs and no violence – the Lyceum was the pillar of respectability, just lots of young kids jiving and having a good time.

The 45

Teenagers broke free from parental control – they escaped the traditional family evening gathering around the radiogram.

The introduction to the UK of the jukebox's offspring – the 45rpm disc in the mid '50s, as a replacement for the out-of-date, heavy and crackling 78, was a huge leap forward for the British record industry as it signalled the dawn of hi-fi.[1] 45s were young, modern, compact and just made for teenagers. In youth clubs throughout the country, a new generation of disc jockey was born. However, whereas in the States 45s were a cheap and disposable commodity, used to launch an artist or promote an album, in the UK the 45 single was typically regarded as a luxury item and as such carried a thirty three per cent purchase tax levy. This upped the price of 45s to about four for a pound, at a time when the average weekly wage was less than eight pounds a week. Nevertheless, 45s sold well and it was teenagers with money to spend who bought them down at their local record shop or 'Gramophone Lounge'.

Portable record players were also available at the time, and the Collaro Conquest, and later the Dansette, made affordable through hire purchase, offered the teenager mobility and the chance to play their choice of music, wherever and with whoever they wanted.

A particular favourite of Wheel disc jockey Roger Eagle – the flip to Bobby Bland's 1957 hit 'Farther Up The Road'. Both 78rpm and 45rpm versions of the disc were pressed by Duke in the States.

Considering the almost total disregard for black music by the music press of the day and the zero air-time afforded by the BBC to UK issues of black American recordings, it's no surprise the public's awareness and exposure to Rhythm & Blues was slow. The successful sales of black American releases in the UK was a virtual impossibility due to lack of exposure. James Brown, for instance, had twenty six chart hits in the States before his first in the UK, in September 1965. Much depended on the major UK record companies and a handful of label executives with balls enough to take a chance and release the R&B product, none more so than London. Considering the highly stacked odds against record companies making decent sales, British labels issuing these records should be commended for not throwing in the towel. Without London, it's hard to see how the minority and very underground R&B/rock and roll scene of the mid '50s could ever have got off the ground.

The BBC with its monopoly of the airwaves was perfectly positioned to control or suppress what they considered unsuitable for teenage ears. Successful sales of black American records released in the UK were, due to the total lack of air-time exposure, a guaranteed impossibility. Shows on the BBC like *Easy Beat* with Brian Matthews pandered to live renditions by home-grown artists of black American music. Firstly to appease the Musicians Union, and secondly to showcase British performers.

The interest shown by Decca and EMI in R&B – that is its suitability as a product for the British market – was of course profit driven, R&B was big business in the States, so why not the UK? The respectable sales of rock and roll records in the UK in the mid to late '50s suggested that there was the possibility of repeating the success with R&B.

In June 1959, in an attempt to appease the imagined anarchic threat of the 'teenagers from hell', the BBC launched *Jukebox Jury*, copying the American TV show of the same name.

The compere, an old school presenter called David Jacobs, chaired a panel of celebrity 'has-beens' in their forties – grateful for a chance to revitalise their flagging careers by appearing to be 'with it'. It was an ideal opportunity on prime time TV to bad mouth any record that didn't neatly fit in to their idea of white pop. What few black records were reviewed were rubbished, and provided the panel with an ideal opportunity to score points with middle-aged viewers at home.

The panel of so-called experts gave uninformed judgements on the week's latest record releases, eventually voting on whether the record would be a 'Hit' or a 'Miss'. Phil Scott can remember quite clearly the panel rudely dismissing Bo Diddley's 'Pretty Thing' as rubbish and a definite 'Miss' (guaranteed if the BBC had anything to do with its promotion), and then dying with embarrassment on Bo's behalf when after the verdict was unleashed, Bo Diddley appeared from behind the studio screens. The same treatment was given to Howlin' Wolf when *Jukebox Jury* reviewed 'Smokestack Lightning'. Roger Eagle apologised to Howling Wolf on behalf of the UK public via the following issue of *R&B Scene*. This patronising attempt by the BBC to be trendy, typified the critical condition of popular music in the UK in the late '50s and early '60s.

41

UK Record Companies – Decca (London-American)

Although by 1957–58, the odd R&B hit was being picked up for release in the UK on EMI labels such as Columbia (LaVern Baker and Frankie Lymon) and Parlophone (Little Willie John and Hank Ballard), the real credit for getting Rhythm & Blues and later soul music released in Britain, must go to Decca's subsidiary label – London. First established in the USA by British Decca in 1947 as an outlet for UK produced records, London began issuing releases in the UK in 1949. By 1954 US recordings, licensed to the London label in the UK, outweighed home grown UK productions.

Although EMI had the HMV label and owned the rights to RCA (and Elvis) from the States, successful UK sales in the mid '50s by artists like Chuck Berry, Little Richard and Fats Domino enabled London to eventually take a chance on many lesser known black artists, Marv Johnson and Barrett Strong being examples. London was the first UK label to arrange complete catalogue deals with American record companies like Atlantic and the first UK label to release recordings from independent labels such as Chess, Vee-Jay and Berry Gordy's fledgling labels in the late 1950s.[2]

London and US Atlantic

From 1955 Atlantic began sharing Decca's London logo, and its recordings were released in the UK on the London-Atlantic label, with the legend 'Recorded by Atlantic, New York' printed on the label. Atlantic's music during the early '50s had changed from the hard-edged jazz and Rhythm & Blues style towards a more commercially acceptable style intended to attract both black and white record buyers. The arrangements at Atlantic by A&R supremo Jesse Stone, of records like 'Money Honey' and 'Shake, Rattle And Roll', typified a more mellow and harmonious approach to producing records. Atlantic were the first large independent to recognise R&B's broader appeal and among the first to concentrate on 'modern' Rhythm & Blues, with artists such as Ruth Brown, Jimmy Lewis, Ray Charles, Big Joe Turner, LaVern Baker, Ivory Joe Hunter, Chuck Willis, Clyde McPhatter and groups such as the Dominoes and the Clovers. By no means insignificant, was the appointment to the board in 1953

of Jerry Wexler, an ex-staff writer for *Billboard* magazine. Wexler brought with him an astute and brilliant commercial awareness of the music industry.

London-Atlantic continued having releases alongside London-American, both being part of the same catalogue and sharing the same HL8000 Series matrix. The first release on London-Atlantic was Ruth Brown's 'Mama He Treats Your Daughter Mean'. London-Atlantic continued until May 1964, the final release being Solomon Burke's 'Goodbye Baby'. In May 1964, the famous black Atlantic 4000 series was launched which gave Atlantic/Atco its own label identity, with the first release being the Drifters' 'Under The Boardwalk'. In 1966, Atlantic (UK) was bought out by Polydor and releases were issued on the plain red Atlantic label. Polydor at the same time launched the UK Stax label, which included material from US Volt, and eventually created the UK Atco label. Polydor promoted its releases in a magazine called *Soul Messenger* for Uptight an' Outasight, their appreciation society.

London's dominance in the record industry eventually came under pressure from a most unlikely source, J. Arthur Rank's Top Rank label. Rank's entertainment empire included film production and distribution as well as the Odeon and Gaumont cinema chains which in the mid '60s, were ruthlessly bastardised into bingo halls as cinema audiences declined with the advent of television.

In 1959, with considerable sums of money to invest, the Top Rank label competed with London in the States for material to release on this side of the pond. Top Rank released many pop records and a number of superb R&B records including Jimmy Reed tracks from a link up with the Vee-Jay label. Although Top Rank hit pay dirt in the charts on a number of occasions, most notably with Gary U.S. Bond's 'New Orleans' and 'Quarter To Three', overall they lost a fortune.

Eventually, in 1962 Rank sold out to EMI and Rank's last single was 'Just Got To Know" by Jimmy McCracklin. EMI switched all Top Rank's existing US record licensing deals to their newly launched label, Stateside. The first record was 'Palisades Park' by Freddy Cannon. US record companies now had two major UK record companies after their product.

Other UK Labels

In 1961, Decca's London-American label was still the biggest player in the UK. For years Decca had been issuing recordings from US labels such as Specialty, Imperial and Chess on their London label, and was the first UK company to taste success with black artists, notably Chuck Berry and Little Richard in the rock and roll boom years. However, Decca (London), ceased its connection with the Chess and Checker label after August 1960, their last Checker release being Little Walter's 'My Babe' and their final Chess release, Etta and Harvey's 'If I Can't Have You'.

Pye owned Pye International, Nixa and had previously issued Mercury products. Noting London's success, Pye were keen to get into what they judged to be a potentially lucrative UK Rhythm & Blues market. With money in the bank from successful record sales with Lonnie Donegan, Pye record executives flew to Chicago in 1961 to meet Phil and Leonard Chess with the intention of negotiating a deal to issue the Chess/Checker catalogue in the UK on a new label – the Pye International R&B Series. From then on Chess/Checker acts such as Bo Diddley, Howlin' Wolf and Sonny Boy Williamson, possibly regarded as risky or too 'black' by London for the UK market were issued on Pye's new label and made good sales, if judged over months rather than weeks. In January 1965, Pye gave Chess their own UK label, the gold Chess 8000 Series. The first issue was 'Hey Good Lookin' ' by Bo Diddley.

Philips, the last major company to introduce 45s, owned Fontana and Mercury. From November 1961, Fontana briefly took over from London and issued four Motown singles, the Marvelettes' 'Please Mr. Postman', the Miracles' 'What's So Good About Goodbye', Eddie Holland's 'Jamie' and the Marvelettes' follow-up single 'Twistin' Postman'.

EMI owned HMV, Parlophone, Columbia, Capitol, Regal-Zonophone and later Stateside, which from October 1963 until March 1965 issued forty five Tamla and Motown 45s. EMI, following Dave Godin's advice, waited until October 1964 when Stateside succeeded in achieving their first Motown hit ('Baby Love' by the Supremes) before giving Tamla-Motown its own label. EMI also owned United Artists, Liberty and MGM.

Last but not least were the courageous indie labels of the day, like R&B records, named after owners Rita and Benny, which operated out of their record shop in north London. Others included Esquire, Ember and King (no connection to the US label of the same name). These labels had only a small number of genre releases that were niche marketed as jazz, blues and Rhythm & Blues.

The London-based Oriole label was an independent with a difference, it had its own pressing facilities, and in 1962 took over from Fontana to release approximately twenty records from Gordy's Tamla and Motown labels, plus a couple of albums, before the contract moved to EMI's Stateside.

CHAPTER THREE
Manchester 1958–62

The year of 1958 marked a watershed for entertainment in the heart of Manchester's city centre – teenage tastes and the demand for beat groups, jukeboxes and jive music influenced a massive youth culture change.

FOR THE FIRST TIME SINCE THE EARLY '50S, THE ESTABLISHED TRAD BANDS, WHICH HAD FORMED the backbone of live music in Manchester's clubland, found themselves competing for bookings with fresh-faced and energetic beat groups. However, there were still scores of pubs that accommodated local jazz bands in the city centre, despite the effect that the jukebox had made on live music. There were also a good number of well supported jazz clubs in and around the city centre, like the Cromford Club, Club Southside, Thatched House, Band On The Wall and the Manchester Sports Guild (MSG). But by the late 1950s, the popularity of trad had peaked in Manchester.

City centre coffee bars like the Mogambo, the Zanzibar and future Mod haunt the Cona, on Tib Lane, attracted teenagers from the suburbs. In response to the teenage demand for jive records in 1958, the Plaza Ballroom on Oxford Street in Manchester, traditionally a dance band venue, began advertising lunch-time 'Disc Only' sessions. During the week, school-kids and young working teenagers could spend their time jiving for sixpence or on Saturday afternoons catch the bus into Manchester to attend 'Marathon Jive Sessions' for one shilling and sixpence.

PLAZA MECCA DANCING
LUNCHTIME DISCS 12 - 2pm
OFF THE RECORD
The greatest record session in town
7 - 11pm 2/6
TOMORROW
HERMAN'S HERMITS

JOHNNY PETERS AND THE JPs
Package Show 7 - 11.30

Manchester, like Liverpool, had dozens of groups eager to play at youth clubs, church hall dances and the new coffee bar clubs. And whilst the Court School of Dancing wanted the teenage trade that flocked to hear the local beat groups, they weren't too keen on the trouble that followed the Teddy Boys around. The management at The Court advertised their 'Beat Group Nights' with caution: 'People Will Not Be Admitted Wearing An Exaggerated Style Of Dress'. At the Station Hotel in Salford, the landlord also showed concern and displayed a similar warning above the entrance door: 'No Characters Admitted'. The Bodega Club, long established as a top city centre jazz haunt, was quick to recognise the growing demand for beat music and copied the Plaza's idea by putting on lunch-time jive sessions, which included a meal in the 1/6d admission price. The club also started 'Pop Shop' sessions on a Friday night with local outfits like Paul Beattie and the Beats.

45

'Some people put the whole Manchester club scene down to Jimmy Savile, who quickly realised that you didn't have to put a group on to create a dance – you could just play records.'

CHRIS LEE

Shake Bama-Lama & The 2Js

Kids wanted more than a church organised 50-50 dance which usually ended up in a mass brawl.

Although 'mainstream pop' was in a critical condition, in Manchester's coffee bar clubs it was a different story. There was a huge demand for more 'meet and jive' places and by the start of the '60s new coffee bar dance clubs began to open, usually in converted basements under the city. Early examples of Manchester coffee clubs included Guys And Dolls on Kennedy Street, the Continental, La Ronde, and the Three Coins on Fountain Street, which opened on 12th December 1961, later to be managed for awhile by the future owners of the Twisted Wheel, the Abadis.

Six months earlier, on 1st July 1960, in the cellar of an old warehouse off Albert Square on Lloyd Street, the 2Js Coffee bar and jazz club opened. Owner Jack Jackson, who also ran the Mogambo coffee bar on Lower Mosley Street, described the 2Js (a name not too dissimilar to Soho's 2Is club) as 'The Most Luxurious Jazz Club In The North'. During the day the club functioned as a coffee bar selling sandwiches and coffee to city office workers, but after 6.30pm it became an unlicensed jazz club. It wasn't too long before Jackson, tempted by the prospect of attracting teenage money, started promoting the 2Js as a 'Teenage and Teetotal Club'. The 2Js was a great success, teenagers flocked to the new club in their hundreds, and by October, Jackson was booking groups to fill the interval between the sets played by trad bands. Unfortunately not everybody accepted the intrusion of beat groups and their followers. There was resentment in some quarters, and a few skirmishes between the regular diehard jazz followers and the new beat fans.

In an attempt to please everybody, Jackson adopted a 'Trad and Pop' policy and introduced late night sessions. On a Saturday night the club would feature for example, the Louisiana or Sunset Jazz Band until 11.30pm. The club would then close for thirty minutes and re-open at midnight, for the teenage membership who would 'jump and jive' to enthusiastic versions of 'Lucille' or 'What I'd Say' by local groups like the Fourtones. The 2Js continued into 1961 but hit financial trouble and Jackson's novel 'Trad and Pop' experiment ended in June. For a short time 'Disc Only' sessions replaced live music (the last pop act, Johnny Kidd and the Pirates appearing on 28th June) but by July 1961 the 2Js had closed.

London 1960 – Home-grown R&B

Whilst trad jazz was doing its best to co-exist with the emerging beat groups in Manchester and Liverpool, in London a group of jazz players were sowing the seeds of what was to become the British Rhythm & Blues movement. Back in 1957–58, bandleader Chris Barber had made a series of tours with visiting Blues singers such as Bill Broonzy and Muddy Waters. The tours had a tremendous impact on two of Barber's Band, guitarist Alexis Korner, and banjo player Cyril Davies, both who had been with Barber since the early 1950s. Korner and Davies, both like-minded spirits, were eager to pursue the 'new' blues music coming out of America and started a club called the London Blues and Barrelhouse Club on Thursday nights at a Soho pub called the Roundhouse, playing a hybrid of jazz and blues. Despite appearing with touring artists like Sonny Terry and Brownie McGhee, Memphis Slim and again Muddy Waters, the venture was too far ahead of its time and failed to sustain enough support.

47

They returned to the Chris Barber Band, which by early 1960 had started to feature a Rhythm & Blues spot in the band's repertoire with Ottilie Patterson on vocals. By 1961 the R&B spot was attracting larger audiences and this encouraged Korner and Davies (by now playing harmonica) to once again break with the Barber Jazz band to form Blues Incorporated. Opposition from orthodox jazz musicians to the amplified sound of Blues Incorporated[1] forced Davies and Korner to seek-out more suitable premises and on 17th March 1962, Korner and Davies opened the Ealing Rhythm & Blues Club in a basement below a tea shop near the local Ealing underground station.

The Marquee Club

Every band wanted to copy the 12-bar blues of Jimmy Reed and everybody wanted to pose with a harmonica.

The Ealing Club had become the focal point in England for Rhythm & Blues and attracted many future British rock stars. By the summer of '62, the success and popularity of Blues Incorporated led to a residency at the famous Marquee Club in Soho. First opened by Chris Barber and Harold Pendleton in May 1962 in Oxford Street, the club later relocated to Wardour Street, with John Gee replacing Chris Barber. At the Marquee the line up for Blues Incorporated changed almost weekly. Mick Jagger, Keith Richard, and Dick Taylor, who had been together in a band called the Blue Boys, and regular visitors to the Ealing Club, drew much inspiration from watching the early performances of Korner and Davies. Eric Clapton, a member of another Rhythm & Blues outfit the Roosters, was one of many young British blues players who also guested with the band.

With ambitions to form his own band, occasional member Brian Jones, started rehearsing with Jagger, by now one of Blues Incorporated's featured vocalists, and fellow musicians Keith Richard and Dick Taylor. A radio commitment at the BBC Studios for Blues Incorporated in June 1962 without Jagger and other fringe members, proved to be a timely opportunity for Jagger, Richard, Jones and Co. On the same day as the Blues Incorporated broadcast, 'Brian Jones and Mick Jagger and the Rolling Stones' made their Marquee debut playing a Chuck Berry and Bo Diddley influenced style of Rhythm & Blues. By the end of '62 with new recruits, pianist Ian Stewart, Bill Wyman and Charlie Watts, the fledgling Stones were making demos and touring the country.

In November of 1962, original co-founder Cyril Davies left Blues Incorporated to form the Cyril Davies All Stars, and concentrated on playing a more earthy style of Chicago Rhythm & Blues. Alexis Korner, whose preferred style was the post-war electrified Blues of Chicago, replaced Cyril Davies with organist Graham Bond, another musician from the old jazz school.

48   Although it is impossible to generalise, beat groups, after

MARQUEE
90 Wardour St., London, W.1
Thursday, April 30th
LONG JOHN BALDRY
and the HOOCHIE COOCHIE MEN featuring ROD STEWART
Friday, May 1st
THE YARDBIRDS
THE AUTHENTICS
Saturday, May 2nd
JOE HARRIOTT QUINTET
MORRISSEY/ GARRICK
Sunday, May 3rd
JAZZ 625
CHRIS BARBER
CHAMPION JACK DUPREE
Admission by ticket only
Monday, May 4th
MANFRED MANN
MARK LEEMAN 5
Tuesday, May 5th
BLUE BEAT
THE BLUE BEATS & GIRL SATCHMO
Wednesday, May 6th
HUMPHREY LYTTELTON

initially being inspired by the acoustic skiffle of Donegan, had progressed via the Fender guitar, the white rock and roll of Presley and the black rock and roll of Little Richard. In truth, like the early Rhythm & Blues bands,[2] their inspiration came from a music that had derived from the post-war amplified R&B of North American cities like Memphis, Chicago and Detroit. In time, beat groups and the early Rhythm & Blues bands would fuse into one, and by the mid 1960s form the backbone of the British pop music scene.

Origins Of Mod

'The student crowds that attended the all night 'trad' raves of the late '50s, early 60s at the Alexandria Palace were strictly anti-Pop. They wore CND badges, baggy jumpers, sugar sack shifts, open-toed sandals and jeans. Nicknamed 'leapniks' by the performing musicians they would leap up and down, out of time with the beat, from one foot to the other like performing bears.'
George Melly

The modern jazz fans who attended clubs like the Flamingo in the late '50s were very much into a jazz form influenced by Charlie Parker's New York bebop, which had originated in the New York jazz clubs of the late 1940s, and the West Coast 'Cool Jazz' of Gerry Mulligan. They had absolutely nothing in common with their trad jazz counterparts. The worlds of the impoverished student 'traddie' and the hip, semi-sophisticated, rather aloof mod jazz fan were poles apart.

An early example of this cultural division was illustrated at the Albert Hall in the late 1950s, at a National Jazz Federation concert, the first part of which was dedicated to trad and the second part modern jazz. The trad fans, in the main college students, left after the first half of the concert having absolutely no interest in what was to follow. In a similar show of indifference a large proportion of the mod jazz fans refused to take their seats until the trad fans had left. Amongst the modern jazz fans were a number of short-haired youths in smart four button continental Ivy League suits with velvet collars.

The Mod's intrusion into the modern jazz scene was probably more down to the appeal of its exclusivity and cool image. Almost certainly, the birth of the Mod movement was helped on its way by the reaction to trad, and the square and staid state of British pop in general. Maybe it just happened to be the time when males began to look to fashion as a way of expressing themselves – when youths started dressing up to go out at night. Obviously an extension or progression from the Ted era – identifying or bonding within a group by dress code.

By late 1960 there was a small teenage element within the modern jazz fraternity which frequented the late night jazz clubs of London's West End. They were attracted for a variety of reasons: modern jazz was a minority music, defiantly anti-pop, was way out of the reach of the masses, and so became an 'in' crowd thing. It was perfect for the initiated, fashion conscious late night clubbers and after-hours crowd. Modern sophisticated American jazz, ultra cool and underground – in complete contrast to the very un-cool trad scene and it's bearded and scruffy beer swilling 'ravers'. The example set by these early 'modernists' laid the foundations of what, by mid 1963, was to be the youth culture in the capital – the Mod scene of the West End.

Just as important was the Mods' appearance and image; handcrafted shoes, back-combed **49**

hair, Italian single breasted box jackets and narrowed trousers cut with a small 'V' at the bottom of the seam. Meeting up at cliquish coffee bars and jazz clubs such as the Flamingo, the prototype Mod possibly numbered no more than a couple of dozen. Their world was all about being seen about the West End. The spectacle of these pioneers of teenage fashion swaggering around like peacocks in their 'bum freezer' jackets, must have caused quite a stir – a reaction they would surely have appreciated.

The Oasis 1961

In the late summer of 1961, the old 2Js premises were bought by three businessmen who had strong links with the Manchester jazz scene – Hugh Goodwin, Rick Dixon and John Orr. And on 4th November, after considerable refurbishment, the club reopened as the Oasis Coffee Bar and Dancing Club. Advertised as 'Manchester's Most Fab Club for the Young' – right from the start the aim of the Oasis management was to attract a teenage membership. The battle for supremacy between the beat group and the jazz band was over. The new '60s teenager wanted beat music, and despite the Oasis management's personal interest in jazz, from a commercial viewpoint, the potential income from teenagers couldn't be ignored so the Oasis went 'pop'. Rick Dixon also ran an artist booking agency, and used contacts he had made whilst being involved in the jazz scene to book groups for the club. The large number of up-and-coming beat groups available in Manchester alone, was too good to pass up on. One month after opening, the Oasis started auditioning and booking local talent as support to top American acts, the first of which was Gene Vincent.

Since the late '50s, Manchester's beat groups had been travelling to Liverpool to appear at clubs like the Cavern, competing on the same northern circuit as their Merseyside counterparts. But beat group traffic travelled both ways up and down the A580, and one of the first of the Liverpool groups to appear at a packed Oasis in January was Derry and the Strangers. Later that month Dixon, via Liverpool impresario Brian Epstein, booked the Beatles. Virtually unknown at the time outside of Liverpool, the Beatles made their first of several appearances at the Oasis on 2nd February 1962.

Manchester 1962

As in London, the Twist had replaced the jive as the latest dance at city centre clubs like the Oasis. It was by far the most popular of the many dance crazes that had started to arrive from America. The Bodega quickly cottoned on but still struggled to shake off its jazz connections.

Bodega Club – 'The With It Place', Cross Street, Manchester
4th October 1962 'Twist & Trad Night'
Olympics, Dakotas and Wayne Fontana

There was a time when guys politely asked girls to dance – then bang.

Despite the dance floor revolution caused by the Twist, the early '60s working class Northern teenager-about-town was still a rock and roller at heart. Girls still sported back-combed 'beehive' hairstyles, wore pretty skirts and stilettos and males still had the look of the late 1950s – shirt collars turned over the outside of the jacket collar, 'winkle-pickers', sideburns and semi-Ted hairstyles. As in most provincial cities, teenage fashion in Manchester was desperately looking for a direction. In less than eighteen months it would find its way; as in central London, teenage fashion would be redefined by a new generation of kids, the Mods. For the moment though, in the coffee bar dance clubs and dancehalls of Manchester, teenagers were quite happy being teenagers – listening to pop records, entering 'Grand Twist Competitions' and jiving to local beat groups at clubs like the Oasis.

More and more teenage clubs opened in Manchester to cater for the demand, not least future Mod haunt the Jungfrau which opened in Cathedral Street on 30th November 1962.

**JUNGFRAU BRITAIN'S FIRST
SWISS COFFEE DANCE CLUB
OPEN NIGHTLY**

By the time the Oasis had celebrated its first birthday in November 1962, the club was publishing its own magazine *Teen Scene* and had hired a DJ called Mac Magonagall Lacey – the Oasis claimed to be 'Manchester's Top Teenage Attraction'.

**Saturday 8th December 1962
OASIS – OASIS
The Beatles (Love Me Do)**

The Plaza Ballroom on Oxford Road, attempted to get 'with it' and stop the teenage defection to coffee bar dance clubs. The following example was probably by accident Manchester's first 'All-Dayer'.

**Plaza Oxford Street
Gigantic Boxing Day Marathon
26th December 3pm–11.00pm
Records – Discs – Jive – Twist 3/-**

Towards the end of 1962, Manchester was considered a safe enough bet by promoters, to stage a Rhythm & Blues concert, featuring nine acts, at the city's prestigious Free Trade Hall. Manchester's clubland was by now the busiest outside of London and regarded by touring American artists as the most important call after the capital. Although still sticking with the safe 'Jazz Package' label, the Manchester show was the latest of an increasing number of live Rhythm & Blues concerts to be staged in the UK (most were held in London) since the late '50's and early '60's. It could only help increase public awareness, and in particular, teenage interest in Rhythm & Blues. The line-up at the Free Trade Hall boasted several top American R&B stars. **51**

'**Manchester kids have always had an obsession with black American music, ever since the mid '50s when both black and white musicians from Burtonwood US Air Force Base, began living and playing in the city .'**

CHRIS LEE

Free Trade Hall Manchester
JAZZ PACKAGE
Helen Hulme, Sonny Terry and Brownie McGee
Memphis Slim, John Lee Hooker, Willie Dixon
Jump Jackson and T-Bone Walker
9 Top R&B Stars
Saturday October 21st 1962...TV seats...7/6d

In an enthusiastic article in the *Manchester Evening News*, prior to another R&B concert at the Free Trade Hall, jazz columnist Jack Florin perfectly judged the mood of the city by hailing the arrival 'at last' of Rhythm & Blues to our shores. At the show on Sunday 9th December 1962, Louis Jordan appeared with Chris Barber and Ottilie Patterson to a packed house, with the admission price a mere three shillings and sixpence. The show, cautiously billed as 'Anglo-American Jazz Unlimited!' was the city's second major R&B concert in less than three months, clearly underlining the fact that promoters now regarded black music as a viable commercial proposition.

Manchester – Late Nights

The first club in Manchester to feature R&B was the Bodega Jazz Club, with Alexis Korner's Blues Incorporated appearing in March 1963 and Cyril Davies' All Stars on Saturday 7th July 1963. Advertising in the *Manchester Evening News*, the Bodega described Rhythm & Blues as 'The Most Exciting Sound Of The Century', and began holding 'R&B Only' nights every Wednesday.

The first club since Jack Jackson's 2Js to hold regular and legal All-Nighters[3] was the Three Coins. What had primarily started out as late night jazz sessions back in October 1962 (for example Johnny Dankworth 6th October 1962) developed into all-nighters, featuring a mixed bill of local trad outfits and beat groups. Then eventually the appearance of London-based white R&B and jazz groups (15th March 1963 Graham Bond, 15th June 1963 Blues Incorporated). 'Ravers' down at the Three Coins and the Bodega were, in the main, older jazz fans and duffle-coated college students.

6th March BODEGA – Tonight and every Wednesday – R&B
'The Most Exciting Sound Of The Century' as those who packed
the Bodega, last Saturday to hear A K Blues Inc. will agree!

'The El Rio, Macclesfield, had Wheel connections via Jack Abadi, it was tiny, a real coffee dance club. I saw the Beatles there, it was packed and as the crowd got more hostile John Lennon leaned forward and punched one of them in the face – then total mayhem broke out.'

BRIAN SMITH

CHAPTER FOUR
The Left Wing Coffee House

JUST OFF ALBERT SQUARE, AROUND THE BLOCK FROM THE OASIS ON LLOYD STREET (EX-2JS Club), in yet another converted basement cellar on Brazennose Street, was the Left Wing Coffee House. The Left Wing had been open since the late '50s and had once housed Socialist reading rooms. Like the Oasis during the day, The Left Wing was just another coffee bar selling salad rolls and drinks to students and city centre passing trade, but at night the club became transformed into a bohemian stronghold for 'cats in the know' – hep talking beatniks, art students, early CND members and Socialists, pseudo-intellectuals and bearded folkies. The Left Wing ignored the temptation to cater for rock and roll, it was strictly 'underground', an anti-pop haunt that featured live 'finger in the ear' folk music and poetry readings. Although it was not the type of coffee bar club to openly seek commercial success, on one rare occasion its

The Left Wing Coffee House

owner, Andrew Capp, in an attempt to attract more female members, placed the following advertisement in the *Manchester Evening News*, which summed up The Left Wing perfectly:

TONIGHT LEFT WING
BRAZENNOSE STREET
ALBERT SQUARE
FEMININE TYPE CATS
REDUCED RATE

It might have been an idea to advertise more often, as although the Left Wing was successful and unique in its role as a socialist meeting place, it just wasn't a viable concern and by the end of 1962, in complete contrast to its famous neighbour the Oasis, it went to the wall.

The Twisted Wheel Club – Brazennose Street 27th January 1963–11th September 1965

The beatnik, folk and protest crowd moved on and, in January 1963, the run down and by now liquidated premises of the Left Wing Coffee Bar were leased by a family of businessmen from West Didsbury, the Abadi brothers. Competition for any new coffee bar club in Manchester was fierce, especially from the Oasis, which reigned supreme. In fact the owners of the Oasis **55**

Live on stage at Jigsaw, Manchester. Roger Eagle was keen to book Bo Diddley for the Wheel but the Jigsaw offered more cash

did not regard the reopening of the Left Wing, or its new owners, as a threat. They gave it a couple of months and predicted that it would soon be back up for sale.

Nothing could have been further from the truth, for the purchasing of the Left Wing by the Abadis was not just an act of blind faith. After deciding that a career in the club business would be more interesting than the one he had in the rag trade, Ivor Abadi had gone into partnership with his elder brother Jack[1], who had been involved in the club business since 1957. The Abadi brothers were astute businessmen and had every intention of making a success of their new venture. Ivor, a shrewd man with a head for financial matters, spent the next few sleepless nights with Jack mentally organising the new venture. One job was to think of a name for the club and after much head scratching (The Spinning Wheel and the Rolling Wheel were names considered) it was Ivor who finally came up with the name the Twisted Wheel. Immediately, the club underwent a massive transformation. Its cavernous walls were painted and the lighting improved, the club's famous wooden cart wheels were cleverly installed within the cellar walls, dividing the club's network of interconnecting rooms. The installation of the wheels in the walls not only added to the club's distinct decor, they also enabled members to see through the large spokes into adjoining rooms, increasing the sense of space and size of the club.

Within two weeks the Twisted Wheel was ready. Although open for business for a couple of nights a week earlier, the Abadis proudly announced the club's official opening as Saturday 27th January 1963. Opened by local pop star Karl 'Wimoweh' Denver, those present at the Twisted Wheel on launch night were to witness the first of many appearances by Dean West and the Hellions, a typical 'gold lame' beat group.

For the first nine months, the Wheel, like many other coffee clubs at the time, played host to an abundance of similar beat groups. The original bohemian Left Wing crowd did not return. The Twisted Wheel was a new club with a new crowd of teenage beat music fans and a management more in tune with the commercial potential of teenage pop music (like the Oasis) rather than folk, poetry and protest. This was the first of several changes in the club's music policy, and others would follow.

Derek Leckenby, formerly of Herman's Hermits, who helped make sandwiches and would later become a doorman, recalls one lunchtime when a customer called Geoff Mullin came in and suggested to the new owners that they should play records, which after a brief discussion the brothers agreed to. The management of the Wheel were keen to get their new venture up and running, and so Geoff Mullin became the first Wheel disc jockey. After a couple of successful lunchtime sessions, Mullin began playing a mixture of rock and roll and pop records in the evenings. Within a matter of days a DJ area had been installed at the back of the club. The first advert for the Twisted Wheel Club was placed in the entertainment section of the *Manchester Evening News* within days of opening.

Twisted Wheel Sunday Club 27th January 1963
Free for Members 7.30–12 Midnight

Saturday 2nd February
Tonight Twisted Wheel - Non Stop Dancing – 7.30–1.00am
Manchester's Newest & Most Unusual Atmosphere

Throughout the spring and summer of 1963 the Wheel, like other beat clubs in Manchester featured live music on Friday, Saturday and Sunday. Groups from the city like Brent Wade & the Wanderers, Danny & the Dominators, Wayne Fontana & the Jets – and for three shillings on Friday 22nd February, the Hollies, fast becoming one of Manchester's top groups. Other attractions included Liverpool's Rhythm & Blues Incorporated, the Spidermen and Four Most, Sheffield's Pontiacs and Birmingham's Renegades. During the week 'Disc Only' non-stop dancing sessions were hosted by the strangely named Peter (Bongo) Von Dort. But the Abadi brothers' biggest coup was only a matter of months away. Their luck or instinct in employing an unknown out-of-town DJ called Roger Eagle would lead to the second change in the club's music policy in less than a year of opening – from beat to Rhythm & Blues.

Just around the corner, the Oasis continued to book the top available acts and by the late summer of 1963 membership was in excess of 32,000.

Tuesday 26th November – Stamford Hall, Altrincham
Rolling Stones – 6/-
Wednesday 27th November – Memorial Hall, Northwich
Rolling Stones – 6/-
Thursday 28th November – Wigan's Empress Ballroom
Rolling Stones 5/-
Friday 29th Nov – Baths Hall, Urmston
Rolling Stones – pay at the door

The Rolling Stones found there was plenty of work available outside of the home counties. After quitting the residency at the Crawdaddy Club in Richmond[2] to tour the provinces as support act to Bo Diddley and Little Richard, on August 30th 1963, the Rolling Stones appeared to a packed Oasis. On the same night the Wheel could only boast the Marauders from Stoke. However, the Oasis' reign at the top was almost over; within a month the Wheel would begin to hold weekly R&B All-Nighters and six months later lay claim to the title of King of Clubs.

Fri 30th Aug - OASIS - ROLLING STONES
Fri 30th Aug - Twisted Wheel - Marauders

September 1963 – Roger Eagle

It was from a chance visit to the Twisted Wheel that a young Roger Eagle got his chance to make a mark on the Manchester music scene. One year earlier, Eagle had travelled to Manchester from Oxford by motorbike to start work at the Kellogg's factory on Trafford Park. Walking into the Wheel one lunchtime clutching a bundle of Chuck and Bo, Chess and Checker albums (bought from Ancill's), Roger Eagle took a seat amid the hiss and chatter of the lunchtime trade. Approached by one of the Abadi brothers he was asked whether he knew anything about 'that' Rhythm & Blues music. Eagle who had never deejayed before in his life, couldn't believe his luck. His enthusiasm and knowledge of music impressed the Abadis and Eagle bluffed his way into becoming resident disc jockey for one pound a night.

Roger Eagle's musical taste had been nurtured during the mid '50s, aged fourteen, listening to Rock and Roll on the Alan Freed Show (broadcast on American Forces Network in Frankfurt) and the Gus Goodwin Show on Radio Luxembourg. Other early influences included his main man Little Richard, saxophonist Gerry Mulligan, George Lewis, Bunk Johnson and Kid Ory. Like many other kids his age, Eagle liked jazz and from time to time listened to skiffle, but his main passion before discovering Rhythm & Blues was rock and roll. Eagle's own words however perfectly describe who his most major influence was: 'I was originally a rock and roll nut until I heard Ray Charles' 'In Person' and 'Live At Newport' LPs in the back end of the '50s. For me 1958 was the year rock and roll died.'

At the time Roger occasionally visited the Cona coffee bar on Tib Lane, which within twelve months would be the biggest Mod hangout in Manchester after the Wheel. At the Cona, it was common practice for kids to take in their own records to play and Eagle was no exception. Here, and at the nearby Town Hall pub, Eagle soon found himself meeting up with like-minded people. Naturally enough when Eagle landed the job at the Twisted Wheel, the Manchester R&B Mafia followed him. Eagle was behind the decks, the music policy was Rhythm & Blues – Manchester was about to redefine the appreciation of black music in the UK.

Within six months of landing the job at the Wheel, Roger Eagle's DJ reputation was second to none. His boundless energy, enthusiasm and dedication helped to transform the Twisted Wheel's stature and future place in music history from just one of Manchester's coffee bars to the number one R&B club outside of London.

On Saturday 28th September 1963, the Abadis opened the Twisted Wheel for the first of its legendary 'All-Nighters' with the Graham Bond Quartet, and an unknown Spencer Davies playing an inspired 12-string and harmonica blues set. Spencer Davies had been spotted by Ivor Abadi playing in a pub in Birmingham and was encouraged to try his luck at the Twisted Wheel. It was the start of a long association with Spencer Davies, soon to form the Spencer Davis Quartet.

Spencer Davies at the first Wheel All-Nighter supporting Graham Bond

In fact, the Abadis as Sandburne Enterprises Limited, turned down the chance of managing Spencer Davis. Although they already had a number of groups on their books, including the Blues Giants and Ivan's Meads, they did not consider themselves as serious artist managers. Managing Spencer Davis simply didn't fit into the family's future business plans.

Gonna Wait Until The Midnight Hour

'They had this tall guy deejaying, he looked more like a Teddy Boy than a Mod, but he had the dance floor in the palm of his hand – it was Roger Eagle.'
Eddie Barnett

At the first all-nighter, Roger Eagle played records that had never been heard of before in Manchester. 'Help Me' by Sonny Boy Williamson – the first record to be played at a Twisted Wheel All-Nighter, 'Wednesday Night Prayer Meeting' by Charlie Mingus, 'Tell The Truth' by Ray Charles and 'Road Runner' by Bo Diddley. R&B had arrived big time in Manchester.

Twisted Wheel – 'Late Night Rhythm and Blues'
Every Saturday from 12 midnight

Grand Opening Saturday September 28th
Exclusive first ever appearance by the North
of England's answer to Ray Charles
The Graham Bond Quartet!

Word spread like wildfire that the Wheel was the place to go to, and the place to be seen at. It became a home for its own teenage misfits and not just another twist and jive dance club. As the popularity of R&B increased, the demand for pop and beat music waned and many of the beat fans either moved on or changed their taste.

There was no serious Mod scene as yet in Manchester, but within six months, much to the horror of parents, the Twisted Wheel would become synonymous with rebellious teenagers, 'All-Night dance raves', black music and amphetamines. It would become the home for the first northern 'in' crowd and the northern centre for teenage fashion – other clubs just couldn't compete. The Twisted Wheel's strange cavernous atmosphere and distinctive decor was unique. The vision and business skills of the Abadi brothers, together with Eagle's musical awareness, **59** forged the most perfect combination in Manchester's clubland. Unfortunately, the Wheel began to attract the attention of the press and Manchester's Vice Squad.

Recollections of Brazennose Street – Ken White

As a former member of the 5 Dimensions who were a popular live act at the Wheel, Ken remembered the first All-Nighter at Brazennose Street. White later played at the Whitworth Street Wheel with the Score.

'I joined the 5 Dimensions in July 1963 and went straight into gigging with little or no rehearsal. At that time we were just a five-piece band with Rod Stewart as singer and harmonica player. Within two weeks we'd been placed with a singer from Birmingham called Jimmy Powell. This was the brain-child of our agent Malcolm Nixon. The group had very little say in the matter – it was take it or leave it if we wanted to work. Not long after Powell had joined, we had a Saturday night booking at Leeds University. When I asked at the end of the gig whether any arrangements had been made for staying the night, I was told we were going to Manchester to a great new club. I was the rookie in the band and just went along with everything. I had come straight out of a pop band playing Bobby Darin songs and the like, into what was then the new musical world of Blues and Rhythm & Blues.

'How anybody knew about the Wheel is a mystery to me – maybe the 5 D's had played a gig there already or were booked to play a future date. Anyway, we drove to Manchester and arrived well after midnight and people were still queuing to get in. Powell managed to blag his way in, so we didn't pay. It was dark and sweaty and I thought it was a bit weird, but it had a superb atmosphere, felt great and the music was brilliant. I had never been to any club quite like it. Later we played the Liverpool Cavern and other similar cellar clubs and I realised that it wasn't so unusual.

'My first visit to the Wheel was in fact for the first All-Nighter. Jimmy Powell got chatting to a guy there he knew from Birmingham called Spencer Davies – he was appearing that night on harmonica and 12-string guitar. Spencer told Jimmy that back in Birmingham he was rehearsing and putting a band together and that he had this young fifteen-year-old kid lined up for vocals, guitar and piano. He was talking about Stevie Winwood, of course.

'When the main band of the evening appeared on stage, I was shocked – they were totally unlike anybody I had ever seen before. They were called the Graham Bond Quartet and weren't an R&B band at all, just a bunch of 'old jazzers' trying to get a gig by playing 'Got My Mojo Working'. I didn't like them then, or later, which of course doesn't mean anything – just my taste at the time. I'm sure that they were good players – in fact certain of it. Bond was big, moustachioed, with long greasy hair. He played organ and sang poor vocals – blues shouting I suppose. Jack Bruce played stand up double bass and Dick Heckstall-Smith was on tenor sax – thinning on top with a silly jazz/beatnik goatee. Ginger Baker on drums looked the epitome of all jazz drummers. He took drugs (shock horror!) and was thin with close-cropped hair and a haggard face.

60   'After the All-Nighter, people congregated at a nearby café which we called the 'Greasy

'The hippest of the hip at the time, was John Mayall, who along with Victor Brox, was inspired by West Coast cool, and played jazz and R&B – they all wanted to be black. One day John painted himself with potassium permanganate but turned green instead of brown.'

CHRIS LEE

THE TWISTED WHEEL CLUB
26 Brazennose Street, Manchester 1
*
Late Night Rhythm & Blues
SATURDAY . 13th JUNE . 1964
(FROM 12 MIDNIGHT)
JOHN LEE HOOKER
PLUS
JOHN MAYALL BLUES BREAKERS
* MEMBERS ONLY . . . 7/6 *
*
MEMBERSHIP CARDS MUST BE PRODUCED WITH THIS TICKET

Spoon' – I don't think that was its actual name, but the food certainly was! I saw a few frightening sights at that café.

'People coming down from the pills they had taken to keep them awake. Miserable, depressed, dirty and scruffy teenagers mingling of course with drunks and all the various flotsam and jetsam that hang around a city in the early hours of the morning. I think the café was mainly used by people in the newspaper trade. In later days though it became a regular thing, especially if we had played the Wheel, to end up back at Roger Eagle's flat at Wilbraham Road on the Sunday morning – to listen to records or just crash out.'

R'N B IN THE NORTH-EAST

NEWCASTLE *(Home of the Animals)*
every Friday
CLUB A'GOGO

WHITLEY BAY *(By the sea)*
every Sunday
AGO GO'S CLUB

MIDDLESBRO'
every Wednesday
THE SCENE CLUB

Biggest attraction for the North-East in June
JOHN LEE HOOKER
at Middlesbro' — June 4th
at Newcastle — June 5th

'I remember Eric Clapton coming back to my flat with this pretty little Mod girl. He just sat there disinterested listening to Freddy King records.' **Roger Eagle.**

Brazennose Street Wheel – 1963 continued

The day after the Wheel's first All-Nighter, the Place in Hanley, Stoke-on-Trent, opened up its doors to Rhythm & Blues for the first time. Black dance music had reached the provinces. Other pioneer clubs included the Three Coins in Leeds, the Esquire in Sheffield, the Club-A-Go-Go in Newcastle-upon-Tyne and the Scene in Middlesborough. With British artists for all these clubs being booked mainly from the established and thriving London club scene.

The Twisted Wheel All-Nighters were held every Saturday from 'Midnight 'til Dawn'. It was the perfect after-hours meeting place for working groups like the Dimensions, Paramounts or Hollies (who used to rehearse at the Wheel), who earlier on a Saturday night may have been appearing at any one of dozens of clubs in the city centre.

The second All-Nighter on the 5th October saw the return to Manchester of John Mayall, who with the Blues Breakers made the first of many appearances. The eccentric Mayall, a former graphic artist from Manchester, had been playing blues guitar since the mid '50s, having formed his first group the Powerhouse 4 just after completing his National Service. Encouraged by Alexis Korner, Mayall had visited London, where he had formed the Blues Breakers, and later recorded his first album live at the famous Klooks Kleek Club.

On the same night as the club's second all-nighter, the Bodega, eager to get on the R&B bandwagon announced an 'R&B Rave Nite' with Cyril Davies' All Stars, the Velvettes and Long John Baldry. Essentially a pop club, the Oasis attendances were still the best in Manchester, though the Twisted Wheel was proving to be a serious threat to business. Occasionally however, the Wheel's closest neighbour and biggest rival, came up trumps.

Oasis – This Monday 28th October 1963
'The Bo Diddley Show' – In person
Bo Diddley
Bo Diddley
Bo Diddley
Bo Diddley
with Jerome and the Duchess
Country Gents – Beatmakers
Pay at the Door. Please come early.

The newly-formed Spencer Davis Group[3], featuring teenage protégé Stevie Winwood, appeared twice during the first three months of the All-Nighters starting, first on 26th October and on the weekend of the Kennedy assassination, Saturday November 23rd 1963. Repeat appearances by Graham Bond, John Mayall and the Blues Breakers together with Jimmy Powell and the 5 Dimensions, Liverpool's Roadrunners and the Rockin' Berries were the more significant bookings for the rest of '63.

Twisted Wheel – Early Session – The Renegades
Saturday Oct 12th – Late Night Rhythm and Blues
Recording Stars – 'Jimmy Powell and the Dimensions'
From Midnight Members Only 6/-

Twisted Wheel
Wed Oct 16th – Bongo Von Dort
Thursday 17th – Free For Girls

Twisted Wheel – Friday Oct 18th
By Popular Request The Nashville Men
Tomorrow Night Dance in Manchester's
Newest and Most Exciting Dance Hall

Saturday October 26th Twisted Wheel Presents
Early Session – Hellions
Late Night Rhythm and Blues
Every Saturday from 12 Midnight
TO-NIGHT TO-NIGHT
Spencer Davis Quartet
Members Only 6/-

London 1963 – The Flamingo

In Soho the Mod scene had expanded. By late 1961, the smart suit and short hair Ivy League look adopted by a number of the original mod jazz crowd, began influencing the dress style of working class teenagers who had started to head up West at weekends, from the suburbs of London and the home counties.

By 1963, long queues outside clubs like the Marquee and Flamingo in the West End, and the Crawdaddy in Richmond typified the success Rhythm & Blues was having in the capital.

The Marquee was buzzing and its reputation had spread throughout the country. Marquee favourites Cyril Davies and the All Stars, recognised as probably the best and most authentic sounding of the early British R&B bands, had a cult following and toured the UK extensively (on 7th July 1963 at the Bodega, Manchester), occasionally with the newly formed Rolling Stones in support.

In 1963 the Flamingo Club, for years the home of respectable British jazz artists such as Tubby Hayes and Ronnie Scott, introduced all-night jazz and Rhythm & Blues sessions. The Mods claimed it as their own and attendances at the Flamingo increased as the club became the place to be seen.

The resident band was Georgie Fame & The Blue Flames. Fame, from Leigh in Lancashire and one time member of local group the Dominoes (later the Beat Boys) had been playing in London since 1959, performing in Larry Parnes 'Rock and Trad' shows. Parnes had hoped to groom Fame for stardom along the same lines as Billy Fury, but by the end of 1962 Fame and his band had headed south and were busy working the London jazz club scene. Securing a residency at the Flamingo, Fame and his combo added a jazzy, sophistication to the blues of Mose Allison, the R&B of James Brown and Ray Charles and Jamaican bluebeat – in total contrast to the hard-edged hollering of Blues Incorporated, Cyril Davies and similar bands around the corner at the Marquee. Fame was now managed by Rik Gunnel, who was gathering quite a brood of stars around him – including Zoot Money, John Mayall and Chris Farlowe.

At the 'All-Nighter', Mods and jazz fans mingled with West Indians, late night party animals and students. The All-Nighter also attracted a number of black US servicemen, who, temporarily stationed in the South of England, would introduce the latest American dance styles to the club. Live or on record, jazz, soul or R&B, if it was 'cool' or you could dance to it, it was played at the Flamingo.

Amphetamines were already on the scene around the

West End jazz haunts well before the Mods arrived and were freely available. Drinamyl tablets, better known as 'Purple Hearts', had been available on prescription since their introduction by Smith, Kline and French in 1951. The whole nature of the All-Nighter, the driving beat of R&B, the temperature and long periods of energy-sapping dancing encouraged the misuse of 'Purple Hearts' or 'Blues' (pronounced blue-ees). Amphetamines were as much a part of the scene as the clothes you wore or the way you danced.

The teenage abuse of amphetamines, and crimes involving the supply or theft of amphetamines, would become such a problem, not only in London but in every major city, that in 1964 the Misuse of Drugs Act was passed by Parliament, making it an offence to carry prohibited drugs without a prescription.

By the end of '63, the Flamingo was hosting the top all-night Rhythm & Blues session in the country. Although still essentially a jazz club that pandered to R&B on a Saturday at the 'All Nighter' (later also on Sunday afternoons), its membership would have seemed sophisticated in comparison to the crowd attending the early Twisted Wheel All-Nighters. Before the arrival of the first Manchester Mods, mostly upwardly mobile Jewish youths, the early '64 crowd at the Wheel was as primitive as you could get. A mixed bag of genuine R&B and rock and roll fans, curious late

TWISTED WHEEL
26 BRAZENNOSE STREET
MANCHESTER 2
presents
Late Night R & B
(Every Sat. from 12 midnight)
MEMPHIS SLIM
and
ZOOT MONEY'S
BIG ROLL BAND
MAY 9, 1964
Members only 7/6d.

night young clubbers, runaways and out-of-town dossers. After the start of the Brazennose Street All-Nighters, the Wheel became totally committed to Rhythm & Blues (apart from mid week 'Pop Nights with Bongo'). Modern jazz never featured.

Although the Flamingo attracted a large number of West Indian and black American servicemen, local black youths rarely attended the Twisted Wheel. There was no sinister reason behind this, it was just that Manchester's Afro-Caribbean population already had a very lively jazz, bluebeat and ska scene in Moss Side at illegal shebeens and at clubs like the Reno and Nile.

London 1964 – The Scene Club – 'Put On Your Hi-Heal Sneakers'

'Stepping into Ham Yard still gives me the goose bumps.'
Jimmy Donnelly, early London Mod.

There were only a few venues the early style-conscious London teenager would go to. Sure the trend-setting prototype Mods had already begun to colonise cafés and shops in the West End, but as far as clubs went, apart from the 'All-Nighter' at the Flamingo and the Marquee, which in the main catered for jazz and the early British R&B groups, that was it.

Towards the tail end of 1963, two completely different types of club opened – La Discotheque on lower Wardour Street and the Scene Club situated in Ham Yard off Great Windmill Street. Ham Yard has a long and notorious history as a location for avant-garde music venues. In 1948, the Club 11, with Ronnie Scott and Johnny Dankworth, survived for two years before being closed for drug misuse. It was also known as the Cy Laurie under George Melly and the Piccadilly Jazz Club. The Scene and La Discotheque were the first clubs in the country aimed solely at the quickly expanding Mod scene.

La Discotheque, and in particular the Scene Club, provided the blueprint for hundreds of **65**

'Manchester differed from London in the sense that there were no specific mod clubs, they tended to be music-led. Some places like the Jigsaw had a mixture of music, one week they would have Wayne Fontana on, and the next Major Lance.'

BRIAN SMITH

club owners in the UK to follow.[4] The Mod movement, which a year earlier in late '62 had still been in its infancy, by the end of '63 had become the teenage scene in the West End. The Scene was at its core – the first purpose built club, for young teenage kids to go, to pose and listen to black R&B.

In terms of being a centre for Mods, the Scene and La Discotheque (which played bluebeat as well as Rhythm & Blues records) were at this time about six months ahead of the Wheel. With hindsight, this point is only of minor relevance, as the London Mod scene was very insular, and interested only in what was happening in the capital. Mod haunts in outer London were of little significance, let alone what was happening in Manchester. For now the whole Mod world was centered around Soho and nowhere else mattered…but that would change.

Because of this purist southern Mod attitude, it is not possible to draw too close a comparison between the Scene and the Brazennose Street Twisted Wheel. The Scene was first and foremost a club for Mods that played music Mods wanted to hear. The Twisted Wheel had a more liberal and tolerant membership. By 1964 the Twisted Wheel would have a huge Mod clientele and was by far the biggest Mod club outside of London, but it was never exclusively a Mods-only club. In the north, the love of black music had always overridden the strictest fashion codes.

Record Mirror kept close tabs on these new, less cliquey provincial venues, its weekly columns highlighting the good times at such places as the Wheel and the Esquire in Sheffield or the Place, Hanley. After all, it was a music paper not a fashion magazine. On 11th July 1964 it printed the following quotes about the Place, the membership of which stood at 5,000 in the summer of '64: 'The guv'nor place up north for sound and stage room, they get a really chic and swinging crowd up there' Georgie Fame; 'I like it there. They have a Hammond organ which is especially useful to us, and we find the people who turn up really do come to listen' Spencer Davis; 'It's great, a very good place to play. The audience is very appreciative, and the management always so friendly and helpful – you really feel welcome there' Paul Jones.

The Scene building was much like the Twisted Wheel, essentially a cellar with alcoves and stage, the only difference being that it was far smaller than the Wheel's premises in Manchester. Stairs led down into the Scene from Ham Yard, and a fire exit opened out onto Great Windmill Street. Although the decor was drab and scruffy, with paint splashed on the walls and stone floor, the clothes down there were just the opposite; very smart, hardly any jeans were worn at the early All-Nighters and if they were, they would be white Lee's or Levi's. Handmade mohair suits, suede jackets and full length leather coats were more likely. Smart and cool was the code, non-Mods wouldn't dare venture near the place.

BIG-RHYTHM & BLUES NIGHT
at the **La Discotheque Club**

SPECIAL

PASS

TO

LA DISCOTHEQUE
RHYTHM & BLUES NIGHT
17, WARDOUR STREET, W.1.   GER 4532

THURSDAYS

THE SCENE
Ham Yard (Off Gt. Windmill St.)

Monday
R & B DISC NIGHT with GUY STEVENS

Tuesday
OFF THE RECORD

Wednesday
BUBBLES & THE OUTRIGGERS

Thursday
RONNIE JONES THE NIGHT-TIMERS

Friday
THE CHESSMEN

Saturday
BARRY ST. JOHN

Pete Meaden, one of the early West End 'faces' hung out there. Meaden's claim to fame was as the man responsible for exposing Pete Townsend and future members of the High Numbers, later the Who, to this burgeoning new underground scene.

Owned by Ronan O'Rahilly, who later owned Radio Caroline, and Lionel Blake, the Scene had James 'Doctor Soul' Hamilton as disc jockey and Guy Stevens as the man to make things happen, mainly through his close connection with Chris Blackwell at Island Records. Hamilton was responsible for breaking many great records, not least of all Billy Young's 'The Sloopy' sent over from the States by Jerry Wexler. Between them they were probably the first British club DJs to play imported soul music.

Like Roger Eagle, Guy Stevens' background was rock and roll (he later caused controversy by claiming during an interview that Hitler was the first rock and roller). Nevertheless, Stevens was responsible for some big R&B records, many of which he either sent to or exchanged with Eagle. Because Stevens worked with Blackwell, and ran his Sue label, and with the subsequent links to the States, the music was only a week or so behind America. Plenty of scouts from British labels would wait and watch what the dance floor reaction was likely to be to these US imports, before deciding if they should get a UK airing. West End outlets such as Transat in Lisle Street, Atlantic Imports in Gloucester Avenue and Lee's Record Stall in Earlham Street, were now supplying US imports to both DJs and collectors. British released obscurities could be bought from certain shops around town such as Paul for Music in Cambridge Heath Road, or Lufton's in the West End. Guy Stevens even had one-off, twelve-inch 45rpm demos made especially for James Hamilton, Brian Peters and the other Scene Club DJs and if they packed the floor, within days they would be issued on the famous red and yellow Sue label. The Scene was famous, and influential, and the likes of Motown and Atlantic would send new releases over from the states for the DJs to spin.

At the Scene the dancing was superb. It was a major break from the traditional boy-girl, jive type styles. Dancing was now all about self-expression and was unrestricted freestyle. It was a way to get noticed, almost a ritual. Dancing made you feel good and gained you respect. Being 'cool' to girls was all part of the macho Mod attitude. Being the best dressed was all part of the deal, a way of becoming a 'face'. Being a smart dresser wasn't as easy as it would be a few years later, after the so-called fashion explosion that began according to the hype with 'Swinging Carnaby Street'. In 1963–64, Mod clothes had to be improvised, style was self taught, the only guide to being cool and a snappy dresser came from within the Mod movement itself. Like the originals had done a couple of years before them, Mods bought imported continental suits and made to measure mohairs from back street tailors in the pre-Carnaby West End. Dark glasses, short-cropped hair and Italian polo shirts, desert boots and thin knit sweaters completed the look.

Most Mods worked during the week, made good money, and lived for the crazy weekends down the West End. The Mod lifestyle was all about being cool, chromed scooters and parkas, handmade shirts or suits from John Stephens, black music and pills. A typical Saturday night was spent hanging around the West End until the Scene or Flamingo All-Nighter started and dance until 7.00am after dropping anything between twenty to thirty Purple Hearts. After the All-Nighter, the true diehard Mods would stay in the West End, possibly head down to Petticoat Lane, act cool and check out the scene, or hang out at places like Mick's Café on Fleet Street. Then it was a case of dropping more pills and then shooting off to the Sunday afternoon session at the Flamingo which started at 3.00pm. Georgie Fame and the Blue Flames would do a set called 'Twistin' with the Blue Flames' which despite the twist connotation was really an R&B, soul and modern jazz session. And when the afternoon came to a close, the Flamingo was the place to 'come down' from the amphetamine-fuelled weekend before work on Monday.

March of the Mods

What brought the attention of the Mod to the national press was not the fashion, culture, style or music of the modern '60s teenager, but the riots with Rockers at English seaside resorts during the Whitsun Bank holiday of May 1964. The contrasting lifestyles of the Mods and the Rockers made them an easy target for the press; short and clean hair versus long and greasy hair, scooters as opposed to motorbikes, Rhythm & Blues compared to rock and roll.

The press were up to what they do best – creating public hysteria over the lawlessness of modern youth, just as they had done eight years earlier when they had reported on the violent behaviour of Teddy Boys. Mods and Rockers were irresistibly newsworthy, ideal copy for the papers. The new '60s teenager was violent too, no different to the bikers from hell who belonged in the last decade. An easy story for the press, who could fuel the anger of their readers. At a stroke the press sent the Mod movement into orbit. When the fuss over the 'Beach Battles' at Brighton had subsided, the Mod movement proper was about two-years-old.

By the time Rediffusion's *Ready, Steady, Go!* had reached its first birthday in August '64, the Mod movement had spread to other major cities like Manchester. The inspiration for the dancing on *Ready, Steady, Go!* came from the Scene Club, and on several occasions the show's **69**

'Granada TV did a couple of things in those days, one was particularly good, called "The Blues & Gospel Caravan" which was filmed at a railway station in Chorlton, re-christened "Chorltonville". It featured Muddy Waters, Cousin Joe, Sonny Boy, Brownie and Sister Rosetta. It was reviewed by Roger Eagle in R&B Scene.'

BRIAN SMITH

producer Vicki Wickham recruited teenage dancers directly from the club to appear. By late 1964 the Mod movement in London had come of age and this inspired the media to claim that London was the epicentre of the Swinging Sixties and the fashion capital of the world.

Prior to then, teenage fashion had been in the dark ages, the fashion industry yet to realise that there was a serious teenage market. It was the Mods who gave the industry direction and the Mods who made the British rag trade sit up and take notice. *Ready, Steady, Go!* with its OpArt imagery, and the 'fabulous' Cathy McGowan became the launch pad for scores of British Beat groups. Mary Quant, who had opened her first 'Bazaar' on the Kings Road in Chelsea as early as 1956, became a household word along with John Stephens who had opened his first shop in Carnaby Street in 1958.

Though possibly more important to the Mods were fashion traders like John Simons. Simons was greatly influenced by the American Ivy League look of the mid to late '50s, the modern jazz scene and had been involved with Mod fashion as a trader on Petticoat Lane. As co-owner of the Ivy Shop in Richmond, Simons was one of the first outlets to stock the complete Mod wardrobe – mohair suits, Madras cotton button-down shirts, straight leg chinos, penny loafers and Levi's jeans.

Rather than being seen as a product of *Ready, Steady, Go!* and media hype, it was the Mods who should have been credited with inspiring a whole teenage industry, Carnaby Street and all. The majority of teenagers probably believed the bull they read in the Sunday newspapers – that England was a really swinging place. But the hype promoted by the media, and subsequent nationwide growth of the Mod industry meant absolutely nothing in clubs and coffee bars up and down the country. They were enjoying the real deal.

Soul On 45

The availability of black music on record signalled the start of another musical revolution. The secondhand attempts at playing black music by veterans of the earlier London jazz scene were now old hat. Kids wanted the genuine article. Many bands struggled to impersonate the sophistication of the new black music coming from across the Atlantic. They tried to master the new musical intricacies, but few succeeded in capturing the degree of quality that was now being issued on vinyl. For the new and discerning crowd the club DJ was king and collecting R&B records on Sue, Atlantic or Motown became an obsession for hundreds of kids throughout the country.

'If you wanted to make it as an R&B band in England, you had to be accepted by the kids at the Wheel in Manchester first.'

ELTON JOHN

CHAPTER FIVE
Meanwhile Back in Manchester – Twisted Wheel 1964

THE ABADIS QUICKLY REALISED HOW LUCKY THEY HAD BEEN TO SECURE ROGER EAGLE'S services. Artist selection for All-Nighters was influenced greatly by Eagle's recommendations, and by the start of 1964 the Wheel, in terms of membership and reputation, had become the fastest growing club of its kind in the north of England rivalling the Flamingo and Marquee as Britain's top R&B venue.

The first All-Nighter of the New Year showcased the Downliners Sect, and for the following week's All-Nighter the club announced the appearance of the Cyril Davies' All Stars. It was a fantastic scoop. The Wheel crowd had been waiting months for Davies and his band, and it was to be his first visit to Manchester since his July '63 appearance at the Bodega. However on the same day the advertisement was placed in the *Manchester Evening News*, Cyril Davies, co-founder of the British R&B movement, collapsed and tragically died, of what was later confirmed as leukaemia.

Long John Baldry stepped in to sing with the All Stars and fulfilled the Wheel booking. He later changed the name of the band to the Hoochie Coochie Men. On the night, Baldry invited the young Rod Stewart to join him on stage as second vocalist; up until then, Stewart had been appearing with semi-pro Birmingham outfit, the Dimensions, an extremely popular act at the Wheel. The night was a sellout and one of the best All-Nighters the Brazennose Street Wheel ever had.

> Tue 7th Jan 1964
> Twisted Wheel – Twisted Wheel
> This Saturday 11th January
> Cyril Davies and his All Stars

Advert was changed on Saturday 11th January 1964 to:

> Twisted Wheel – Twisted Wheel
> To-Night – Early Session – The Beat Boys
> All Nighter – Long John Baldry with Cyril Davies' All Stars

A repeat appearance by Baldry and Davies' All Stars on 11th January was followed by Jimmy Powell and the 5 Dimensions' second visit on the 18th of the month, Graham Bond on the 25th, and John Mayall and the Blues Breakers on 1st February.

73

Getting Mighty Crowded

8th February 1964 was a significant date in the Twisted Wheel's history. Booked to appear at the All-Nighter were pseudo Rhythm & Blues outfit Manfred Mann, at number five in the charts the same week with '5–4–3–2–1'. As far as the Abadis were concerned, Manfred Mann was just another booking, and it was totally fortuitous that they had rocketed to fame in the meantime. There was no way they could have imagined that before Tony Kay & the Huckleberries had finished the early Saturday session, there would be a queue stretching from Brazennose Street, around the block at Ridgefield continuing all the way to Queen Street.

By midnight the Wheel was packed, well beyond its capacity and the queue outside was still growing. The Abadis were told by a worried police sergeant to lock the club's doors and mounted police were called to disperse the disappointed crowd. Open just over one year, the Twisted Wheel had broken all attendance records for any club in Manchester. That night somewhere between 4–6,000 people had been locked out. Inside the club for Phil and Ivor, the size of the crowd awaiting the appearance of Manfred Mann was only part of the problem as the band had yet to turn up.

By 2.00am there was still no sign of the group and backstage Ivor and Phil argued over who should tell the crowd. There was no back-up group and it was too late to arrange a stand-in. There was also the risk of being accused of running a hoax, or worse the possibility of a full-scale riot. Salvation came as Ivor Abadi steeled himself to walk onto the newly-built stage to inform the audience; word filtered through that the Manfred Mann group, held up by the crowd outside, had just entered the club from the back.

Despite having just undergone its first extension the club was absolutely packed solid. Lead singer Paul Jones took a peep at the size of the crowd and told Ivor Abadi that the stage was too small and there was absolutely no way they were going to play that night. Ivor bluntly told the group that of course they would have to play even if it meant standing on each other's heads – if they didn't, then they would never play Manchester again. To the relief of all concerned Manfred Mann performed and went down a storm.

Recollections of Brazennose Street – Eddie Barnett

Eddie Barnett who later went on to open one of Manchester's top boutiques, Barnett Man on Corporation Street, was one of the Brazennose Street crowd.

'We were in the Jungfrau on Cathedral Street when the police raided it. We were told to get outside while they searched it. I think they found a few blues then they told us to clear off. We walked along Deansgate and turned into Brazennose Street which was pretty well lined up from one end of the street to the other with scooters. People were coming out of the Clef D'Or club at the bottom of Brazennose Street, a club for wise guys and the like and we followed them onto Queen Street joining the queue for the Wheel All-Nighter which stretched all the way back as far as Albert Square. Outside the Wheel, I could hear harmonicas

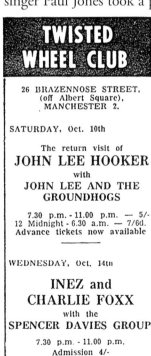

blaring playing '5–4–3–2–1'. Inside I can remember dancing to 'Woolly Bully', 'Midnight Hour' and 'See-Saw'.'

Eddie became a regular part of the early Mod crowd down at the Wheel and recalled some of the fashions; button-down shirts and narrow knitted ties, sideburns and Levi shrink-to-fit jeans, BOAC airline shoulder bags, bowling alley shoes and navy macs. He also remembered a dodgy black guy from Nottingham known as 'The Duke', selling lengths of tonic suit material from the boot of his car outside the Expresso Bongo next door to Ralph's Records near Victoria Station. Eddie and his friends would take the material to Jewish tailors who happily made up superb mohair single-breasted suits. These would be proudly worn at the next All-Nighter, usually with a brightly coloured silk handkerchief hanging from the breast pocket.

John Lee Hooker
in Roger's office at the Wheel

A supply of pills for the All-Nighter was a must and Eddie recalled that on a Saturday afternoon, after his regular pre-All-Nighter haircut it wasn't unusual for the hairdresser to slip him an envelope of Blues…'Something for the weekend Sir?'. But not all drug activity went unnoticed. The Manchester Vice Squad were well aware that All-Nighters went hand-in-hand with amphetamines. On one occasion after an All-Nighter, Eddie went by cab to the flat of some friends in Prestwich, Mick and Phil B. Despite pushing a wardrobe against the door they failed to halt a raid by the 'Squad' who had been tipped off by the taxi driver.

Brazennose Street – continued

By 1964, Eagle was one of the biggest club promoters of live Rhythm & Blues in the country. He would use his knowledge of R&B to flatter and impress visiting American Blues artists playing at places like the Free Trade Hall, to persuade them to appear at the Wheel.

If a local beat group, or one of the London based R&B bands wanted to appear at the Wheel, it was Roger Eagle they had to get past, as he was the one the Abadis listened to. The Twisted Wheel had already earned the reputation of having the most critical audience of its kind in the UK and many artists bombed in front of its discerning membership. As Elton John later commented (he appeared at the Wheel in Bluesology): 'If you could make it at the Twisted Wheel you could play anywhere.'

On 15th February 1964, the Wheel secured its first booking of an American artist, Sonny Boy Williamson backed by the Animals. It was the first of many top-line acts that the Wheel would book over the next six years. No doubt it must have blown Sonny Boy's mind hearing Eagle warm up the audience with his records like 'Help Me' and 'Don't Start Me Talking', after all this wasn't Chicago it was the north of England…the home of the Beatles.

WELCOME
TO
BRITAIN

INEZ & CHARLIE FOXX

with your great new disc

HURT BY LOVE

b/w CONFUSION SUE WI - 323

Personal Appearances

July 2nd: Scene at 6.30
Cavern, Liverpool.

July 3rd: Ready, Steady, Go
Manor House Club.

July 4th: Flamingo, London.

July 6th: Morris, Shrewsbury.

July 7th: Attic Club, Hounslow.

July 11th: Saturday Club.

MOCKINGBIRD

INEZ &
CHARLIE
FOXX

ISLAND RECORDS LTD., 108 CAMBRIDGE ROAD, LONDON, N.W.6

'Roger – like a lot of us – was probably a closet fan of the early Beatles.' Brian Smith

By March 1964, the Beatles had already had four Number One records and Merseybeat was beginning to dominate the hit parade. And while most of the world's press seemed to be permanently camped on Liverpool's Matthew Street outside the Cavern, for the Abadi brothers and Roger Eagle it was business as usual.

The success of the Beatles was of little interest to the Wheel's membership, and successful and popular as the Cavern was, for many Liverpool teenagers the Wheel was where it was at. Every week they would make the eighty-mile round trip for the all-night session at the Twisted Wheel to hear the sound of authentic R&B.

Arriving at Heathrow from a triumphant tour of the USA, the Beatles were met by the usual army of press photographers and orgy of female fans. If Eagle had seen George Harrison standing at the top of the aircraft steps, proudly holding aloft a copy of Major Lance's 'Um, Um, Um, Um, Um, Um' album on Okeh, he might have had second thoughts about committing, what must have been considered by many as an act of sacrilege – the ritualistic burning of the Beatles' second album on the Wheel stage.

By March '64, the crowd at the club had changed dramatically. After just over a year of business, the Twisted Wheel's membership was estimated at over 14,000 by Manchester Police – the Wheel was booming. On a Saturday night, kids would travel from all over the country to get to the All-Nighter – from North Wales, the Midlands, Staffordshire and Yorkshire, from as far north as Scotland and as far south as Cornwall.

The long-haired young dossers and runaways, with their rolled-up sleeping bags, had been using the All-Nighters for shelter, and were now being made unwelcome by the new 'in' crowd. By the summer, the last of them had moved on to non-Mod clubs like the notorious Heaven and Hell, and the Manchester Cavern on Cromford Court, which opened on 23rd May.

I Dig Your Act

'Manchester had become probably the biggest centre in Europe for clubs. I counted over two hundred in the immediate Manchester area from 1960 to 1966.' C.P. Lee

Other clubs with an eye on the Wheel's success copied its lead. The Jungfrau, for example, one of the better clubs in the city and which at the time had become very popular as a pre-All-Nighter venue with the new Manchester Mods was quick to get in on the act.

Jungfrau – Big 3 All Niters Experiment
North's £5000 Group Talent Contest
All Niters starting Sat 22nd February
Midnight – 6am – The Stylos 5/-

Evidence of the sudden mushrooming interest in R&B all-nighters and the Mod trade is clearly illustrated by a sample of advertisements placed in the *Manchester Evening News* entertainment's column over a two month period from March to May 1964.

Saturday 21st Feb – Jungfrau
R and B – The Sheffields 5/-

Wednesday 26th Feb – 3 Coins
Thursday is R&B Night
+ Manchester's only Blue Beat
Session 2/-

7th March – Jungfrau
Saturday All Niter –
Rhythm and Blues
From the Star Club Hamburg –
The Roadrunners (Liverpool)

March 13th – Grand Opening
Coffee Bar Dance Club – Top 20
Hollinwood

Saturday 14th – Jungfrau
Rhythm and Blues All Nighter
Nashville Teens

Wednesday 18th – 3 Coins
Thursday is R&B Night –
Ray Terret

Friday 20th – The Oasis
'Manchester's Answer
To The Cavern'

Saturday 21st – Jungfrau – The
Paramounts 'Little Bitty Pretty
One' – 'Poison Ivy' plus Rhythm
and Blues Music 6/-

Saturday 21st March
Grand Opening – Back Door Club
Bow Lane – Back of Cona
Coffee Bar

Manchester's Greatest
All-Nighter – The Stylos
Members Free – Guests 5/-

Thursday 2nd April – Bodega
'Another Fab Gear Night'

Saturday 11th April – Jungfrau
The Sheffields – All Nighter –
The Rats

Sunday 12th April 1964 – Oasis
LITTLE RICHARD
LITTLE RICHARD
12/6d

Thursday 23rd April – 3 Coins
'Welcome All Mods'
Great Rhythm and Blues Night
'We Set The Fashion'
7.30–Midnight

Thursday 23rd April – Bodega
'Put On Your Hi Heel Sneakers
Because Tonight is Mod Night'
Remo Sands and the
Spinning Tops

Saturday 25th April – 40 Thieves
Midnight – Dawn – The Tuxedos

Sunday 26th April – La Cave
'Meet the Mods from France,
Germany, Spain, Italy and
Switzerland'
Life is great at La Cave –
Girls 2/6d Boys 3/6d
Church Street – Piccadilly
Manchester

Saturday 2nd May –
Heaven & Hell
All Night 7pm–7am 5/-
Saturday 9th May –
Stamford Hall Altrincham
'Fontana's Newest Sensation' –
The Pretty Things

Saturday 16th May 'The Place'
Hanley Staffs
All Nighter 8pm–4am – Victor
Brox Croxier and Blues Giants
The Syndicate + Neil Davis 4' –
Sunday – Spencer Davis Quartet
'The Largest Collection Of
Authentic R And B Discs In
The Country!'

Saturday 23rd May – Cavern
Grand Opening – Capacity over
2000!

'Roger received a letter from a blues player in Chicago called L.C. McKinley. Although we'd never heard of him he'd heard about the Twisted Wheel. He wanted work.'

BRIAN SMITH

Manchester Mods

The Deansgate end of Manchester city centre, from Victoria Station up to St. Annes Square and Albert Square was where local Manchester Mods like Eddie Barnett hung out, in the days before pedestrianisation and construction of the Arndale Shopping Centre monstrosity.

The build up to the weekend's activities would start at coffee bars as early as Wednesday, to discuss who was on, who was going, and, more importantly, who had the pills.

Saturday afternoons were spent cruising around Manchester on chromed Lambrettas before the wearing of crash helmets was made compulsory, through the busy shopping traffic on Market Street and Piccadilly, before meeting up at the Cona on Tib Lane or the Mogambo on Mosley Street. Early on Saturday night the Mod crowd would head down to the Jungfrau where, like the Cona, there was lots of space to park their scooters. At about 11.00pm, it was time to make the short trip down Deansgate to Brazennose Street, ready for the Wheel All-Nighter.

There was a strong Jewish element amongst the new 'in' crowd and the Wheel had become the place to be seen for upwardly mobile Jewish teenagers from Manchester suburbs like Prestwich and Whitefield. They had the money and formed the backbone of the early Mod scene in the city. Invariably from good middle class backgrounds, they were the early pioneers of fashion in Manchester and took a great pride in their appearance. In their handmade shoes and suits they competed with each other as to who looked the sharpest. An added bonus for young Jewish Mods from respectable families was that the Wheel All-Nighter didn't start until midnight, the end of the Jewish Sabbath.

In the city centre, an existing infrastructure of Jewish businesses quickly recognised the potential trade and were soon able to cater for the Mods. Back street tailors could knock out made-to-measure suits in whatever style was required. Ralph's Records near Victoria Station, owned by Ralph Mendleson, and Barry's Records on Blackfriars Street, owned by Barry Ancill, supplied records to the Wheel and anyone in the know. Barry knew what the new generation wanted to listen and dance to. Denny Dewhurst, owner of Denny's Hairstyles, was a popular guy on the scene, his hairdressers on Deansgate was the place for the right hairstyle, just as you wanted it, done from a sketch you took to the shop.

```
HARD   DRIVE
SOUL-PAIN
VICTOR   BROX
BLUES   TRAIN
```

R&B Scene

Roger Eagle, was considered important enough by the Abadi brothers to be given his own office at the back of the club. From here, Eagle produced and edited one of England's earliest Rhythm & Blues magazines. First issued in June 1964, and priced one shilling, the publication's original title *R'NB Scene*, was later changed to *R&B Scene*. Assisted by close friends Roger Fairhurst, then president of the Chuck Berry Fan Club, Dave Wagget, responsible for the artwork, and a very accomplished staff photographer called Brian Smith, *R&B Scene* ran for two years. As well as articles from Roger Eagle, there were regular contributions from Mike Leadbitter and Eagle's inner circle of fellow Wheel R&B enthusiasts like Mike Bocock and Bob Groom. Financed by **79**

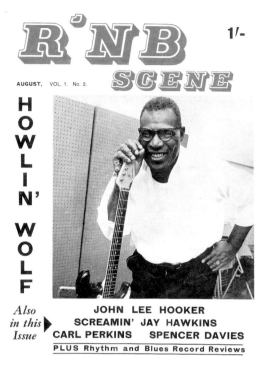

R'N'B SCENE

1/-

AUGUST, VOL. 1. No. 2.

H
O
W
L
I
N'

W
O
L
F

Also
in this ▶
Issue

JOHN LEE HOOKER
SCREAMIN' JAY HAWKINS
CARL PERKINS   SPENCER DAVIES

PLUS Rhythm and Blues Record Reviews

the Abadis and initially using the club's address 26, Brazennose Street, the magazine was another first for the Wheel and predated every other publication of its kind. *R&B Scene* was true grass roots stuff and absolutely unique.

Through his editorial, Eagle communicated to his readers his enthusiasm and passion for Rhythm & Blues. It was a club-based magazine aimed at teenage R&B fans, who until then had had to rely on the sleeve notes of LPs to learn more about their music. The kids who bought *R&B Scene* more than likely obtained their first copy over the coffee bar at the Wheel or at one of a number of similar R&B clubs that stocked the magazine, such as the Scene in Middlesborough or the Esquire in Sheffield. It also advertised in the national music press which indirectly helped promote the Wheel too. Although *R&B Scene* was not put together by some fancy publishing company it was amazingly professional both in its appearance and content, and quickly attracted advertisements from record dealers as far away as California. Rhythm & Blues music was still very much a minority taste, but through his magazine, Eagle and his gang enthusiastically preached the word as best they could. *R&B Scene* was a typical example of how people discovered black music in the early days – not by media hype, but by word of mouth.

Unselfishly, Roger Eagle allowed similar minded clubs to place ads in *R&B Scene* for free. No doubt, Ivor would have flipped if he had known.

Say Man

Without doubt Eagle was the driving force and inspiration at Brazennose Street, and such was his commitment to black music, that by 1965 the Twisted Wheel was the biggest R&B club outside of the United States. Roger Eagle was clearly the main man, yet his claim that single-handedly, week in, and week out, he deejayed for seven hours at a time, is not altogether correct. After the first few editions of *R&B Scene*, Roger did begin sharing the deejaying with friend, Neil Carter, another self confessed R&B nut and fully paid up member of Eagle's inner circle. Ivor Abadi also recalls Roger getting more involved with the visiting performers. They would alternate All-Nighters or would split the night's session between them.

In one of our interviews, Roger recalled that in 1963–64, there weren't enough R&B records available to fill a seven-hour stint. However by '64, London and Pye had released enough decent records to disqualify this argument, and the probable reason why Roger played black rock and roll, was simply that he liked it. Roger always was 'his own man'.

Similarly, he had absolutely no qualms about playing a smattering of off-the-wall novelty records such as 'Scratchy' by Travis Wammack, or fringe pop records like 'Liar Liar' by the Castaways and 'She's About A Mover' by the Sir Douglas Quintet. All great records in their own right, and with years of hindsight it's very easy for us to be smartarses. Information on the availability of current black record releases was limited in those days; the exceptions being the odd specialist record shop such as Dobell's in London or Barry's in Manchester, the occasional favourable review in *Record Mirror* (usually by Norman Jopling), and of course, the inimitable *R&B Scene*.

Brazennose Street – continued

The odd non-typical Wheel booking was still being made. On Friday 1st May for instance, Millie 'My Boy Lollipop' Small appeared. The Saturday night early sessions were usually filled by a local or up-and-coming beat/R&B group like the Beat Boys or the much underrated Renegades. For the All-Nighters however, the Abadis aimed to get the best possible touring

acts available. Appearances through March and April of 1964 included Jimmy Powell and the Dimensions, the Spencer Davis Group, John Mayall, Graham Bond, Long John Baldry, the Alex Harvey Soul Band, the Animals and Georgie Fame. Roger Eagle must have been thrilled to get Memphis Slim for the All-Nighter of the 9th May, but at the same time despondent to learn that one of his idols, Little Richard, was to appear in front of a sell-out crowd the following night at the rival Oasis Club.

There had always been a demand for good rockin' black dance music at the Wheel. Even amongst the foot tapping older Rhythm & Blues crowd, who went to the All-Nighters by the score to appreciate top American Blues artists such as John Lee Hooker, Jimmy Reed and Memphis Slim. But the membership and mood of the club was changing. For some of the new crowd, the interruption of their All-Nighter, even by top draw US Blues artists like John Lee Hooker, was a 'come down'.

By the spring of 1964, an ever increasing Mod membership began demanding more and more soul music, the new black music of America, and they just loved the records played at the Wheel All Nighter – Eagle spoiled them. In fact, Eagle was probably the best in the business at gauging exactly what records his young dancing audience wanted. For more and more of the new kids, the fresh new sound of highly charged soul music had overnight become the main attraction.

'Before I discovered the wonderful world of the soul 45, it was a big shock at the time, to witness the reaction of a group of teenagers, to the appearance on stage of John Lee Hooker. Roger Eagle had hardly finished the courteous 'Live on stage at the Twisted Wheel we proudly present the great John Lee Hooker' when they coolly walked away. I use the word 'they' deliberately – until that night, my first at the

Wheel, I had no idea who these kids were or where they were coming from. They were Mods of course and from another planet.

'The Mods just drifted away from the stage and vanished into the dark of the deejay room. There they danced in their own inimitable and unique way to the sounds the DJ was laying down: 'Shop Around' by the Miracles and 'The Way You Do The Things You Do' by the Temptations. Hooker struggled to compete above the sound of the records, I could clearly see he was being distracted. Half way through 'Dimples', a big record for him in 1964 and probably the reason he was on tour, he suddenly stopped playing: 'Damned if I'll carry on.' Mumbling into his microphone, Hooker pleaded: 'Could somebody please turn that jukebox down?'

'A significant number of the crowd, Hooker or no Hooker, had only one intention in mind, to dance all night. This could well be the point when the Twisted Wheel moved on from the hard-edged R&B and Chicago Blues to the fresh and energetic sound of soul music. The new crowd wanted black dance records like Sugar Pie Desanto's 'Soulful Dress', 'Hurt By Love' by Inez & Charlie Foxx, the Miracles' 'Mickey's Monkey' or 'Can I Get A Witness' and 'You're A Wonderful One' by Marvin Gaye. No disrespect was intended to the great John Lee – it was simply that they wanted to dance. Live R&B was fine if it was snappy and uptempo, but if it brought you down – then forget it.'
Phil Scott

Eagle usually obtained his records from Barry Ancill's on Blackfriar's, Guy Stevens at the Scene or shops like Dobell's in the capital. After Mike Bocock from Bolton showed him how to obtain imports, he also started ordering directly from the States. His good friend and fellow rock and roll fan, Guy Stevens also helped him obtain discs from the USA. Stevens, who had been placing ads in Eagle's *R&B Scene* for the Sue Appreciation Society regularly sent Eagle copies of early British R&B 45s as well as US Sue and other American imports. Sue imports were among the first danceable soul records to be heard at both the Scene and the Wheel, roughly a year before Motown burst onto the British club scene. Eagle also received 45s directly from American record companies like Ronn and Jewel. Being the enthusiast that he was, Eagle constantly pestered American record companies for copies of records that hadn't been released in the UK.

After sending a letter to Don Robey at Duke praising the vocal skills of Bobby Bland, Eagle found himself in receipt of a demo of Bland's 'Yield Not To Temptation'. Robey ensured that Eagle's praise for Bland was quoted on the back of Bobby Bland's next Duke album 'Ain't Nothing You Can Do' along with fellow Bland convert Brox Croxier (Victor Brox[1]).

Mr. Smith, Mr. Kline and Mr. French

The arrival of the Mods and Motown wasn't the only change at the Wheel.

For whatever reason, whether just to keep awake, have the energy to survive the sweltering temperatures of a crowded club, the stamina to dance from midnight 'til dawn, or just for the buzz of being 'blocked', all-nighters went hand in hand with pep pills. This wasn't just the case at the Wheel, or for that matter any other all-nighter. The main reason kids went was to be one

T-Bone Walker backstage at the Wheel

of 'the crowd'. Kids loved the Wheel because it was 'their place' and they could hear exclusive records not being played anywhere else. Kids didn't go to the Wheel for the pills, they were merely a by-product of the scene. The real buzz was being with people of a similar mind, in on the music and fashion. The opinion most kids held down at the Wheel was, if you took pills – so what? And if you didn't, which admittedly wasn't an option for many, well that was OK too. Not that the Abadi brothers tolerated drugs on their premises anyway. On the occasions when the Vice/Drug Squad wanted access to the Wheel, they would always willingly oblige.

The 1964 Drugs (Prevention of Misuse Act) was certainly taken up by the Manchester Vice Squad.

'I remember absolutely crapping myself on my second or third visit to Brazennose Street. I was standing by the coffee bar waiting for Spencer Davis to come on stage. The music was deafening, James Brown's 'Night Train'. 'Miami, Florida, Atlanta, Georgia, Night Train…NIGHT TRAIN'. The sound of the thumping bass suddenly went off and everyone was looking around in amazement. Lights started flashing. The club lights came on and in an instant the Wheel was swarming with police. A few plain-clothed police chased after a number of youths who'd rushed to the toilets. I was searched and questioned by one of the squad and asked if I was in possession of any pills. Given the all clear, I was then given a slip of paper with 'C' CHECK CHARLIE on and left alone. I cherished that slip of paper for years. The comical thing about the bust was that during the searches Roger Eagle played 'There's A Riot Goin' On' by the Coasters. The police left the club after about twenty minutes empty handed, Eagle's flashing lights obviously providing enough of a warning for anybody who may have been in possession, to dump their pills.'

ANONYMOUS EYE WITNESS

Little Walter on stage in October '64, after having drunk an entire bottle of whisky on the way to the club

Sat 16th May – Twisted Wheel
All Nighter – Spencer Davis Quartet

With or without amphetamines, the new Wheel crowd were high, alive and wanted to dance. In the rooms off from the stage, acting cool and clicking their fingers they danced on through the night to records like 'Aw Mercy' by Booker T & the MG's and 'Getting Mighty Crowded' by Betty Everett that blared out from the deejay room.

Despite the unrest in some quarters over the live acts, the Wheel carried on booking the best possible performers in the country. One of many appearances by Georgie Fame and the Blue Flames was on Saturday 30th May. The Wheel crowd were well aware of the reputation Fame had in London, especially with the Mod crowd down at the Flamingo and were well-up for this All-Nighter and packed the place.

The first visit by John Lee Hooker on Monday 6th July was followed two days later by a brilliant double booking – Inez & Charlie Foxx backed by Stevie Winwood and the Spencer Davis Group. Inez and Charlie, together with their producer Juggy Murray, were taken north by Guy Stevens.

Wednesday 8th JULY – TWISTED WHEEL
Inez and Charlie Foxx plus The Spencer Davis Group - 2/6d

Noting the popularity of the Spencer Davis Group with the Wheel crowd, Roger Eagle saw to it that they were quickly re-booked for the All-Nighter of the 18th July.

The demand for top groups was also enough to guarantee a return mid week booking on the 22nd July for the Yardbirds who had gone down a storm at the Wheel on their first appearance in early June. Taking a break from the Crawdaddy in Richmond, Surrey, the Yardbirds obviously thought the Wheel an important enough gig to travel up north mid week, even though admission price for the night was only 2/6d.

During the same week the following ad appeared in the *Manchester Evening News*.

Thursday 23rd July – Bodega
'Manchester's Only Licensed Rhythm and Blues Club'

Times were changing, and more and more city centre clubs were applying for late drink licences (until 2.00am). Obviously from a business perspective the profit made from selling alcohol was far greater than that from selling cokes and coffee. Club owners at the time were very nervous of the scrutiny certain coffee bar clubs were getting from the police. They were also beginning to get bad vibrations that there would soon be wholesale changes that would affect the running of clubs in Manchester, a result of the ambitions of a certain Chief Superintendent. The Abadi brothers would find applications to the licensing authorities for a licence to sell alcohol continually refused.

Another Saturday Night

If you were serious about your soul music in the '60s, in the immortal words of *Ready, Steady Go!* 'Your weekend starts here!' That would mean an all-nighter, in London probably the Scene or La Discotheque. You would then go on to hang around on Saturday, buying a few records or a shirt generally building up for the Saturday All-Nighter. If like David Meikle you travelled down to Manchester from Glasgow the records would come from Barry's or Ralph's and the shirt from Barnett Man or Ivor's Boutique. But as soon as the shops closed, you would make for one of the scores of coffee bars to talk records, clothes and possibly score some gear. You might even take in an early session at one of the other clubs in town.

Memphis Slim

KEY TO CITY CENTRE GUIDE TO COFFEE BARS AND CLUBS OF 1960s MANCHESTER

1. Twisted Wheel '63–'65
2. Twisted Wheel '65–'71
3. Blue Note Club
4. Can Can Coffee Bar
5. Cona Coffee Bar
6. Guys & Dolls Club
7. Rails Club
8. Jigsaw Club
9. Jackie's Explosion Club
10. 3 Coins/Beat City/Stax Club
11. Macarlo Coffee Bar
12. Clef D'Or Club
13. Mogambo Coffee Bar & Stork Club
14. Wishing Well Coffee Bar
15. Annabel's
16. Annabel's
17. Parakeet Coffee Bar
18. Auto Club
19. Kardomah Coffee Bar
20. Original Kardomah Coffee Bar
21. Empire Grill (Egg & I)
22. Continental Coffee Bar
23. Oskar's Pub
24. 2Js/Oasis
25. Bodega Coffee Bar/Club
26. Rowntrees
27. Expresso Bongo Coffee Bar
28. La Cave Coffee Bar
29. Mr Smith's Club
30. Portland Lodge Club
31. Takis/Rotters Club
32. Nicky the Greeks Café
33. Zanzibar Coffee Bar
34. Normandie Coffee Bar

'The police busted the place a few times, one big one was the last night at Brazennose Street – which was madness, you couldn't even get into the place.'

KEN WHITE

CHAPTER SIX
Out With The In Crowd – Recollections of Brazennose Street
Phil Scott

'As a rebellious young fifteen-year-old, I imagined the Wheel to be dingy and dangerous... a dimly lit club that was strictly off limits. Some kind of mad and warped place – the type of place every parent in Manchester (certainly mine) dreaded to think you'd go to.'
Phil Scott

WHETHER BY ACCIDENT OR DESIGN, IT WAS THE ACTUAL CHOICE OF THE NAME THE TWISTED Wheel that did it for me...I don't think there has been a more suitable name for a club ever since. The name Twisted Wheel was perfect and it fired up my imagination well before I had the bottle to go. It conjured up images of some kind of secret underground scene, a club full of weird people who stayed up all night digging strange music. I was right, but there was much more to the place than that.

It was a warm summer night in August 1964. I had been to the Oasis on Lloyd Street and I'd had a brilliant night and wasn't ready for catching the last bus home. I'd first heard about

---

MANCHESTER CITY POLICE (INFORMATION ROOM).

999 Call	Time *21.00*	Date. *14 . 4 . 64*

From *Anonymous Male* ____ MOSS SIDE .

Message
" *You know the Twisted Wheel. The mods and Rockers are there* "

Received by : ▓▓▓

Action Taken *Radio A.6.* — *all quiet at the moment. Will pay passing attention* "

Copies :- A & File.

▓▓▓

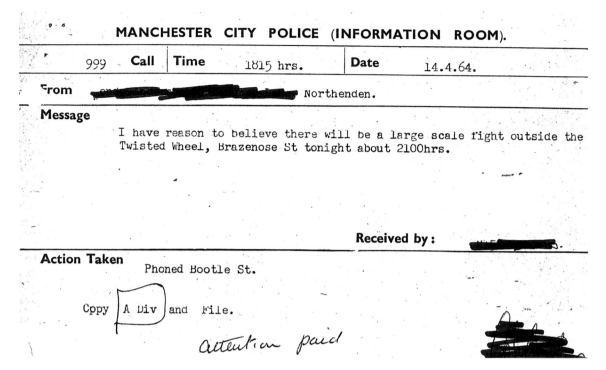

the Wheel from some kids at school, it was just around the corner from the Oasis and had the reputation as the place to go. The Wheel was a fascination to lots of us at the time and its notoriety was incredible. Such was my preoccupation with the place, every night instead of doing my homework I would scour the *Manchester Evening News* for any snippets I could find about the Wheel and that grown up world down town. 'Drug Squad Raids Club', 'Strange Looking Teenagers', 'Girl Sold Purple Hearts In Café', 'All Night Rave-Up','Pep Pill Family Had 800 A Day On NHS'… The urge was too strong to resist, I knew I would go the first chance I could.

Forgetting about the all-night bus, I turned off Albert Square and into Brazennose Street, right on the stroke of midnight – the impact was unforgettable. I had walked into a different world. There must have been between two to three hundred people milling around the top end of Brazennose Street. Further down, outside the entrance to the Wheel on the left of the street I could see the head of the queue. Stretching from the Wheel, almost the whole length of Brazennose Street were rows and rows of scooters. They were all decked out in sparkling chrome crash-bars and floridas, spotlights and carriers. Although I noticed quite a number of Vespas the majority of the scooters were Lambretta TV 175s and LI 150s. Some had fur covered backrests or small racing fly-screens with logos like 'Wolfy' or 'TV' Club, all were kitted out with racks of wing mirrors. Gleaming machines, sparkling under the street lights, it was a wonderful sight. Their owners hung around in ex-US Army fish-tail parkas, the hoods of which were trimmed with fox fur. Under their parkas I noticed they were wearing smart mohair suits. At the entrance to the Wheel I saw a group of odd looking youths with short cropped hair, some were wearing full length leathers, others ankle length, semi-transparent navy blue plastic macs.

I walked past the entrance, looking for the end of the queue. A couple of boozed up sailors who had obviously had a heavy night on the town came staggering past on the opposite side of the street. I could hear them slagging off some of the scooter crowd, calling them 'poofs' and taking the piss. In a flash, three or four of the crowd rushed across the street and beat the shit out of them. Luckily the sailors sobered up quickly enough to leg it.

'Mods were the nice guys, the rockers were the not so nice guys.' Ivor Abadi

I eventually found the end of the queue, which by now stretched from Brazennose Street, around the corner at Ridgefield onto Queen Street. Asking myself what the hell I was doing there, I nervously waited in line. Eventually I reached the entrance to the Wheel, I could feel the hot air and smell the coffee coming from inside the club. Proceeding downstairs, I came to a dark red velvet curtain, above which there was a sign 'ARE YOU 18 YEARS OF AGE?' I was politely asked my age by a smartly dressed man who was standing by the till. I later found out he was the owner, Ivor Abadi.

I lied about my age, completed a membership form, paid the girl on the desk my six shillings and entered the Wheel for the first time. It was a fantastic feeling, my first sight of the inside of the Wheel. Years later, lots of people I spoke to clearly recalled their first experience of walking into the Wheel, I understand why.

Sat 29th Aug – Twisted Wheel
Early Session – Little Boy Blues
All Nighter – John Lee Hooker and The Groundhogs 6/-

I made my way to the counter of the coffee bar on my left. I must have looked a real jerk that night with my long hair and green US Army combat jacket, really out of place. The club was packed with the strangest looking crowd of people I'd ever seen. One guy was walking around in what looked like a bright silk boxing robe and sandals, another youth in Polaroids, who had strutted in behind me, was wearing a long green fishtail US army parka, trimmed on the back and around the hood in fur. Underneath he was wearing an immaculate fawn mohair suit, his hair unlike mine, was short, neat and spiky. Everyone seemed to know him. I later found out that his nickname was Wolfy and he was the leader of a scooter crowd from out of town.

A couple of smart looking kids in polo shirts and jeans came over to me, and after weighing me up, asked if it was my first visit to the Wheel and if I normally went to a place called Heaven and Hell. I knew all about the club they meant, it was a dive of a place with a notorious reputation, frequented by deadbeats and scruffs. Situated on the other side of town, the Heaven and Hell also had all-nighters but it was a club that attracted undesirables – a place where kids could 'doss' down for the night on mattresses. Wheel kids would not be seen dead near the place. I assured them that I wasn't a member of Heaven and Hell and loved the Twisted Wheel, which seemed to satisfy them. They walked away after telling me that if I ever wanted to come down to the Wheel again I had better smarten up my act and get a haircut. A few weeks later I ran into those two guys again. My shoulder length 'Rolling Stones' hair was gone, I now had a crew cut. I was wearing a striped Madras jacket, Levi jeans and bowling alley shoes (courtesy of Oldham Top Rank Bowl). They just nodded their approval in an 'I told you so' sort of way **91**

Buddy Guy

and carried on dancing. I was part of the crowd.

A group of girls with really short hair danced together on the crowded dance floor just in front of the stage. There was still the odd one or two down at the Wheel that night who still had rocker type 'bee-hive' hairstyles and were not yet into the Mod thing. But they all could dance. Naively, I thought the girls with the short hair were lesbians, but I was miles out, they were Mods and just as style conscious as the guys. One girl I remember was wearing a thick string 'grandad' vest, dyed red. She wore this over a bikini top. A lot of the kids down there in the pre-boutique days, had tailored their own clothes to create what they couldn't buy in the shops – their own individual look. Smart or cool looking improvised clothing, the first real teenage fashion scene in Manchester. There were some fabulous dancers at the Wheel that night. In the middle of the dance-floor all the action seemed to revolve around a young Jewish guy. He was wearing what looked like to have been originally a white waiter's jacket. The edges of the jacket were trimmed with neat black stitching and on the back someone had painstakingly embroidered the Twisted Wheel motif, above the motif were emblazoned the words 'Twisted Wheel Club Manchester'. He was the best dancer I had ever seen, and up with the best I have ever seen since.

I am convinced that if he was on the soul scene today, dancing just as he did back then, he would still look the business. Looking back it was the first time I had ever seen the highly stylised and freestyle rhythmic dancing that was later to be uniquely associated with the soul crowd at the Whitworth Street Wheel and later the Northern Soul Scene.

Although a few years later the Whitworth Street Wheel crowd, as far as dancing went, were in a league of their own, and remained the best in the UK for years, it's worth remembering that in the Manchester of 1964 the majority of kids were still jiving. It's still puzzling what inspired the dances the kids at Brazennose Street did. Sure there were comparable dancers in London, notably at the Scene Club and the 'All Nighter' at the Flamingo, but dancing to soul music in the UK was still very much in it's infancy. Considering there were few black artists on the TV or cinema, and therefore no examples of footwork from Jackie Wilson or James Brown to copy, it has always amazed me how this form of dancing ever got started in the first place.

These dancers had it all. Cool and expressive, brilliant footwork, the occasional frenzy of acrobatics, leg splits and twists, spinning and sliding, swerving like Dervishes. Skating sideways on one foot…a backdrop…a spin, I think the kids down there just got in with the beat and made up the moves as they went along. They were mesmerising to watch and the atmosphere they generated in that club was electric.'

Brazennose Street – continued.

'At heart I was a Teddy Boy amongst a load of Mods.'
Roger Eagle

As for Roger's thoughts on the Mods – well, strangely enough, he always regarded himself as a Teddy Boy. (Keith Rylatt regularly sent articles and photos on Teddy Boys to Roger, years after the Twisted Wheel on Whitworth Street had closed.) In Roger's own words: 'I was always a pretty smart dresser, but some of the kids down there were years in front of anything I have ever seen since. We kind of had a mutual respect. They loved the records I used to play and I reckon that's why they liked me. I never invented the Mod Scene down at the Wheel it just happened. Saying that though I'm really glad I was a part of it all.'

Roger Eagle always believed that kids down at the Wheel, and at other similar clubs, could generate enough demand to turn a record into a hit. The teenage voice could be as powerful as any radio station. Mainstream pop shows like the BBC's *Top Of The Pops* obviously had massive clout but they weren't the only ones to influence what would become a hit, and nobody would be seen dead watching *Top Of The Pops*. Club deejays certainly could influence the potential sales of records, but really it was the kids down at the clubs who created the demand for soul records, well before they were played on mainland radio. For example, Roy C's 'Shotgun Wedding' was a massive club generated hit.

Long John Baldry

Not many kids had a car in those days – they got to Manchester anyway they could.

By the late summer of 1964 the Wheel was booming, with attendance figures higher than at the Oasis. There were acts on four, sometimes five nights of the week and the demand to get into the Wheel, especially for the weekly All-Nighter was incredible. The prospect of travelling to Manchester and dancing all night attracted many kids of a similar mind from all over England. Hitchhiking lifts or arriving by train, the Wheel and the All-Nighter was the perfect escape for teenagers. Out all weekend, no worries about finding a B&B for the night, do the All-Nighter, come down and get the train back home in the morning…brilliant!

Fortunately, the Abadis already had plans drawn up to expand the capacity of the club. More floor space was urgently required for the dancers, and more room was desperately required to accommodate the hundreds of people that were being turned away every week from lock-out All-Nighters. The last Saturday before that expansion work got under way saw the return of John Lee Hooker almost one year after the first All-Nighter.

The money spent on the extension was well justified. Wheel members had been asking the management for more big name acts and, although the Abadis and Eagle were putting on the best names available, the extension allowed in more people and justified bringing in the top names. Even during the week, the club would pack people in: Tuesday 15th September the Pretty Things 4/-, Friday 25th the King Bees, Sunday 27th the Zombies – bands that normally would get a top billing on a Saturday night, were quite happy to play week days at the Twisted Wheel.

> **Saturday 5th September Twisted Wheel**
> **'Grand Opening Night – We Take Pleasure In Announcing**
> **That The Premises Have Now Been Extended – Enabling Members**
> **To View Groups In A New Large Area.**
> **Planned For The Future Are Most Of The Country's Top Groups'**
> **To-Night! Memphis Slim – Georgie Fame – The Sheffields**
>
> **Sat 3rd Oct – Twisted Wheel**
> **Early Session – Bluesounds 5/-**
> **All Nighter – Little Walter/Alexis Korner 7/6d**
>
> **Sat 10th Oct – Twisted Wheel**
> **Early Session – Diamonds 5/-**
> **All Nighter – John Lee Hooker and the Groundhogs 7/6d**

Eagle would always 'get his man' for the All-Nighter. Top British bands who appeared at the Wheel such as the Kinks, the Moody Blues, the Animals and the Yardbirds often went on to become Top 10 record stars. However, Roger Eagle had his own agenda. Acts with sudden found 'pop' status and the rich trappings of fame was one thing – but for him it didn't meant a thing; he much preferred to push the Abadis into booking artists like Little Walter or Jimmy Reed.

One band of future superstar status that at the time failed to make any impression at all on the Abadi brothers were the Small Faces. In the words of Philip Abadi: 'The worst band we had ever seen at the Wheel'. The Faces, who had been playing at a Working Men's Club in Sheffield, had driven over to Manchester in their van with the prospects of a Wheel booking. An unsuccessful audition for the Abadis on Friday 2nd October 1964 was cut short after a couple of numbers. Unceremoniously they were given the thumbs down and compensated with a pound note for petrol for the return drive back to Sheffield.

Wed 11th Oct – TWISTED WHEEL – The Soul Sisters & The Spencer Davis Group 2/6d

One band that always commanded 100 per cent attention was the Spencer Davis Group. The Wheel crowd just adored the Birmingham outfit playing Bobby Parker's 'Watch Your Step', the Malibu's 'Strong Love' or the Soul Sisters 'I Can't Stand It'. The group's second release (on Fontana in November '64) was a cover of the latter, originally issued in the UK on Sue some six months earlier. They had broken away from the stereotypical white interpretation of Chicago Rhythm & Blues and instead played what the young kids now wanted to hear, soul music. The Spencer Davis Group belonged to the Mods – close your eyes and Stevie Winwood could have been black and from Detroit.

The Wheel management couldn't ignore the increasing demand for soul acts. On Wednesday 14th October 1964 Inez & Charlie Foxx returned (2/6d) and on Sunday 1st November, riding high with her massive club hit 'Soulful Dress', Sugar Pie Desanto took the place by storm (4/-). On Wednesday 11th November, the Soul Sisters appeared backed by the best in the business – the Spencer Davis Group, the price of admission two shillings and sixpence. Kids were certainly getting value for money. If you tot up the last three acts mentioned, in today's money you could have seen the lot for less than fifty pence.

Wed 14th Oct – Twisted Wheel – Inez and Charlie Foxx

The Rolling Stones, who Roger Eagle described as 'a bloody good backing band' turned up at the Wheel on Brazennose Street, one Saturday night after they had appeared in Liverpool. The Stones had been to see Duane Eddy in concert, and were standing at the bar with their hangers-on, surrounded by gawping girls. All of a sudden, Roger began playing the original versions, in the same order, of all the tracks on the Stones first album. Eagle commented 'The Stones knew very well what I was doing – I was reminding them that we had been playing those records for ages at the Wheel and that in Manchester we knew where it was at.' Roger fondly remembered selling a copy of *R&B Scene* to Brian Jones.

Search for Jay

For months, enquiries by Roger Eagle and company as to the whereabouts of Screamin' Jay Hawkins, with the intention of getting him over to the UK, had yielded nothing. However by the second issue of *R&B Scene* in August 1964, Eagle had a scoop: 'According to Don and Dewey[1], Screamin' Jay Hawkins is alive and well and performing as resident MC/house pianist at a club in downtown Honolulu – for those of you who ever find yourselves shipwrecked in the Pacific…etc. etc.' Staff photographer, Brian Smith, had relayed this valuable information to the rest of the gang at *R&B Scene*. The search for Jay was over.

Roger Eagle, ever the eccentric, had always held a passion for off-the-wall performers like Link Wray, Bunker Hill and John Zacherle. The prospect of booking the oddball Screamin' Jay Hawkins, with his 'Mojo Bones' and 'Voodoo Spells', must have really fired up his imagination. Everyone at *R&B Scene* was instantly put on a mission; to try and persuade Screamin' Jay Hawkins to visit England and appear at the Wheel.

Amazingly, letters posted to Hawaii from a grey and wet Manchester in the desperate hope that Jay would respond finally paid off. On 27th October 1964, Jay's new manager, John Cann, contacted *R&B Scene* and it was agreed that the magazine would plug the tour and Jay would **95**

Screaming Jay was a comedian and bloody good mimic, and one night before going on at the Wheel he phoned his agent Don Arden, from Roger's office, pretending to be John Lee Hooker, who Arden also had on tour. In a totally convincing voice, complete with stammer, Jay told him he was in jail and pleaded with Don to come and get him out. When Don asked him in a state of panic "Which one?" Jay simply said "I don't know man, just come and get me out!".

BRIAN SMITH

appear at the Wheel. If nothing else this story illustrates the clout Eagle and his inner circle of R&B nuts had – 100% enthusiasm getting a well deserved result.

At the Wheel in the meantime, it was very much business as usual – the Moody Blues and Sonny Boy Williamson (7th November 1964). Another visit from Eagle's favourite London band the Yardbirds (14th November) and on the 21st November for both the early and All-Night sessions, US Bluesman Jimmy Reed. On the 23rd November 1964, early R&B pioneer Alexis Korner began a Monday night residency that would last for two months and finish on 25th January 1965.

Sat 21st Nov – Twisted Wheel
Early/Late Sessions – Jimmy Reed

The final two most notable dates for the diary of '64 must be the one act that the Wheel got and the one that got away. Despite having a massive following with the Wheel R&B hierarchy, featuring in an article in *R&B Scene* and optimistically being listed as a forthcoming winter attraction to the Wheel, the great Howlin' Wolf never made it to Manchester. Instead the up-and-coming Place in Hanley had the honour.

Thursday 10th December – 'The Place' Hanley
Howlin' Wolf

The one that didn't get away, was over the Christmas holiday period and wrapped up '64 perfectly, the return of Sonny Boy Williamson this time backed by the impressive Spencer Davis Group.

Sat 26th Boxing Day – Twisted Wheel
Early/Late Sessions – Sonny Boy Williamson
Spencer Davis Group/Soul Seekers

Manchester 1965 – Heavy Times
Tuesday 4th January – 'Drug Taking Soars' – UK Shock Report.
'DRUGS GO' – Drug peddlers are believed to be behind a raid on a Manchester chemist in which more than 3,000 'pep pills' and sedatives, including 'Purple Hearts' were stolen. The tablets in small tins were stolen from Victor Kays, Preston Street, Hulme.
Manchester Evening News

Tuesday 26th January – 'Drugs Prescription Altered By Woman'
20 Drinamyl tablets (purple hearts) altered to 50
Manchester Evening News

Manchester Vice/Drug Squad had been aware of the increasing problem of drug abuse in the city since 1964, and as a result focused much of their attention on teenage clubs, All-Night raves and pep pills. As well as the usual weekly Twisted Wheel All-Nighter, the weekend of the 9th May 1964 saw the following action in Manchester.

Fri 8th – Forty Thieves – Midnight till Dawn – The Tearaways
Sat 9th – All-Nighter – Ocean Fortic – Union Street off Church Street
Sat 9th – Oasis All Nighter – Manfred Mann – Starting 12 Midnight 7/6d
Sat 9th – Heaven & HellClub – All Nighter – 'Syndicate Rhythm and Blues' – 2/6d
– including breakfast 5/-

Although the rise in the number of coffee bar dance clubs pleased the northern teenager, this was alarming news to the the city's Chief Constable, James McKay. Something had to be done to halt what he considered to be 'the moral decay of the innocents'.

Aided by the newly passed act of Parliament, The Misuse of Drugs Act 1964, McKay commissioned one of his senior officers, Chief Superintendent Dingwall to investigate Manchester's coffee bar club scene, with the intention of finding enough evidence to enable him to become the country's leading crusader against what he perceived to be a moral menace. Ultimately McKay would persuade the government to introduce legislation that provided his officers with far greater authority.

That some form of control was needed there is no doubt. Poor conditions – bad ventilation, inadequate lighting and proper sanitation – were commonplace, and ignored by a lot of club owners. But McKay's ultimate intention was to completely close down the teenage coffee dance clubs.

As the law stood, coffee bar clubs were private members clubs and could choose when and how long they opened. Since they did not serve alcohol they did not need a drinks license. As a result it was easy to meet the legal requirements for owning this type of club. Not surprisingly, on occasion this attracted the criminal element.

The welfare of underage teenagers attending late night coffee bar clubs which were also the haunt of unsavoury characters, was of course a legitimate cause for concern. However, Chief Constable McKay's hidden agenda, government legislation and the end of clubs, failed to take into account the fact that thousands of law-abiding teenagers in 1964 had an alcohol free and non-violent outlet for their energies.

As far as the authorities and in particular the Manchester police were concerned, with a membership of 14,000, the Twisted Wheel had quickly become a cause for concern. For the nearby Bootle Street nick, home of 'A' Division, the Wheel was placed within the top ten most troublesome venues on their patch. 'A' Division, to be fair were on the front line, with the majority of the city's two hundred coffee dance clubs in their manor, not to mention the illegal gambling dives, strip joints and shabeens. Manchester by now easily rivalling Hamburg as the good-time capital of Europe. Part of the 'growing menace' was possibly that kids were travelling from all over the North to the Wheel's by now legendary All-Nighters. From Stoke, Sheffield, and Liverpool in as early as spring 1964.

Neighbouring police forces were also showing some interest. Bradford City Police had become alarmed at the numbers that were travelling to the Wheel on Saturday nights (reported in early 1964 as 'by the coach load') and the associated crime that went with it. In particular, the theft of Drynamyl (Purple Hearts), Dexedrine (Dex), Durophet capsules (Black Bombers) and Benzedrine (Bennies) from chemists' shops en route to Manchester. Suburban chemists in Manchester were being cleaned out, often within an hour of closing on Saturday evening.

Amphetamine and hash were the favourite soft drugs of the coffee dance club's all-night crowd, which of course attracted immediate attention from the city's underworld. The Kray twins are alleged to have visited Manchester in that same year, to check out the club scene with a view to colonising it. Legend has it that the police and members of the 'Quality Street Gang' met the Krays at Piccadilly station, entertaining them at a city centre hotel, before escorting them back to the station to catch the train home. Whether this is a true version of events or just another urban myth is unclear, but it does help to illustrate the depth of lawlessness that prevailed in Manchester.

A sad by-product of places open all-night were runaway teenagers[2], and a number of young people who had been reported as 'missing from home' turned up at the Wheel. Bootle Street police station's ledger from 1964 illustrates this, with twelve entries under the Twisted Wheel Club alone. Kids ranging in age from fourteen to sixteen were picked up on Sunday morning at such places as Lower Mosley Street bus station for being 'under age'. In almost every case their parents hadn't the slightest idea where they were. One seventeen-year-old girl, Sandra from Manchester, has the following entry: 'Mother seeking advice – girl frequents club and says she gets Purple Hearts'.

By late spring 1964, Chief Constable McKay had become alarmed about the perceived problems on his doorstep. He decided to act and set in motion a series of short, evidence gathering sessions. One strategy was to raid clubs with the new Drug Squad (formerly the Vice Squad) – the Wheel would in time get visits from 'Sergeant Plummer's Purple Hearts Club Band'! But one of his most amusing exercises was sending in his 'Mod Squad' – police cadets who 'were able to affect the dress and deportment of the persons frequenting Coffee Clubs'. In other words, police cadets wearing what they perceived to be hip clothes, complete of course, with a note-pad to make observations. The following report was submitted to McKay by a member of his undercover team, a young WPC. Accounts like it would be included in a future report that was to have draconian consequences:

> Eleanor B – 'I am Policewoman number 1234 in the 'A' Division of Manchester City Police.
>
> At 12 midnight on Saturday 14th March 1964, acting upon instructions and in company with Policewoman number 5678 Christine F, I went to the 'Twisted Wheel Coffee Club', 26 Brazennose Street, Manchester. This club is held in a cellar. After standing in a queue outside for sometime, we were asked by a member of staff if we were members. We replied 'No' and were told to form another queue for non-members.
>
> At 12.30am we entered the premises and went down some stairs. When we reached the bottom of the stairs we were asked to sign a membership form. We each signed our correct names and addresses and Policewoman F paid our membership fee, 2/6 each, and our entrance fee, 6/- each, and we were handed a membership card.
>
> We went along a passage to a room with a bar, where coffee, soft drinks, soup, sandwiches, cakes and cigarettes were being sold and Policewoman F purchased two coffees, 1/- each. This room was reasonably well lit but very

Subject:— "ALLEGED SALE OF "DRINAMYL" TABLETS AT MANCHESTER CLUB".

Sir,

    I refer to the letters dated 20th April, 1964 and 28th April, 1964, from the Chief Constable, Bradford City Police, respecting the above.

    The club referred to, the "Twisted Wheel" is situated at 26. Brazenose Street, City, and occupies the basement part of an office block. The owners, are three brothers, ██████ ██████ ██████, and ██████████. The membership is said to be fourteen thousand, a large number of which, reside outside the Manchester area. Yorkshire, Derbyshire, Cheshire, etc. These members apparently organise coach trips to attend. (This appears to be ███████ connection) The club caters for teen-agers, 16 to 20. years. (Although the uniform branch say that many youngsters below that age group are found in the club)

    The club premises are divided into six rooms, four of which have no furniture whatsoever, members apparently stand or lie on the floor. One room is used for the sale of soft drinks and refreshments and the other accommodates a three-piece band. The lighting arrangements throughout the club, are very poor indeed. (This is by design) These conditions would certainly assist any member, who wishes, to traffic in drugs. Even if the maagement were concerned about this possibility, (which I very much doubt) I cannot see how they could prevent such a practice, if it does exist. The conditions at this club, in my opinion, are ideal for such a purpose.

enquiry. He stated, "No member of the club had been found indulg[...] in such a practice and if they were, they would immediately be disqualified as a member. He admitted, that there had been rumours to that effect on several occassions, amongst members of the club, but nothing definite had come to light, when enquiries were made by the staff. Membership had however, been withdrawn from on member (Name not known) who appeared on television (Seene at 6.30.) who alleged that drugs could be obtained at that club. He promised to inform the police as soon as any suggestion was made, that members were selling or bringing drugs into the club.

Current observations are being taken on these premises, by both the Plain Clothes Dept, and the Policewomens Dept, in an effort to obtain evidence of drugs, to date, these enquiries and observations have been negative. This is largely due, to the conditions that exist at the club .

There has been one offence, recently reported in the Manchester area, concerning the the larceny of drugs, they were five hundred "Adrinamyl" tablets from a chemists shop in ▓▓▓▓▓. This occurred between 5.30.pm 31st December, 1963 and 8.30.am 1st January, 1964. Crime Report '▓▓▓▓. refers.

Apparently a ground floor window was broken and the person responsible, reached through and stole a jar containing the tablets. No person was arrested or suspected of this offence. ▓▓▓▓ ▓▓▓▓ has been interviewed (Bradford City C.I.D.) but denies being responsible.

Observations and enquiries will continue, in an effort to clear this matter up. The "A" Division Plain Clothes dept, have promised to inform this department if their observations prove to be successful.

crowded with only about five tables with four chairs round each.

There were five other rooms in the Twisted Wheel, used by the members, and being cellar rooms they were small and could be reached through various passages and doorways. There were two doors marked 'Private', I think one door led to the kitchen and I believe the other led to the Manager's office.

In the largest room a group was playing and people were standing around listening. It was very dark and crowded and couples were lying on the floor around the sides of the room. It was impossible to pass through because there were so many people asleep or couples kissing and cuddling.

In the smallest room it was also very dark and there was no seating accommodation, just a heap of bodies all round the room, all lying and sitting on top of each other. It was difficult to tell which limbs belonged to which bodies. Some couples lay kissing and cuddling, covered up with their own coats, the floors were concrete and there were no coverings.

In one room where records were being played there were several tables and chairs and boys were fast asleep lying with their heads pillowed on the tables. The average age of the members was about 17 years to 20 years but some looked about 14 or 15 years old. There were a lot more boys than girls and it was difficult to distinguish the sexes as the boys and girls were dressed in blue jeans and many of the boys had long hair.

Along one passage there were two Ladies and one Gents toilet. About 3am I heard boys coming out of the Gents complaining that the light in the toilet had gone out. The corridor floor then began to get wet and there was a very unpleasant smell.

At about 4am we saw a boy with a cut face and it appeared that there had been a fight in another room. A member of staff was with this youth trying to find the person responsible and at one point it looked as if there was going to be a 'free for all' in the room when some boys were accused of cutting the youth's face.

Because of the darkness and the moving from room to room, it was difficult to estimate the number of people there; I would say approximately 250. There was only one Fire Exit, which was in the room where the group was playing. I also noticed that because there were no tables, empty bottles were left on the floors of the rooms.

We spent our time wandering from room to room. At about 4.30am Policewoman F purchased two soft drinks.

At 5.10am the group stopped playing and it was announced that two more records would be played and then everyone had to leave.

At 5.25am people began to queue at the cloakroom for their coats and we slowly drifted out with most of them although there were still plenty of people in the premises when we left.

At 12 midnight on Saturday 21st March 1964, I again visited the Twisted Wheel with Policewoman Christine F. At 12.15am we showed our membership

Chief Constable

Date...... 16th April, 1964

Subject.... Sale of Drinamyl Tablets at Club

Sir,

I have to report that on Friday, 3rd April, 1964 I arrested ████████, 17 years, on a charge of shopbreaking and larceny. This youth has become a drug addict, taking drinamyl tablets. He broke into a chemist's shop in this city on two occasions and stole drinamyl tablets.

When he was interviewed regarding this matter, which he admitted, he informed me that he first began taking drinamyl tablets in January this year. He stated that he had been to a club in Manchester, known as the Twisted Wheel Club and had been offered drinamyl tablets there. On the first occasion he bought only a few, but on the next occasion he bought in the region of one hundred tablets. He began taking these tablets regularly and became addicted to them, so much that he had to break into the chemist's shop to steal these tablets.

Extensive enquiries have been made in clubs and coffee bars in this city and a number of teenagers have been interviewed. Many of them admit taking drinamyl tablets. On each occasion, when asked where they obtained them, they informed me that it was at the Twisted Wheel Club in Manchester. I have checked this story with a number of persons and I am satisfied that they have been telling the truth.

Every Saturday night a bus leaves Bradford and goes to the Twisted Wheel Club in Manchester, taking with it a large number of teenagers. This bus does not leave Manchester until around 8 a.m. on Sunday morning. The teenagers who go on this bus inform me that drinamyl tablets are handed round in the club and are offered for sale. The present price is 5d each. Most of the teenagers are students.

I suggest a copy of this report be forwarded to the Chief Constable, City Police Office, Manchester informing him that the club is being used by teenagers and that drinamyl tablets are being sold there. It would appear that these tablets will have been either stolen or obtained on false prescriptions.

(AT)

Signed:

Our ref. 64/2475/25

Your ref. ...... -

Forwarded to the Chief Constable, City Police

CITY OF BRADFORD POLICE

CRIMINAL INVESTIGATION DEPARTMENT

H. AMBLER
Chief Constable

12459

Date......22nd May, 1964.

1301/6
116

Subject.............Interview – ▮▮▮▮▮▮▮▮

Sir,

I have to report that a telephone message was received from
Detective Sergeant ▮▮▮▮▮ of Manchester City Police, stating that a
Chemist shop had been broken into in ▮▮▮▮▮▮▮, Manchester, during
the night of the 31st December 1963.

Entry had been by breaking a rear ground floor window and by
inserting 2 pieces of wood had lifted out a bottle containing 500
Drynamyl tablets. These tablets are similar to those which are
known as "Purple Hearts".

The request was that ▮▮▮▮▮▮▮▮▮, a drug addict, of ▮▮▮▮▮▮
▮▮▮, Bradford, be interviewed regarding this offence in view of the
fact that he was a frequent visitor to Manchester.

On Saturday, 16th May 1964, I saw ▮▮▮▮▮▮▮▮ at the Town Hall,
Bradford. I interviewed him regarding this offence and he informed me
that he had not been in Manchester on the night of the 31st December,
1963 and had, in fact, spent the evening at his home ▮▮▮▮▮▮▮
▮▮▮▮▮ watching television. I checked his alibi and found that this
is correct.

I am satisfied that he has no connection with the offence at
Manchester.

I respectfully suggest that a copy of this report be forwarded to
the Chief Constable, Manchester City Police, for his information.

signed: ▮▮▮▮▮▮.

D.C.▮▮▮.

noted
re attached
▮▮▮▮
▮▮ ▮▮/Sgt.

Our ref. .....▮▮▮▮▮.....................

Your ref. ....

Forwarded to ....The Chief Constable,..............

....Manchester City Police,.......

.........South Street, MANCHESTER.

26 MAY 1964
C.I.D. ADMIN.

Chief Constable. ▮

City Police Headquarters,
Town Hall, BRADFORD 1.

Date ...25th May 1964..............

cards. I paid 6/- each for entrance fees and we were allowed in the premises. On entering, I bought two coffees from the bar.

The conditions this time were much the same as the previous visit, except that it was more crowded and the tables and chairs had been taken out of one of the rooms and so there were more people sitting and lying on the floor.

I also saw on two occasions two youths produce beer bottles from their pockets and drink out of the bottles. There was some empty beer bottles on the floor.

On this occasion at about 12.30am Police Sgt M and Policewoman M visited the club and questioned the younger looking members. At 5.10am Sgt M visited the club and at 5.50am Policewoman M visited the premises.

At about 6.00am I left the premises with Policewoman F as most of the members were leaving.

ELEANOR B. 'A' DIVISION

McKay's champion in his moral crusade was Chief Superintendent Alan Dingwall, who had presented a sub-section on the problem of 'Coffee Beat Clubs' in the Chief Constable's Annual Report, 1964. He hoped that his drastic recommendations 'might become a blue print remedy for other local authorities and Chief Constables throughout the country'.

The immoral antics of the youth of Manchester had become an obsession, with McKay and Dingwall. They had no concept whatsoever of the social needs and lifestyle of urban kids of the mid sixties, describing the clubs in question as 'places free from adult supervision...places where teenagers can stay all night if they so desired'. The 'Beat Club problem' began to totally overshadow other city centre problems such as gambling, illegal drinking, prostitution and vice dens. Extracts from the report began to illustrate this obsession: 'Some of the clubs are owned and managed by persons of known criminal record and inevitably attract persons of similar character'. It goes on to say 'Older women and many coloured men were frequenting the clubs'. A moral frenzy was being whipped up throughout the latter part of '64 and early '65.

In spring 1964, on Granada TV's early evening news magazine, *Scene At Six Thirty*, a youth who had recently been arrested for possession appeared standing outside the Wheel. He alleged that drugs could be obtained at the club and promised to 'inform the police as soon as any suggestion was made, that members were selling or bringing drugs into the club'.

From an internal Bootle Street report dated 15th May 1964 – 'ALLEGED SALE OF DRINAMYL TABLETS AT MANCHESTER CLUB'.

The Guardian got caught up in the frenzy, reporting on the 'teenager problem, drugs and coffee bars'. Members of the media were taken by the police to 'see at first hand, evidence that the worst of these clubs were being used for drug peddling and harbouring young prostitutes, absconders and teenage tramps'.

The end result was the unprecedented Manchester Corporation Act, 1965. McKay and Dingwall had succeeded. They had built up such an emotive and spectacular case against the clubs, that their recommendation for a new law to be brought in was passed by Parliament. In layman's **105**

CITY OF BRADFORD POLICE

CRIMINAL INVESTIGATION DEPARTMENT

Date.....9th October, 1964. ...

Subject......The Twisted Wheel Club, Manchester.........................

Sir,

    I have to report that on the 21st September, 1964, ▮▮▮▮▮▮, 16 years, 5▮, ▮▮▮▮▮ Lane, Bradford, and ▮▮▮▮▮▮ 17 years, 36, ▮▮▮▮▮▮ Crescent, Bradford, were arrested and charged with breaking and entering the chemist's department of a local shop from where they stole 500 Drinamyl tablets, 500 Dexadrine tablets, 300 Durophet capsules, 24 Benzedrine tablets and 30 Krameria and cocaine lozenges. They are at present remanded in custody for medical reports.

    The two boys were believed to be addicted to this type of drug and enquiries have been made with a view to ascertaining their previous sources of supply.

    During these enquiries it was alleged by ▮▮▮▮▮'s mother that he had been in the habit of frequenting the Twisted Wheel Club, Manchester and she believed drugs of this type were being circulated there. She had no evidence at all to support this.

    I suggest a copy of this report be forwarded to the Chief Constable City Police Office, Manchester, for his information and any action he think necessary.

Signed: F. ▮▮▮▮▮

21003

MANCHESTER CITY POLICE
13 OCT 1964
C.I.D. ADMIN.

Our ref. .....▮▮▮▮▮▮.....................

Your ref. ....

Forwarded to The Chief Constable,..............
              City Police Office,.....................
              MANCHESTER.

Chief Consta

terms, the new law would enable the respective city authority to fully control all clubs in its area.

The Bill gained Royal Assent in the summer of 1965 and became law on January 1st 1966. Police could now freely enter and inspect any club without a warrant, and also had the power to implement the aspect of the Act which enabled them to recommend a prison sentence for the owner, if drugs were found to be being consumed on the premises. It is no wonder then that by the summer of 1966 only a handful of the original two hundred plus coffee dance clubs were still in existence. The majority had either shut down or converted into 'respectable' licensed places of entertainment.

But someone forgot to tell Manchester's 'in' crowd. The summer of 1966 was the peak of the Mod scene in the north of England, and the police and council activity simply fuelled their excitement and anticipation of good times. Raids, arrests and drug squad searches, all made for an exhilarating summer.

The police, however were not resting on their laurels and another story emerged that would keep media and public anxiety at fever pitch. Mod Eddie Barnett was in the Jungfrau on Cathedral Walk one night and recalled a drugs raid which culminated in the club being shut down for the night. The customers were told to disperse and after meeting up with other Mods, Eddie learned that they too had been in clubs that had been raided. The story given to them by the police, and the reason behind the raids, was that a senior police officer's son had died from an overdose of black bombers. They alleged that he had earlier been at an All-Nighter. Apparently the lad had become so unwell that his friends had driven him round the city centre, throughout the night. Eventually they had dropped him off at casualty where he was pronounced dead upon arrival.

Derek Howe, another influential Mod on the scene confirms the story and even recalls newspaper coverage of the event, but like the alleged visit of the Krays, it's been impossible to confirm. Chris Lee who researched the whole of this era of Manchester youth culture, spent weeks on the case but was unable to establish any official record of the death.

One big question certainly remains unanswered – if the Twisted Wheel Club was so notorious and the hub of so many problems, why was it never closed down? More to the point, why at the very height of Chief Constable Mckay's campaign was it allowed to close down in Brazennose Street and open up, the following week in Whitworth Street? It would have been an ideal opportunity to close the Wheel for good. One possible theory was that with cooperative owners, one big club containing all of the miscreants would be easier to control.

Last Days at Brazennose Street

The efforts of the previous year involving the possible appearance of Screamin' Jay Hawkins finally paid off. On Friday 19th, and for both sessions on Saturday 20th February, Screamin' Jay Hawkins appeared at the Wheel backed by local band the Falling Leaves. Hawkins was a sensation and treated like royalty during his visit by Roger, Brian Smith, Roger Fairhurst and company. He was lauded in *R&B Scene*, a frequent visitor to Eagle's flat, a riot down the local curry house and even had tea with deejay Neil Carter and his mum.

Saturday 20th February – Twisted Wheel
Early/Late – Screaming Jay Hawkins + Falling Leaves

Alexis Korner

Screamin' Jay Hawkins made his final appearance at the Wheel on the Easter Monday of 19th April with the Blues Set. Unfortunately the loveable, but naïve Jay, as he was affectionately known, had innocently got himself involved with a ruthless UK booking agent. After either a dispute over money or a problem over fulfilling dates, it is alleged that a revolver was held to his head and a very terrified Jay fled the UK. No doubt he would have loved to have made more appearances at the Twisted Wheel but it wasn't to be. After all of the effort in persuading Jay to come over to England (which in part revived a flagging career), it was sad to hear that he had gone into hiding somewhere in the USA, still fearing for his life.

On the 6th March, the Twisted Wheel scooped again. Live on stage was the legendary Buddy Guy, supported by a young Rod Stewart and the Soul Agents. Up-and-coming white R&B outfit the Cops 'N Robbers played the early session.

After Buddy Guy, Champion Jack Dupree performed on the 20th March. Dupree had been persuaded to come over to Manchester from Paris by Ivor Abadi who had seen him perform whilst on holiday. The calibre of artists appearing at the Wheel was outstanding – Friday 26th March Spencer Davis Group, Saturday 27th March T-Bone Walker backed by John Mayall and on the 3rd April Larry Williams and Johnny 'Guitar' Watson.

April 1965 – 'POLICE PATROLS PEN 500 MODS ON BEACH. WE WANT BLOOD IS SHOUTED' SOME OF 70 ARRESTED HAD DRUGS

Motown Generation
'I remember playing an advance US copy of the Four Tops 'Reach Out I'll Be There' (UK release Oct 1966) for at least six months before it was released in the UK.'
Roger Eagle.

By 1965 the sound of Motown was being played in virtually every club in every city of the UK. All-Nighters at the Twisted Wheel were no exception, the difference being that at the Wheel they would be playing Motown records well in advance of them being released in this country.

Friday 5th Feb – Beat City Mini Ballroom
MOTOWN NIGHT

Although there were still plenty of scooters parked up outside the Wheel, and many to be seen cruising around the city centre, by Easter 1965 scooter numbers had fallen. There also seemed to be a new breed of teenager attending the Wheel – kids who were more into the soul music that was now being played, rather than the Mod thing. They were smart dressers, but more Fred Perrys, Ben Shermans and Levi's jeans, than mohair suits and knitted ties. They were casual and cool and spent most of the night up on the dance floor, well into the sounds. It was becoming obvious that these kids – the younger element at Brazennose Street (like Barry Tasker and Paul Davis) would make the move across town to the new Twisted Wheel on Whitworth Street after the original Wheel closed. They went on to be part of a new 'in' crowd, the Whitworth Street 'Soul crowd', while many of the scooter crowd and hard core R&B fans of the original Wheel never made the trip, it all ended for them so to speak, the night Brazennose Street closed.

Phil Scott considers the final six months at Brazennose Street (March–September '65) to be the best months in the club's relatively short, but celebrated history.

'Certainly the quality of artists had vastly improved since the extension to the club made back in September 1964, although to be fair, it was always the Twisted Wheel's policy to put on the very best acts available. By March of the following year, the Twisted Wheel's stature as the number one R&B club in the UK was undeniable. The Wheel was regarded as the major venue by visiting black US artists, an increasing number of who were performing in the UK...the Swinging '60s, 'England swings like a pendulum do', the Beatles and all that.'

The Wheel's R&B crowd was respected by artists and regarded as the one to please. By April '65 the Wheel was at its peak as a Mod club, rivalled only by the Scene in the capital; it had the most original of 'in' crowds, the snappiest dressed teenagers and the best dancers by far in the country. And the Twisted Wheel had the boldest and best deejays in the country in Eagle and Carter, two guys out on a limb, in a league of their own. Deejays who 'played 'em first'. The combination of all these factors together with, in the Wheel's own words, 'A Most Unusual Atmosphere', just about clinched it. The final six months at the Twisted Wheel on Brazennose Street was as good as it got. The club had it all.

Ever since the Wheel had opened, the Abadis had struggled with the property's short lease. It had to be renewed every twelve months, and despite the increasing interest shown in the Wheel by the Manchester Police,

Alex Harvey

or anybody else for that matter, it was for this reason alone that the decision was made to seek other premises. On Friday 13th September, the Abadi brothers made public their intention of closing down Brazennose Street. At first it seemed to many that it would only be closed on Fridays – surely the All-Nighters would carry on? But unbeknown to the Wheel faithful, plans had been made in advance of the closure to open a new club on the other side of town. The Wheel would continue, although for some it would never be the same. The All-Nighters had started in September '63 and the grand extension had opened in September 1964. On Friday 13th September 1965, club members would now read of the closure of their beloved Brazennose Street haunt in the *Manchester Evening News*.

NOTICE
TWISTED WHEEL CLOSED TONIGHT &
EVERY FRIDAY UNTIL FURTHER NOTICE

TWISTED WHEEL MEMBERS' NOTICE
GRAND OPENING OF NEW TWISTED WHEEL PREMISES
SATURDAY SEPTEMBER 18TH 1965 – SPENCER DAVIS GROUP
AT 6 WHITWORTH STREET. OPP FIRE STATION MANCHESTER

THE CLUB IN BRAZENNOSE STREET WILL CLOSE AFTER THE
ALL-NIGHT SESSION ON SATURDAY SEPTEMBER 11TH 1965
FEATURING JOHN MAYALL

Complete listing of all acts advertised in the Manchester Evening News that appeared at the Twisted Wheel Brazennose Street

1963
JANUARY
Saturday 27th – Dean West and the Hellions

1963

FEBRUARY
Friday 1st – Dean West and the Hellions – Non Stop Dancing 7.30–1.00am
Thursday 7th – Dean West and the Hellions 7.30–11.30pm 2/6d
Friday 8th – Trevor Fayne and Original Phantoms
Sunday 9th – Brent Wade and Wanderers 2/6d
Friday 15th – Freddy and the Dreamers 7.30–12.00 Midnight 3/-
Saturday 16th – Wayne Fontana & Jets 7.30–1.00 am
Sunday 17th – Eddie and Cymerones
Friday 22nd – Hollies
Saturday 23rd – Antones
Sunday 24th – Danny and the Dominators – 3/-

MARCH

Friday 1st – Dean West & Hellions 7.00–12.00 Midnight 3/-

Saturday 2nd – Country Gentlemen – 7.30–1.00am

Sunday 3rd – Danny & Dominators

Friday 8th – Marty Barry & Teenbeats – 7.00–12.00 Midnight 5/-

Saturday 9th – Renegades – 7.30–1.00 am

Sunday10th – 7.30–12.00 midnight – Cymerones

Friday 15th – Nashville Men 3/-

Saturday 16th – Renegades (Birmingham's top group) 7.30–1.00am

Sunday 16th – Lee Paul and the Boys – 7.30–12.00 Midnight 3/-

Friday 22nd – Johnny Martin and the Tremors

Saturday 23rd – By popular request M/c's leading rhythm group – The Hollies

Sunday 24th – Hellions

Friday March 29th – Country Gentleman 3/-

Saturday March 30th – Ricky Dene and Fantoms

Sunday March 31st – Eddie and Cymerones 3/-

APRIL

Friday 5th – Nashville Men

Saturday 6th – Terry Slade with Peter York and the Pontiacs

Friday 12th – Frank Kelly

Saturday 13th – Renegades

Sunday 14th – Don Curtis and the Coasters

Monday 15th– Deek Rivers & Big Sound

Friday 19th – Jasons

Saturday 20th – Valiants

Sunday 21st – Fourmost

Friday 26th – Nashville Men

Saturday 27th – Sean Campbell and the Tremeloes

Sunday 28th – Eddie and the Cymerones

MAY

Friday 3rd – Hollies

Saturday 4th – Rhythm & Blues Inc. (from Southport) 3/-

Sunday 5th – Renegades 3/-

Friday 10th – Original Phantoms

Saturday 11th – Hellions

Sunday 12th – Johnny Martin & Tremors

Friday 17th – Bry Martin and the Marauders 3/-

Saturday 18th – Spidermen (Liverpool)

Sunday 19th – Wayne Fontana and the Jets – 3/-

Friday 24th – Hollies

Saturday 25th – Renegades

Sunday 26th – Eddie and the Cymerones
Monday 27th – Four Just Men
Friday 31st – Pontiacs (Sheffield)

JUNE
Saturday 1st – Country Gents – (Decca recording artists)
Sunday 2nd – Nashville Men
Monday 3rd – Mike Cadillac and Playboys
Friday 7th – Dynachords
Saturday 8th – Hellions
Sunday 9th – Merseybeats
Monday 10th – Gay and the Guys
Friday 14th – Hollies
Saturday 15th – Danny Havoc and the Ventures
Sunday 16th – Coasters
Monday 17th – Bry Martin and the Marauders
Friday 21st – Emperors of Rhythm – 3/-
Saturday 22nd – Renegades
Sunday 23rd – Sunday Club – Beat Boys – 3/-
Friday 28th – Coasters
Saturday 29th – Nashville Men
Sunday 30th – Four Most

JULY
Monday 1st – Hollies – 4/-
Friday 5th – Lance Harvey and the Statesmen – 3/-
Saturday 6th – Pontiacs
Sunday 7th – Country Gentlemen – 3/-
Friday 12th – Coasters
Saturday 13th – Hollies
Sunday 14th – Renegades
Friday 19th – Methods
Saturday 20th – Nashville Men
Sunday 21st – Beat Boys – 3/-
Friday 26th – Marauders 4/-
Saturday 27th – Country Gentlemen
Sunday 28th – Pontiacs

AUGUST
Friday 2nd – Lance Harvey and the Statesmen
Saturday 3rd – Cymerones
Sunday 4th – Incas – 3/-
Monday 5th – Phil J Corbett and Coasters

Friday 9th – Rhythm & Blues Incorporated

Saturday 10th – Methods

Sunday 11th – Renegades

Monday 12th – Marauders

Friday 16th – Country Gentlemen

Saturday 17th – Hellions

Sunday 18th – Beat Boys

Friday 23rd – Lance Harvey and Statesmen

Saturday 24th – Rain Makers

Sunday 25th – Emperors of Rhythm

Saturday 31st – Renegades & 12 String Spencer Davis (R & B Guitarist) 7.30 pm

Sunday 31st – Nashville Men

SEPTEMBER

Monday 2nd Sept – MEMBERS NOTICE

Management wish to announce starting tomorrow admission on Tuesday 1/-

Friday 6th – Original Phantoms

Saturday 7th – Coasters

Sunday 8th – Dynachords

Monday 9th – Marauders

Friday 12th – Lance Harvey and the King Pins – 3/-

Saturday 13th – Lance Harvey

Friday 20th – The Escorts

Saturday 21st – The Hellions

Sunday 22nd – Sunday Club – Country Gents

Monday 23rd – The Marauders

Friday 27th – The Nashville Men

Saturday 28th September

Early session – The Renegades plus plus plus

Spencer Davis 12 string R&B guitarist

Late Night Rhythm and Blues

Grand Opening – from 12 midnight

Graham Bond Quartet plus Spencer Davis 12 string-R&B guitarist

Members only 6/-

Sunday 29th – Lance Harvey and the King Pins 3/-

OCTOBER

Friday 4th Tonight – Decca Recording Artists – 'They Say' – The Mojos

Saturday 5th – Decca Recording Artists –'That's My Plan' The Beat Boys

Saturday October 5th Tonight – Late Night Rhythm and Blues

John Mayall's Blues Breakers from Midnight – Members Only 5/-

Sunday 6th – Gerry De Ville and the City Kings – Members Only 3/-

Friday 11th – Paul Stevens Emperors of Rhythm

Saturday 12th Renegades plus Late Night Rhythm and Blues
From Midnight – Jimmy Powell and the Dimensions Members Only 6/-
Sunday 13th – Sunday Club –Tony Kay and the Huckelberries
Wednesday 16th – Bongo Von Dort
Friday 18th – By Popular Request – The Nashville Men
Saturday 19th Early Session – Rainmakers
12 Midnight – Graham Bond Quartet plus Spencer Davis 12 string Rhythm and Blues guitarist
Friday 25th – Decca Recording Stars – 'They Say' The Mojos
Saturday 26th Early Session – Hellions
Twisted Wheel Presents Late Night Rhythm and Blues every Saturday from 12 midnight
TO-NIGHT TO-NIGHT
Spencer Davis Quartet Members Only 6/-

NOVEMBER
Friday 1st – Decca Recording Artists – The Beat Boys
Saturday 2nd – Early Session – The Avalons
Late Session – Tonight London's Top R&B Band John Mayall's Blues Breakers
Sunday Club – Decca Recording Artists – Country Gentlemen
Friday 8th – Oriole Recording Stars – Buddy Britten & the Regents 3/-
Saturday 9th – Early – The Rainmakers/All-Nighter – Roadrunners (London)
Friday 15th – The Coasters – 3/-
Saturday 16th – Early – The Whirlwinds/All-Nighter - Hogsnort Rupert (London)
Sunday Club – Vic and the Spidermen
Monday 18th – Decca Recording Stars – The Rockin' Berries
Friday 22nd – Decca Recording Stars – The Mojos
Saturday 23rd – Early – Escorts (Liverpool)/All-Nighter – Spencer Davis Quartet
Sunday Club – The Beat Boys
Friday 29th – Nashville Men
Saturday 30th – Early – Vic and the Spidermen/All-Nighter – Graham Bond Quartet

DECEMBER
Sunday 1st – Lance Harvey & the Kingpins
Monday 2nd – Red Caps
Friday 6th – Jeannie and the Big Guys
Saturday 7th – All-Nighter – Jimmy Powell and the Dimensions
Sunday 8th – Renegades
Monday 9th – The Beat Boys
Friday 13th – Twisted Wheel – Buddy Britten and the Regents
Saturday 14th – Early – Carole Kay and the Dynachords/All-Nighter – Rocking Berries
Sunday Club – Whirlwinds
Friday 20th – Jimmy Powell and the Dimensions
Saturday 21st – Early – Avalons/All-Nighter – John Mayall's Blues Breakers
Sunday Club – Marauders

Xmas Eve 24th December 8pm–2am – Buddy Britten and the Regents,
Nashville Men, Chris Nava Combo
Xmas Day 25th December – 7-30pm–12 – Coasters
Boxing Day 26th – Decca Recording Artists - Beat Boys
Friday 27th – Lance Harvey and the Kingpins
Saturday 28th – Early Session – Wailers/All-Nighter – Graham Bond Quartet
Sunday 29th – Country Gents
Tuesday 31st – New Year's Eve – Mojos (Decca) – Whirlwinds – Wailers

1964
JANUARY
Friday 3rd – Rey Anton and the Peppermint Men
Saturday 4th – All-Nighter – Downliners Sect !!
Monday 6th 'Direct From Thank Your Lucky Stars' – Decca Recording Artists –The Redcaps
Tuesday 7th – Ad for Twisted Wheel
This Saturday – Cyril Davies and the All Stars
Friday 10th – Tony Kay and the Huckleberries
Saturday 11th – Early – Beat Boys/All Nighter – Long John Baldry plus Cyril Davies All Stars
Sunday Club 12th – Mal Rider and the Spirits
Friday 17th – Country Gentlemen
Saturday 18th – Early – Lance Harvey & King pins/All-Nighter – Jimmy Powell & Dimensions
Sunday Club 19th – 'Fontana Recording Artists' – Lorraine Gray and the Chapperrones
Friday 24th – Freddie Starr and the Midnighters
Saturday 25th – Early – Carole Kay and the Dynachords/All-Nighter – Graham Bond Quartet
Sunday Club 26th – Marauders
Wednesday 29th – Rockin' Berries
Friday 31st – Tony Dee and the Shake Outs

FEBRUARY
Saturday 1st – Early – Sheffields/All-Nighter – John Mayall and the Blues Breakers
Sunday Club 2nd – Rockin' Berries
Monday 3rd – Red Caps
Friday 7th – Coasters
Saturday 8th – Early – Tony Kay and the Huckleberries/All Nighter – Manfred Mann
Sunday Club 9th – Spidermen (Liverpool)
Friday 14th – Dynachords
Sat 15th – Early – Ian Crawford + Boomerangs/All-Nighter – Sonny Boy Williamson + Animals
Sunday Club 16th – Beat Boys
Friday 21st – Lance Harvey and the King Pins
Saturday 22nd – Early – The Mastersounds/All-Nighter – Graham Bond Quartet
Sunday Club 23rd – Country Gents
Friday 28th – Red Caps
Sat 29th – Early – Galaxies/All-Nighter – Long John Baldry and the Hoochie Coochie Men

MARCH

Friday 6th – Phil's Feelgoods
Saturday 7th – Early – Whirlwinds/All-Nighter – Jimmy Powell and the Dimensions
Friday 13th – The Cyclones
Saturday 14th – Early – Excheckers/All-Nighter – Spencer Davis Quartet
Sunday Club 15th – 2 Acts – The Beat Boys – Tony Dee and the Shakeouts
Friday 20th – Decca Recording Stars – The Young Ones
Saturday 21st – Early – Beat Boys/All-Nighter – John Mayall and the Blues Breakers
Sunday Club 22nd – Red Caps
Saturday 28th – Early – Renegades/All-Nighter – Graham Bond Quartet
Sunday 29th – Jackie Lynton and the Cutters plus The Beat Boys – 4/–

APRIL

Friday 3rd – Lance Harvey and the King Pins
Saturday 4th – Early – Saints/All-Nighter Long John Baldry and the Hoochie Coochie Men
Sunday Club 5th – Marauders
Friday 10th – Rockin' Henry Hayseed
Saturday 11th – Early – Tony Dee + Shakeouts/All-Nighter – Alex Harvey and his Soul Band
Friday 17th – Helene and the Kinsmen – 3/–
Saturday 18th – Early – The Mighty Avengers/All-Nighter – Animals
Sunday Club 19th – The Beat Boys
Friday 24th – Phil's Feelgoods
Saturday 25th – Early – The Madmen/All-Nighter – Georgie Fame and the Blue Flames
Sunday Club 30th – Whirlwinds
Monday 31st – Fontana Recording Artists – The 5 Embers

MAY

Friday 1st – Millie 'My Boy Lollipop'
Saturday 2nd – Early – The Diamonds/All-Nighter – Graham Bond Quartet
Friday 8th – 2 Top Recording Groups – The Beat Boys + Me and Them 4/–
Saturday 9th – Early – Mastersounds/All-Nighter – Memphis Slim – 7/6d
Sunday Club 10th – David John and the Mood 3/–
Thursday 14th – 4 Pennies 6/–
Friday 15th – Malcolm Clarke and the Cresters 4/–
Saturday 16th – Early – The Ramblers/All-Nighter – Spencer Davis Quartet
Sunday Club 17th – The Big 3
Friday 22nd – Johnny Peters and the JP's
Saturday 23rd – Early – The Addicts/All-Nighter – Long John Baldry + Hoochie Coochie Men
Sunday 24th – The Marauders
Friday 29th – Lance Harvey and the Kingpins
Sat 30th – Early – Paul Ryan and the Crescents/All-Nighter – Georgie Flame + Blue Flames

JUNE

Friday 5th – Country Gents / Clayton Squares

Sat 6th – Millie (early)/Cheynes All-Nighter

Sunday 7th – Rockin' Berries

Friday 12th – Mighty Avengers

Sat 13th – Litter (early)/All-Nighter – John Lee Hooker & John Mayall

Sunday 14th – David John and The Mood

Friday 19th – Chris Ryan & The Question

Sat 20th – Renegades/Jimmy Powell

Sunday 21st – Red Caps

Friday 26th – Addicts

Sat 27th – Escorts/All-Nighter – Graham Bond

Sun 28th – Dave Berry & Cruisers

JULY

Friday 3rd – Beat Boys

Sat 4th – Early – Diamonds/All-Nighter – Long John Baldry and the Hoochie Coochie Men

Sunday Club 5th – Marauders

Monday 6th – John Lee Hooker

Wednesday 8th – Inez and Charlie Foxx plus The Spencer Davis Group – 2/6d

Friday 10th – Spidermen 3/-

Saturday 11th – Georgie Fame and the Blue Flames/Early Session 5/- All-Nighter 7/6d

Sunday 12th – Long John Baldry

Wednesday 15th – Jimmy Powell and the Dimensions 2/6d

Friday 17th – The Bluesounds (R and B) 3/-

Saturday 18th – Early – The Abstracts – 5/- / All-Nighter – Spencer Davis Group – 6/-

Sunday 19th – Shades 5 2/-

Wednesday 22nd – Yardbirds

Friday 24th – Herman's Hermits 3/-

Saturday 25th – Early – Powerhouse 6/All-Nighter – Charlesworth Big Blues with Bobby Breen

Sunday 26th – Tony Sheridan and the Bobby Patrick Big Six 3/-

Wednesday 29th – R and B – Hideaways 2/6d

Friday 31st – Alexis Korners Blues Incorporated 3/-

AUGUST

Saturday 1st – Early – Paramounts 3/-/All-Nighter – Graham Bond Organisation 6/-

Sunday 2nd – Addicts 3/-

Monday 3rd – Georgie Fame 4/-

Wednesday 5th – Blues Giants 2/6d

Friday 7th – Ivan's Meads 3/-

Saturday 8th – Early – David John and the Mood 3/-/All-Nighter – The T-Bones 4/-

Sunday 9th – Clayton Squares 3/-

Wednesday 12th – Beat Boys – 2/6d

Friday 14th – Mighty Avengers – 3/-
Saturday 15th – Long John Baldry + the Hoochie Coochie Men/Early 5/- All-Nighter 7/6d
Sunday 16th – Mark Leeman 5 3/-
Wednesday 19th – Shades 5
Friday 21st Country Gents 3/-
Saturday 22nd – Early – The Bluesounds/All-Nighter – Alexis Korner's Blues Incorporated
Sunday 23rd – Phil's Feelgoods
Saturday 29th – Early – Little Boy Blues/All-Nighter – John Lee Hooker + the Groundhogs 6/-
Sunday 30th – Blues Giants

SEPTEMBER
Wednesday 2nd – Little Boy Blues 2/6d
Friday 4th Sept – Twisted Wheel – 5 Shades 3/-
Saturday 5th – Twisted Wheel
'Grand Opening Night – We Take Pleasure In Announcing
That The Premises Have Now Been Extended – Enabling Members
To View Groups In A New Large Area.
Planned For The Future Are Most Of The Country's Top Groups'
To-Night! Memphis Slim – Georgie Fame – The Sheffields
Sunday 6th – Soul Seekers 3/-
Wednesday 8th – Victor Brox Blues Train 2/-
Friday 10th – Ivan's Meads
Saturday 12th – Soul Agents/Jimmy Powell and the Dimensions/Early 5/- All-Nighter 7/6d
Sunday 13th – Renegades
Tuesday 15th – The Pretty Things 4/-
Saturday 18th – Early and Late Sessions/Alexis Korner and The Soul Seekers
Sunday 19th – Clayton Squares
Wednesday 22nd – The Rats 2/6d
Friday 24th – King Bees
Saturday 26th – Early and Late Sessions/Spencer Davies Group/Blues Giants
Sunday 27th – Zombies 4/-

OCTOBER
Friday 2nd –Small Faces 3/-
Saturday 3rd – Early – Bluesounds 5/-/All-Nighter – Little Walter/Alexis Korner 7/6d
Sunday 4th – Me and Them
Wednesday 7th – Alexis Korner's Blues Incorporated'
Friday 9th –Ivan's Meads
Saturday 10th – Early – Diamonds 5/-/All-Nighter – John Lee Hooker + the Groundhogs 7/6d
Sunday 11th – Jimmy Powell and the Dimensions
Wednesday 14th – Inez and Charlie Foxx
Friday 16th – The Boys 3/-
Saturday 17th – Both Sessions – Alex Harvey and the Soul Band/The Plebs

Sunday 18th – Beat Boys
Monday 19th – Alex Harvey
Wednesday 21st – Yardbirds
Friday 23rd – Vic Takes 4 3/-
Saturday 24th – Early and Late Sessions – The T–Bones
Sunday 25th – Cheynes
Wednesday 28th – Kinks
Friday 30th – Ivans Meads
Saturday 31st – Early and Late/5 Shades/Long John Baldry and the Hoochie Coochie Men

NOVEMBER
Sunday 1st – Sugar Pie Desanto 4/-
Wednesday 4th – John Lee's Groundhogs/John Lee Hooker
Friday 6th – Black Abbots
Saturday 7th – Early and Late Sessions/The Moody Blues/Sonny Boy Williamson + others
Sunday 8th – Marauders
Wednesday 11th – The Soul Sisters plus the Spencer Davis Group 2/6d
Friday 13th – Curt's Creatures 3/-
Saturday 14th – Early and Late Sessions – Clayton Squares/The Yardbirds
Sunday 15th – Rockin' Berries
Wednesday 18th – Georgie Fame and the Blue Flames
Friday 20th – Trendsetters
Saturday 21st – Early and Late Sessions – Jimmy Reed
Sunday 22nd – Blues Giants
Monday 23rd – Alexis Korner (begins Monday night residency)
Wednesday 25th – Slants
Friday 27th – Nashville Teens
Saturday 28th – Early and Late Sessions – Spencer Davies Group/Beat Boys
Sunday 29th – T-Bones
Monday 30th – Alexis Korner

DECEMBER
Wednesday 2nd – Blues Council
Friday 4th – Jimmy Powell and the Dimensions
Saturday 5th – Early and Late Sessions – Georgie Fame/Blues Giants 4/-
Sunday 6th – Clayton Squares
Monday 7th – Alexis Korner
Friday 11th – Soul Messengers
Saturday 12th – Early and Late Sessions/John Mayall and the Blues Breakers / Night Style
Sunday 13th – Country Gents
Monday 14th – Friday 18th – Alexis Korner
Saturday 19th – Early and Late Sessions/John Lee's Groundhogs/Joe Cocker Big Blues
Monday 21st – Alexis Korner

Thursday 24th Xmas Eve – Blues Giants + Hipster Image 7pm–2am
Friday 25th – Christmas Day – 7.30pm – 12.00 – Blues Giants/Glowing Embers 7/-
Saturday 26th – Early and Late / Sonny Boy Williamson/Spencer Davies Group/ Soul Seekers
Thursday 31st – New Years Eve – Twisted Wheel
Alexis Korner/Renegades/Blues Giants 7pm–2.00am 10/-

1965
JANUARY
Friday 1st – New Years Day – Beat Boys 7.30pm–11.30pm 3/-
Saturday 2nd – Early – 5 Dimensions – Late – Impullsions
Monday 4th – Alexis Korner
Friday 8th – Blues Herd
Saturday 9th – Early – Sheffields – Late – Crusaiders
Sunday 10th – The Impressions
Monday 11th – Alexis Korner
Friday 15th – M Q Blues
Saturday 16th – Early and Late – John Mayall – The Falling Leaves
Sunday 17th – St Louis Union
Monday 18th – Alexis Korner
Friday 22nd – The Angle
Saturday 23rd – Early and Late – The T Bones – The Fairies
Monday 25th – Alexis Korner
Saturday 30th – Early and Late Sessions – Duffy Powell and the Sorrows
Sunday 31st – Dawn Breakers

FEBRUARY
Saturday 6th – Early – Clayton Squares/Allnighter – Spencer Davis
Sunday 7th – Dawn Breakers
Friday 12th – Blues Giants
Saturday 13th – Early and Late – Rod Stewart and the Soul Agents – 5 Dimensions
Sunday 14th – Blues Herd
Friday 19th – Screaming Jay Hawkins – The Falling Leaves
Saturday 20th – Early and Late – Screaming Jay Hawkins and the Falling Leaves
Sunday 21st – Long John Baldry
Saturday 27th – Early/Late – Zoot Money's Big Roll Band plus Brian Auger Trinity
Sunday 28th – St Louis Union

MARCH
Saturday 6th – Early – Cops 'N Robbers/Late – Buddy Guy – Rod Stewart + Soul Agents
Sunday 7th – Marauders
Saturday 13th – Early and Late Sessions – Alexis Korner plus 5 Dimensions
Sunday 14th – Blues Giants
Saturday 20th – Early – The Habit – Late – Champion Jack Dupree plus the Sheffields

Sunday 21st – St Louis Union

Friday 26th – Spencer Davies Group

Saturday 27th – Early and Late –T Bone Walker – John Mayall

APRIL

Saturday 3rd – Early – Hipster Image + Fossils/Late – Larry Williams + Johnny Guitar Watson

Sunday 4th – Victor Broxx

Saturday 10th – Early and Late – Jimmy Powell 5 Dimensions/John Lee's Groundhogs

Sunday 11th – Blues Herd

Saturday 17th – Early and Late – Graham Bond

Sunday 18th – St. Louis Union

Monday 19th – Screaming Jay Hawkins plus the Blues Set

Saturday 24th – Early and Late – Long John Baldry/Blues Giants

Sunday 25th – Blues Set

MAY

Saturday 1st – Early – Clayton Squares/All-Nighter – Spencer Davis Group

Sunday 2nd – Chevrons

Saturday 8th – Early and Late – Tea Time 4 – John Mayall Blues Breakers

Sunday 9th – 3 Dots and a Dash

Saturday 15th – Early and Late – 5 Dimensions plus – Blues Giants

Sunday 16th – The Gremlins

Saturday 22nd – Early and Late – Fetish Crowd and Brian Auger Trinity

Sunday 23rd – Victor Brox

Saturday 29th – Early and Late – The Action – Blues Set – Champion Jack Dupree

Sunday 30th – St. Louis Union

JUNE

Saturday 5th – Early – Cops 'N Robbers/All-Nighter – Blues Giants – John Lee Hooker

Sunday 6th – Blues Pentagon

Saturday 12th – Early and Late – Rod Stewart – St. Louis Union

Sunday 13th – Big City Blues

Friday 18th – Ivans Meads

Saturday 19th – Early and Late Sessions – Soul Sisters/Brian Auger Trinity

Saturday 26th – Early – Mike Allen Group/All-Nighter – Jimmy Powell 5 Dimensions

Sunday 27th – New Departures

JULY

Friday 2nd – Mike Cotton Sound

Saturday 3rd – Early and Late – John Lee's Grounghogs

Sunday 4th – St. Louis Union

Saturday 10th – Early – Brian Auger Trinity/All-Nighter – Georgie Fame + the Blue Flames

Saturday 17th – Early – Clayton Squares – Late – 5 Dimensions

121

Saturday 24th – Early – The Gremlins/All-Nighter The Ram Jam Band/Inez and Charlie Foxx
Saturday 31st – Early – Ivan's Meads/All-Nighter – Spencer Davis

August
Saturday 7th – Early and Late Sessions – Jimmy Powell and the 5 Dimensions
Sunday 8th – Toggery 5
Friday 13th August
NOTICE
TWISTED WHEEL CLOSED TONIGHT &
EVERY FRIDAY UNTIL FURTHER NOTICE

TWISTED WHEEL MEMBERS NOTICE
GRAND OPENING OF NEW TWISTED WHEEL PREMISES
SATURDAY SEPTEMBER 18TH 1965
SPENCER DAVIS GROUP
AT 6 WHITWORTH STREET. OPP FIRE STATION MANCHESTER
THE CLUB IN BRAZENNOSE STREET WILL CLOSE AFTER THE
ALL-NIGHT SESSION ON SATURDAY SEPTEMBER 11TH 1965
FEATURING JOHN MAYALL

Saturday 14th – Early & Late Sessions – 5 Divisions
Sunday 115th – Blues Division
Saturday 21st – Early & Late Session Graham Bond Organisation
Sunday 22nd – Lobos
Saturday 28th – Early & Late Sessions – John Lee's Groundhogs
Sunday 29th – St Louis Union

September
Saturday 4th – Early & Late Session – St Louis Union
Sunday 5th – Jimmy Powell & 5 Dimensions
Saturday 11th – Last Night John Mayall & the Blues Breakers

'All the groups wanted to play in Manchester, especially the Wheel.'

KEN WHITE – ex-Jimmy Powell & the Dimensions

Brazennose Street Records

LAVERN BAKER (WITH JIMMY RICKS) 'You're The Boss' (US-Atlantic/UK-London)

RITCHIE BARRETT 'Some Other Guy' (US-Atlantic/UK-London)

CHUCK BERRY 'Come On' (US-Chess/UK-Pye International)

BIG SAMBO 'At The Party' (US-Eric)

BOBBY BLAND 'Turn On Your Lovelight' (US-Duke/UK-Vogue)

BOBBY BLAND 'Yield Not To Temptation' (US-Duke/UK-Vocalion)

BO DIDDLEY 'Road Runner' (US-Checker/UK-London and Pye International)

BO DIDDLEY 'Pretty Thing' (US-Checker/UK-Pye International)

BO DIDDLEY EP 'R&B With Bo Diddley' (UK-London)

BO DIDDLEY album 'Bo Diddley Rides Again' (UK-Pye International)

JAMES BOOKER 'Smacksie' (US-Peacock)

BOOKER T & THE MGs 'Green Onions' (US-Stax/UK-London)

JACKIE BRENSTON 'Independent Woman' (US-Chess)

JAMES BROWN 'Night Train' (US-King/UK-Sue)

JAMES BROWN 'Tell Me What You're Gonna Do' (US-King/UK-Ember)

RUTH BROWN 'Mama He Treats Your Daughter Mean' (US-Atlantic/UK-London)

BUNKER HILL 'Hide & Go Seek Pt 1' (US-Mala/UK-Stateside)

BUNKER HILL 'You Can't Make Me Doubt My Baby' (US-Mala)

BUNKER HILL 'Red Riding Hood And The Wolf' (US-Mala)

CADETS 'Stranded In the Jungle' (US-Modern/UK-London)

ALVIN CASH 'You Shot Me Through The Grease' (US-Mar-V-Lus album track)

CASTAWAYS 'Liar Liar' (US-Soma/UK-London)

RAY CHARLES 'I've Got A Woman' (US-Atlantic)

RAY CHARLES 'Tell The Truth' (US-Atlantic/UK-London)

RAY CHARLES (& THE COOKIES) 'Lonely Avenue' (US-Atlantic)

CLOVERS 'Love Potion Number No. 9' (US-United Artists/UK-London)

COASTERS 'Poison Ivy' (US-Atco/UK-London)

SAM COOKE 'Shake' (US & UK-RCA)

GARNELL COOPER & THE KINFOLKS 'Long Distance' (US-Jubilee/UK-London)

CYRIL DAVIES R&B ALLSTARS 'Country Line Special' (UK-Pye International)

SPENCER DAVIS GROUP 'I Can't Stand It' (UK-Fontana)

SPENCER DAVIS GROUP 'This Hammer' (UK-Fontana)

SPENCER DAVIS GROUP 'Washed My Hands In Muddy Water'
   (UK-Fontana album 'Their First LP')

DAYLIGHTERS 'Oh! Mom (Teach Me How To Uncle Willie)' (US-Tip Top/UK-Sue)

DOC BAGBY 'Dumplin's' (US-OKeh/UK-Fontana)

BILL DOGGETT 'The Hully Gully Twist' (US & UK-Warner Brothers)

DOMINOES 'Sixty-Minute Man' (US-Federal/UK-Vogue)

DOVELLS 'You Can't Sit Down' (US-Parkway/UK-Cameo-Parkway)

BETTY EVERETT 'Getting Mighty Crowded' (US-Vee-Jay/UK-Fontana)

FIVE DU-TONES 'Divorce Court' (US-One-Derful!/UK-Stateside)

GENE & EUNICE (WITH JONESY'S COMBO) 'Ko Ko Mo' (US-Combo/UK-Vogue)

DOBIE GRAY 'The 'In' Crowd' (US-Charger/UK-London)
ROY HAMILTON 'You Can Have Her' (US-Epic/UK-Fontana)
HOMESICK JAMES 'Crossroads' (US-USA/UK-Sue)
JOHN LEE HOOKER 'Boom Boom' (US-Vee-Jay/UK-Stateside)
JOHN LEE HOOKER 'Dimples' (US-Vee-Jay/UK-Stateside)
HOWLIN' WOLF 'Smokestack Lightning' (US-Chess/UK-Pye International)
JESSE & BUZZY 'Goin' Back To New Orleans' (US-Savoy)
NAT KENDRICK & THE SWANS 'Dish Rag Pts 1&2' (US-Dade/UK-Top Rank)
J.B. LENOIR (WITH HIS AFRICAN HUNCH RHYTHM) 'I Sing Um The Way I Feel'
    (US-USA/UK-Sue)
LITTLE MILTON 'Let's Boogie Baby' (US-Meteor)
LITTLE RICHARD 'Long Tall Sally' (US-Specialty/UK-London)
LITTLE WALTER 'My Babe' (US-Checker/UK-London and Pye International)
LITTLE WALTER 'Juke' (US-Checker)
MAR-KEYS 'Last Night' (US-Satellite/UK-London)
MAR-KEYS 'Beachbash' (US-Stax)
MARVELETTES 'Please Mr. Postman' (US-Tamla/UK-Fontana)
NATHANIEL MAYER & THE FABULOUS TWILIGHTS 'Village Of Love'
    (US-Fortune/UK-HMV)
PERCY MAYFIELD 'Stranger In My Own Home Town'
    (US-Tangerine/UK-HMV album 'My Jug And I')
JIMMY MCCRACKLIN 'The Drag' (US-Art-Tone/UK-Top Rank)
JIMMY MCCRACKLIN 'Can't Raise Me' (US-Checker/UK-Liberty)
LUKE 'LONG GONE' MILES 'Long Gone' (US-Smash)
CHARLIE MINGUS 'Wednesday Night Prayer Meeting' (US-Atlantic)
MIRACLES 'Shop Around' (US-Tamla/UK-London)
MIRACLES 'You've Really Got A Hold On Me' (US-Tamla/UK-Oriole)
WILLIE MITCHELL 'Stone Face' (US-Hi album 'That Driving Beat')
MUDDY WATERS 'Messin' With The Man' (US-Chess)
OHIO UNTOUCHABLES 'I'm Tired' (US-LuPine)
ORLONS 'The Wah Watusi' (US-Cameo/UK-Columbia)
BOBBY PARKER 'Watch Your Step' (US-V-Tone/UK-London & Sue)
JUNIOR PARKER 'Barefoot Rock' (US-Duke)
BOBBY PETERSON QUINTET 'One Day' (US-V-Tone/UK-Sue)
WILSON PICKETT 'In The Midnight Hour' (US & UK-Atlantic)
ELVIS PRESLEY 'Mystery Train' (US-Sun/UK-HMV)
? & THE MYSTERIANS '96 Tears' (US-Pa-Go-Go & Cameo/UK-Cameo Parkway)
MAC REBENACK 'Storm Warning' (US-Rex)
OTIS REDDING 'Pain In My Heart' (US-Volt/UK-London)
BIG JACK REYNOLDS 'Made It Up In Your Mind' (US-MAH's)
ALVIN ROBINSON 'Searchin' ' (US-Tiger/UK-Pye International)
DR. ROSS 'Numbers Blues' (US-Hi-Q)
124 SAM THE SHAM & THE PHAROAHS 'Woolly Bully' (US-XL/UK-MGM)

SIR DOUGLAS QUINTET 'She's About A Mover' (US-Tribe/UK-London)
BENNY SPELLMAN 'Fortune Teller' (US-Minit/UK-London)
BARRETT STRONG 'Money' (US-Anna & Tamla/UK-London)
SUGAR PIE DESANTO 'Soulful Dress' (US-Checker/UK-Pye International)
HOWARD TATE 'Look At Granny Run Run' (US-Verve/UK-Verve)
RUFUS THOMAS 'Did You Ever Love A Woman?' (US-Stax)
RUFUS THOMAS 'Jump Back' (US-Stax/UK-Atlantic)
WILLIE MAE THORNTON 'Tom Cat' (US-Sotoplay/UK-Sue)
ALLEN TOUSSAINT 'Whirlaway' (US-RCA)
TRIUMPHS 'Raw Dough' (US-Volt)
DORIS TROY 'Just One Look' (US-Atlantic/UK-London)
BIG JOE TURNER 'Shake, Rattle And Roll' (US-Atlantic)
T.V. SLIM 'Bad Understanding' (US-Speed & Checker)
PHIL UPCHURCH COMBO 'You Can't Sit Down' (US-Boyd/UK-HMV & Sue)
PHIL UPCHURCH COMBO 'Pink Lollipop' (US-Boyd album track)
VAN-DELLS 'Slumber Party' (US-Stax)
VIBRATIONS 'My Girl Sloopy' (US-Atlantic/UK-London)
TRAVIS WAMMACK 'Scratchy' (US-ARA/UK-Atlantic)
TRAVIS WAMMACK 'Distortion' (US-ARA)
TRAVIS WAMMACK 'Night Train' (US-ARA album track)
TRAVIS WAMMACK 'Have You Ever Had The Blues' (US-ARA)
TRAVIS WAMMACK 'Don't Cry No More' (US-ARA)
SONNY BOY WILLIAMSON 'Help Me'/'Bye Bye Bird'
   (US-Checker/UK-Pye International)
CHUCK WILLIS album 'The King Of The Stroll' (US-Atlantic)
JOHN ZACHERLE 'Dinner With Drac Pt 1' (US-Cameo/UK-London)

'With English kids I'm always nervous – except in Manchester where they're very enthusiastic and always enjoy themselves, no different from kids in the States.'
JOAN JOHNSON – The Dixie Cups

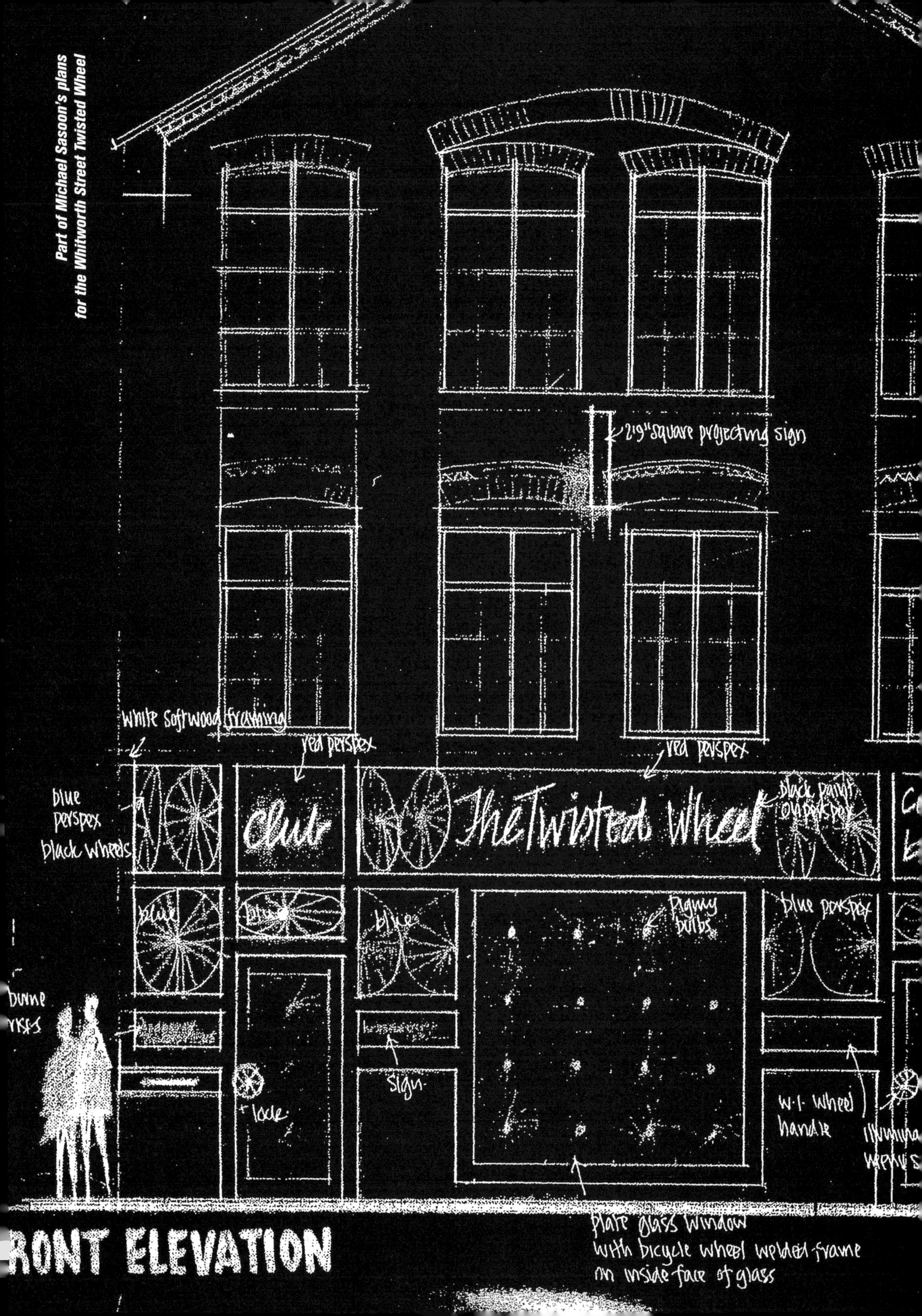

2'9" square projecting sign
white softwood framing
red perspex
red perspex
blue perspex
black wheels
Club
The Twisted Wheel
black paint on perspex
blue
blue
blue
Pigmy bulbs
blue perspex
sign
lock
W.I. wheel handle
RONT ELEVATION
plate glass window
with bicycle wheel welded frame
on inside face of glass

Part of Michael Sasoon's plans for the Whitworth Street Twisted Wheel

CHAPTER SEVEN
The Twisted Wheel Club, Whitworth Street
The Soul Years, 18th September 1965–15th February 1971

Tell Me It's Just A Rumour

RUMOURS STILL ABOUND OF A LAST MINUTE HITCH WITH THE MOVE FROM THE OLD SITE TO the new; a gap of anything up to a month has been reported over the years. Although none of this is true, there very nearly was a problem.

The move from Brazennose Street during the week 12th–18th September 1965 went remarkably smoothly, with plenty of work having already been done at the new premises. The row of buildings on Whitworth Street was directly opposite the fire station, and included the site of the new Twisted Wheel at number six. This was built on one of the oldest parts of the city, namely Shuters Brook. The exit of the club opened out onto Brook Street, named after the stream that had run as far as the old Roman gates originally situated in the London Road and Store Street area. The buildings formerly housed a water wheel powered by the brook.

In late spring 1965, Michael Sasoon, a talented architect from Cheadle, had been commissioned by Sandburne Enterprises to turn the premises into a plush night club, and as can be seen from the proposals presented to Manchester Corporation in June, the intentions were very ambitious. However, they were never fully implemented.

The brothers intended to have a low-key opening of the new club on the evening of Tuesday 14th, but a visit from a Fire Brigade inspector put an end to that. He pointed out that a license could not be granted until an additional fire exit was installed on the west facing gable wall. The door was installed within hours, while Ivor Abadi's solicitors conducted a rapid search to establish who owned this land adjacent to the club. It turned out to be part of the premises of the derelict shop next door, fondly known as the Black Cat café. Jack was immediately dispatched to the estate agents to negotiate a weekly rent for the lot. As it was in

THE TWISTED WHEEL CLUB
6 WHITWORTH STREET, MANCHESTER 1
Tel. CENtral 1179   (Opposite Fire Station)
———
★ GRAND OPENING ★
of New Twisted Wheel Club Premises on
SATURDAY, 18th SEPTEMBER, 1965
THE SPENCER DAVIS GROUP
———
The Club in Brazennose Street will Close on
SATURDAY, 11th SEPTEMBER, 1965
with
JOHN MAYALL BLUES BREAKERS
PLUS
GUEST ARTISTS

ADVANCE TICKETS ARE NOW
AVAILABLE FOR BOTH THESE
DATES

N.B.—See *Manchester Evening News* Dancing Column for further details.

Georgie Fame

such disrepair, a nominal rent of two pounds per week was agreed, but the estate agent remained curious and suspicious. After the deal had been struck, the agent asked why the club wanted a derelict little shop and narrow strip of land, when they had thousands of square feet already? As soon as he discovered why, and how pivotal it all was, within twenty four hours the rent had increased tenfold.

After being told by Phil Abadi to 'piss off', a brand new brick wall appeared on the land some three feet away, blocking the new door. The Fire Brigade made a second visit and, as soon as they discovered the recent addition, again declared that the club could not open. Ivor and Phil assured the officer that the evening's weather forecast predicted unusually high winds, and sure enough, next morning the wall was down. Thursday and Friday saw the builder back, re-erecting the wall, the officer returning and being told once again that the forecast was even worse. Unfortunately the wall did not survive, and as the builder didn't work on Saturdays the fire exit remained clear – the 'wind' having totally removed all of the bricks into a neat pile some distance away. The license was granted and the first all-night session at Whitworth Street went ahead as planned on Saturday 18th September 1965.

The saga of the wall wouldn't go away, and it must have been rebuilt more than a dozen times. The brothers realised that there was no satisfactory way around the problem and finally conceded, asking the agent's solicitor to draw up the necessary legal documentation. On the day they were due to sign, the land owner, gloating with success, had champagne on ice, ready to celebrate raking in twenty pounds per week. Yet Ivor, Jack and Phil never bothered going round to sign the contract. In secret, some weeks earlier, they had arranged with the fire authorities that a different exit could be built under the stage out into Brook Street, which still remains to this day.

18th September – Grand Opening – Twisted Wheel, Whitworth Street
Early Session and All-Nighter – The Spencer Davis Group
Sunday 19th – Twisted Wheel – Peter Jay & Jaywalkers
Saturday 25th – Twisted Wheel – The Action

NEW BIRCH PARK CLUB
'We wish to announce the installment of the fabulous new method of record presentation from the Continent of America'
DISCOTHEQUE – DISCOTHEQUE – DISCOTHEQUE

Sunday 26th September – Twisted Wheel – Lou Johnson

OCTOBER
Saturday 2nd – Graham Bond Organisation
Sunday 3rd – The Who
Friday 8th – Applejacks
Saturday 9th – The Steam Packet
Sunday 10th – St Louis Union
Friday 15th – Mojos
Saturday 16th – T-Bone Walker
Sunday 17th – Boz & Boz People
Friday 22nd – Zoot Money's Big Roll Band
Saturday 23rd – Georgie Fame
& The Blue Flames
Sunday 24th – Jimmy Powell
Friday 29th – Ben E. King
Saturday 30th – Spencer Davis Group
Sunday 31st – Unit 4+2

NOVEMBER
Friday 5th – Cops 'n' Robbers
Saturday 6th – The Action
Sunday 7th – St Louis Union
Friday 12th – The Artwoods
Saturday 13th November – CLOSED
(Possibly closed due to the opening of Jigsaw)
Saturday 13th November –
GRAND OPENING OF JIGSAW
'WITH CLOSED CIRCUIT TV
WATCH YOURSELF DANCING
AND THE GROUPS ON STAGE'

Sunday 14th – Champion Jack Dupree
Friday 19th – Mickey Finn
Friday 19th – Jigsaw Club – Cromford Court
WELCOME TO MODSVILLE
Saturday 20th – Steam Packet
Sunday 21st – Marauders
Sunday 21st – JIGSAW – WILSON PICKETT
Monday 22nd – JIGSAW – WHY NOT TRY THE BIGGEST CLUB IN THE COUNTRY?
THAT'S WHY WE TRY HARDEST TO SATISFY WITH-IT MODS.

Friday 26th – Twisted Wheel – St Louis Union
Saturday 27th – Graham Bond
Sunday 28th – Tennesseans

THE TWISTED WHEEL CLUB
6 WHITWORTH STREET, MANCHESTER 1
Tel. CENtral 1179   (Opposite Fire Station)

AUTUMN PROGRAMME

Sat. Sept. 18	SPENCER DAVIS GROUP
	IVANS MEADS
Sun. Sept. 19	PETER JAY & THE JAYWALKERS
Fri. Sept. 24	FREE FOR MEMBERS
Sat. Sept. 25	THE ACTION
Sun. Sept. 26	Americas Fantastic LOU JOHNSON
	SONNY CHILDE
	THE COOL SCHOOL
Fri. Oct 1	RAM JAM BAND
Sat. Oct 2	GRAHAM BOND ORG.
Sun. Oct 3	HERBIE GOINS
	THE NIGHTIMERS
Fri. Oct. 8	THE APPLEJACKS
Sat. Oct. 9	LONG JOHN BALDRY
	ROD STUART
	BRIAN AUGER, JULIE DRISCOL
Sun. Oct. 10	ST. LOUIS UNION
Fri. Oct. 15	THE MOJOS
Sat. Oct. 16	T-BONE WALKER
Sun. Oct. 17	BUZ & BUZ PEOPLE
Fri. Oct. 22	ZOOT MONEY BIG ROLL BAND
Sat. Oct. 23	GEORGIE FAME
	THE BLUE FLAMES
Sun. Oct. 24	JIMMY POWELL
	THE DIMENSIONS
Fri. Oct. 29	JOHN MAYALL BLUES BREAKERS
Sat. Oct. 30	SPENCER DAVIS GROUP
Sun. Oct. 31	UNIT 4 + 2

DECEMBER
Friday 3rd – Jimmy Powell & Dimensions
Saturday 4th – Twisted Wheel – Spencer Davis Group
Saturday 4th – JIGSAW – MAJOR LANCE – All-Nighter
Sunday 5th – Ivan's Meads
Friday 10th – Electones
Saturday 11th – Champion Jack Dupree
Sunday 12th – Masquerade
(A weekend that saw the Original Checkmates, Jimmy James, the McCoys, Dusty Springfield, the Mockingbirds, the Beatles and the Kinks, all performing in Manchester)
Saturday 18th – John Mayall
Sunday 19th – Steam Packet
Friday 24th – St. Louis Union
Saturday 25th – Twisted Wheel All-Nighter 10/-
Sunday 26th – Ivan's Meads
Friday 31st – Ivan's Meads – Anna Ford (Folk Singer)

'We sometimes doubled the Wheel with the Mojo, but the Mojo had a pole on the stage that was difficult to play around. But it suited Dave Berry who developed that weird stage routine to "The Crying Game" around that pole.'

PETE YORK – drummer with Spencer Davis Group

131

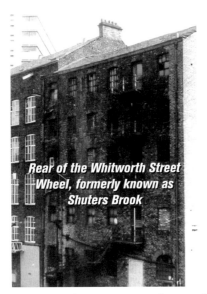

Rear of the Whitworth Street Wheel, formerly known as Shuters Brook

Open The Door To Your Heart

The closing live act at the last All-Nighter at Brazennose Street was John Mayall, who, by the autumn of 1965 was becoming rather old hat. Soul music was now definitely where it was at, and the Impressions, the Soul Sisters, Larry Williams & Johnny Watson and Inez & Charlie Foxx had already played the Brazennose Street Wheel. Perhaps it was fitting that local lad John Mayall, by now a huge name in the British Blues movement, should have had the honour of playing the old club out. Paradoxically, another British white band, Spencer Davis Group, one that had broken away from the traditional Blues school, had the privilege of playing the new club at Whitworth Street in. The Twisted Wheel had outlived the pioneering days of R&B, the original Mods and scooters, the move to Whitworth Street was timely. It was the beginning of a new era.

The announcement that the Brazennose Street Twisted Wheel was to close after the John Mayall All-Nighter was met with disbelief. Girls cried and it seemed that the scene was over. There was some degree of truth in this. The early Mod crowd at Brazennose Street, the ones who were digging the music when it was truly underground, who had endured the piss-taking and the lack of hip clothes in the local stores, were now swamped by the Carnaby Street brigade (in Manchester it was Brown Street). The Mod scene had gone over-ground, mini Mods, targets, Union Jacks, the Who and *Ready, Steady, Go!* The exclusivity of the 'in' crowd was fast evaporating.

It wasn't just in Manchester where things were changing. The Easter riots in Clacton eighteen months earlier in 1964 had heralded the spread of the Mod movement to the youth of Britain, and with it a wider appreciation of black music. The Scene, the Flamingo & All Nighter Club, La Discotheque, the Last Chance Saloon, the Marquee, Tiles, Studio 31, Whisky-A-Go-Go, Nottingham's Britannia Rowing Club, Leicester's Nite Owl, Sheffield's Esquire & Mojo, Leeds' Blue Gardenia, Liverpool's Sink, Newcastle's Club-A-Go-Go, Stoke's Place & Golden Torch, Manchester's Twisted Wheel, had been, or were all now, firmly set in an almost identical mould – Mods, pills, all-nighters, Motown, Stax and Atlantic. But the new Wheel was to be the only one of these clubs to emerge with some individuality.

Whitworth Street was to become host to the stars of the golden era of soul music. The Four Tops, the Miracles, the Impressions, the Drifters, the Supremes, Martha & the Vandellas, Eddie Floyd, Otis Redding, Sam & Dave, Carla Thomas, Aretha Franklin and much more. What placed the Wheel a cut above the rest however, was its appetite for the more cultish acts, such as Oscar Toney Jr, Alvin Cash, the Vibrations, Lou Johnson, Bruce Channel, James & Bobby Purify and Edwin Starr. Also its reputation for playing, what at the time were regarded as obscure records by artists such as Willie Tee, the Dynatones, Rosco Robinson, the Incredibles, Jackie Day, and Bobby Bland.

Whilst the clubs in London attracted kids in the main from London and the home counties, provincial clubs would by and large have a fairly local membership base. The Twisted Wheel was the first club to attract kids from far and wide. The first year at the Whitworth Street Wheel

'The dancing is without
a doubt the highest and
the finest I have ever
seen outside of the USA
– in fact I never thought
I'd live to see the day
where people could so
relate the rhythmic
content of soul music to
bodily movement to
such a skilled degree in
these rigid and
armoured Isles!'
DAVE GODIN

saw members travelling from as far as Carlisle, Newcastle, Hull, Nottingham, Leicester, Birmingham, Worcester and North Wales, as well as from the neighbouring cities of Liverpool, Bradford, Leeds, Sheffield and Stoke.

The transformation of clubs like the Wheel from hard-edged Rhythm & Blues to the hipper soul music didn't happen overnight, it was a gradual process, but by late 1965, the transition was complete. Rochdale's Kubi Club and most certainly the Jigsaw in Cromford Court were typical of clubs that began to pander to the now massive northern Mod scene. Soul music was in demand at virtually every club. Beat City on Fountain Street, Manchester got in on the act and began holding regular 'Motown Nights'. The Jigsaw coined the phrase 'Welcome To Modsville' and even tried to upstage the Wheel by putting on top line acts such as Major Lance and Wilson Pickett.

Twisted Wheel Club Acts for the first six months of 1966

JANUARY
Saturday 1st - Spencer Davis Group
Saturday 8th - Zoot Money's Big Roll Band
Sunday 9th - The Fat Sound
Friday 14th - The Herd
Saturday 15th - Early - Ram Jam Band
Late - Drifters and Ram Jam Band
Friday 21st - Shakespeares
Saturday 22nd - Steampacket
Sunday 23rd - Toggery 5
Friday 28th - Soul Executives
Saturday 29th - Graham Bond Organisation
Sunday 30th - Mike Cotton Sound

FEBRUARY
Friday 4th - Maraccas
Saturday 5th - Georgie Flame & The Blue Flames
Sunday 6th - Ivan's Meads
Friday 11th - Wynder K Frog
Saturday 12th - Early - Alan Bown Set
Late - Doris Troy/Alan Bown Set & Bluesology
Sunday 13th - Outer Limits
Saturday 19th - Charlie and Inez Foxx
Saturday 26th - John Mayall
Sunday 27th - St. Louis Union

MARCH
Saturday 5th - Spencer Davis Group
Sunday 6th - Mike Cotton Sound
Saturday 12th - Steampacket
Sunday 13th - Falling Leaves

Millie Small signing autographs at the Wheel

Saturday 19th – Early – Irma Thomas
Late – Irma Thomas & Wilson Pickett
Sunday 20th – Alan Bown Set
Saturday 26th – St. Louis Union
Sunday 27th – Roll Movement

APRIL
Saturday 2nd – Don Covay
Sunday 3rd – John Evan Band
Saturday 9th – Vibrations
Sunday 10th – The Wheels
Friday 15th – BBC TV TEAM –
'A WHOLE SCENE GOING AT THE CLUB TONIGHT,
FILMING FOR THIS WEDNESDAY'S TV PROGRAMME
WITH THE SOUL AGENTS' – WEDS. BBC1 6.30pm
Saturday 16th – Early and Late Sessions – John Mayall
Sunday 17th – Toggery 5
Saturday 23rd – Lee Dorsey
Sunday 24th – St. Louis Union
Saturday 30th – Chris Farlow

MAY
Sunday 1st – Jimmy Cliff and the Sound System
Saturday 7th – Zoot Money
Sunday 8th – Ivan's Meads
Saturday 14th – Early – Ram Jam Band
Late – Ram Jam Band & Patti LaBelle
Sunday 15th – St. Louis Union
Saturday 21st – The Drifters
Sunday 22nd – Alan Bown Set
Saturday 28th – Georgie Fame & The Blue Flames
Sunday 29th – Silverstones

JUNE
Saturday 4th – Ben E. King
Sunday 5th – The Mickey Finn
Saturday 11th – Early – Alan Bown Set
Late – Alan Bown Set & Ink Spots
Sunday 12th – Boweeval Sound Band
Saturday 18th – Mike Cotton Sound
Sunday 19th – St. Louis Union
Saturday 25th – Roy C
Sunday 26th – Ivan's Meads

Compliments card of dubious origin

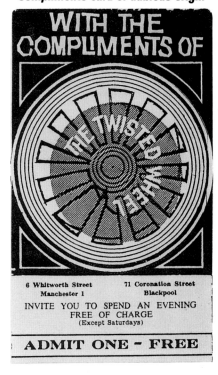

'My parents were horrified at the thought of me going to Manchester, particularly to such an infamous place as the Wheel, so I was forbidden to go.'

CHRIS REA

CHAPTER EIGHT
Bye Bye Blues

FROM LATE 1965, MOTOWN AND SOUL MUSIC BEGAN TO FIGURE MORE AND MORE prominently on the Wheel's deejays' play-lists. While live blues acts still appeared and R&B discs by the likes of Slim Harpo and John Lee Hooker were still popular records, the balance had shifted considerably towards soul dance music. Although he admitted that he 'tipped his hat towards the modern trend', Roger Eagle was not too happy with these changes. Music in Roger's world was Rhythm & Blues. He was very sensitive on this point, he had worked his arse off pioneering R&B, especially in the north of England, and in good faith had moved across town in September 1965 to continue deejaying at his beloved Twisted Wheel. However, he quickly recognised that the music was moving on.

Eagle recalled: 'All they wanted was fast tempo black dance music. I was very restricted at Whitworth Street with what I could play. Ivor was also intervening too much'. At Brazennose Street, Abadi had pretty much given Roger free reign over the music policy, but towards the end he was becoming aware of empty dance floors, when some obscure R&B disc was being auditioned. At Whitworth Street, Ivor began telling Roger to take records off that were clearing the floor. After all this was his new club and he had a new crowd. The R&B eccentrics had been replaced by fresh new faces, in Roger's words often 'too blocked on amphetamines to articulate exactly which Jackie Wilson record they wanted'.

Roger was becoming increasingly dissatisfied with the new rules to the game. He was a forceful character who didn't like being dictated to about a music that he had nurtured and developed over the years. After a visit to the Esquire Club in Sheffield, Eagle remarked that it was refreshing to go somewhere where the music policy wasn't being spoiled by the Mod element. He also snapped a rebuke to the secretary of the newly formed Screamin' Jay Fan Club when *R&B Scene* was described as a 'Mod magazine'.

Roger almost regarded the whole thing as his invention and wasn't going to take orders from the club's owner or the pill heads, who he now felt were making up the

THE TWISTED WHEEL CLUB
6 WHITWORTH STREET, MANCHESTER 1
Tel. CENtral 1179

Christmas Programme 1966

Friday 23rd December

CHRIS FARLOWE · THE THUNDERBIRDS

Two Sessions: 7 p.m. – 11 p.m. — 11 p.m. – 7-30 a.m.

N.B. This all night Session is in place of Saturday, 24th December, because of lack of Transport (Trains & Buses) on Christmas Day Morning.

Christmas Eve

ST. LOUIS UNION . THE GIN HOUSE
7-30 p.m. — 2 a.m.

Christmas Day

THE GIN HOUSE
7-30 p.m. — 12 Midnight

New Year's Eve

SOUL SISTERS · ALAN BOWN SET
COCK-A-HOOPS

1 Session Only: 7-30 p.m.—7-30 a.m.

―――――――――――――――――――――――――――
ADVANCE TICKETS NOW AVAILABLE

POSTAL BOOKINGS ACCEPTABLE (S.A.E.)
No Parking on Whitworth Street, or Minshull Street South PLEASE
CORPORATION CAR PARK AVAILABLE
Aytoun Street, Every Night (No Charge)

membership. Sadly then, in the New Year of '67, the man who had done so much for black music and the Twisted Wheel finally called it a day. As he remembered: 'I was tired of being the one to 'phone for an ambulance, I was bored playing the same Tamla requests over and over again.' It was typical of Roger, that over thirty years later, he could still remember the last record he played at Whitworth Street – 'Funky Broadway' by Dyke & the Blazers. (Suitably avant-garde!)

Roger moved virtually next door to the Blue Note Club on Gore Street, and later deejayed at the Stax Club (old Three Coins & Beat City on Fountain Street) from where he moved to the Magic Village (ex-Jigsaw Club) playing R&B and Funk.

Later Roger would turn his considerable talent and energy into a new scene in Liverpool, opening another pioneering club on Matthew Street, almost opposite the old Cavern, called Eric's. He did, in fact, return to Manchester to deejay in the '90s under the pseudonym of Juke Box Johnson, prior to his death from cancer in May 1999.

120 miles from Manchester, there were enough Wheel regulars to justify hiring a weekly coach. Chris Rea, born in March 1951, was part of the Teesside 'in' Crowd at the time. Like many others, his parents were horrified at the thought of him travelling to Manchester, particularly to such an infamous place as the Wheel and forbad it. In May 1979 however, Chris paid homage to the slightly older kids who had made the journey from the North East to Wheel. On his Gus Dudgeon produced LP 'Deltics' a track entitled 'Twisted Wheel' tells a story that only someone who was close to the scene could do.

Middlesborough had a big Mod contingent, their main haunts being the Scene Club and Mr. McCoy's. The Teesside scene was very working class; apprentices from British Steel, turners, electricians and welders. 'Apo' an amateur boxer and a leading face was a guy who Chris and the others respected, least of all because of his contempt for the plentiful rocker population down at Bar Roma. Chris Rea wrote 'Twisted Wheel' as a tribute to these guys. They typified to him the kids who were part of the Wheel scene – kids who against social class odds showed flair, talent and drive. Jed Platt and Frankie Russell were two such lads, regarded as top Mods, who would go to the Backroom Club in Redcar and then travel to Manchester by coach late on Saturday night. They returned with records, new ideas about clothes and stories about the Wheel. Chris could only dream of eventually being part of their crowd.

One day, Frankie Russell walked into Chris Rea's father's ice cream factory as the new apprentice. He and Chris immediately became friends, and one Wednesday, Frankie asked Chris if he had a midnight blue tonic mohair suit, as that was what they would be wearing that coming weekend down at the Scene. Although he didn't own one, Chris replied that he did, and had to leg it down to Jackson's Tailors to order one on their Express Service.

The Wheel crowd would dance in their own circle at the Scene. That Friday night Chris was not only invited to join the circle, but he was also given the honour of dancing in the centre of it, a privilege normally only granted to top Mods. Chris was resplendent in his brand new tonic suit, hand-made Italian shoes and Ben Sherman. For the next three minutes, as proud as a peacock, he danced solo in the centre of the circle to the

The disc jockey cage in the DJ room.
Basement level looking towards Whitworth Street.

View from the stage towards the raised area.

Coffee bar looking towards entrance and Whitworth Street.

View of the stage from the raised area.

sound of Rex Garvin & the Mighty Cravers. Thirty years later, with a lump in his throat, Chris Rea confessed that all of his platinum discs and sell-out dates at Wembley, amounted to nothing in comparison to those few magical moments, out on the floor, as part of the crowd.

Twisted Wheel Club Acts for the second half of 1966

Prior to their official launch at the Windsor Jazz Festival, Cream performed a warm-up at the Wheel.

JULY
Saturday 2nd – Orlons
Sunday 3rd – Stuart Charles String Band
Saturday 9th – Rufus Thomas
Sunday 10th – Listen
Saturday 16th – Jimmy Cliff and the Explosive Sound
Sunday 17th – Voids
Saturday 23rd – Solomon Burke
Saturday 30th – Joe Tex (Postponed)
– replaced by The Cream (Eric Clapton, Jack Bruce, Ginger Baker)
Sunday 31st – Silverstones

AUGUST
Saturday 4th – Mike Cotton Sound
Saturday 13th – John Mayall & the Blues Breakers
Saturday 20th – Geno Washington & Ram Jam Band
Saturday 27th – Zoot Money's Big Roll Band

SEPTEMBER
Saturday 3rd – Jimmy Cliff & Boz People
Saturday 10th – Alan Bown Set
Sunday 11th – Cock-A-Hoops

Saturday 17th – Steampacket
Sunday 18th – Victor Brox Blues Train
Saturday 24th – The Vibrations
Sunday 25th – Gin House

OCTOBER
Saturday 1st – The Mad Lads
Sunday 2nd – T-Bones
Saturday 8th – Early – The Score/Late – Shotgun Express
Sunday 9th – Action
Saturday 15th – Drifters cancelled – Lee Dorsey
Sunday 16th – Lonely Ones
Saturday 27th – Edwin Starr
Sunday 28th – Roll Movement

NOVEMBER
Saturday 5th – Dixie Cups
Sunday 6th – Victor Brox
Saturday 12th – Ben E. King
Sunday 13th – Wynder K Frog
Saturday 19th – The Coasters
Sunday 20th – VIP's
Saturday 26th – Early – The Score
Late – Score & Mike Cotton Sound

DECEMBER
Saturday 3rd – Alan Bown Set
Sunday 4th – Cock-A-Hoops
Saturday 10th – The Drifters
Saturday 17th – John Mayall
Sunday 18th – Victor Brox
Friday 23rd – Chris Farlow and the Thunderbirds
Saturday 24th – St. Louis Union & The Lemon Line
Sunday 25th Christmas Day – Dawn Breakers
Monday 26th Boxing Day – Boob's Party Night
Saturday 31st Soul Sisters & Alan Bown Set & Cock-A-Hoops

'There are too many Daves about, from now on you can call me Mafia Dave!'
DAVE COOKSON

Greetings From Motown

Steve Pilkington took a close interest in Motown's rise in popularity during '60s Manchester.

'By 1966, Motown, along with Stax and Atlantic, ruled supreme in clubs like the Wheel. Soul music having come a long way since 1964, when it was first heard in the emerging Mod clubs and the original Wheel. Back then, the sound of Detroit certainly didn't dominate the playlists; instead, it was just one constituent part of a highly eclectic mix of music served up by the ground-breaking deejays in those clubs. Typically, this could consist of the cool jazz of Jimmy McGriff, the sax-laden R&B of Big Jay McNeeley, the jumping ska of Prince Buster or the Motor City magic of artists like Marvin Gaye and the Four Tops. However, even then Mod taste was beginning to orientate towards the soul end of the spectrum and contemporary US black vocal groups like the Shirelles, the Temptations and the Chiffons.

'Motown Records began to achieve successful sales by late 1964, generated not least by a new era of teenage clubgoers. In 1964, Motown had thirty one singles released in the UK, by the following year this had risen to fifty three. The slick, melodic, cool sounds of black Detroit were perfect for expressing yourself on the dance-floor, perfect music for the coolest kids on the block. Although it might have once been 'hip' to be seen carrying a copy of 'Authentic R&B' or John Lee Hooker's 'Dimples' LP under your arm, teenage tastes had changed. Instead of raw, earthy R&B classics from Muddy Waters and Howling Wolf, records which we all played at home, down at clubs like the Wheel, the kids wanted to get hold of something upbeat and exciting, records they could dance and get a buzz from – John Lee Hooker didn't lend himself too well to the 'Block'.

'The advent of pirate radio stations certainly helped the cause of black popular music in the UK. In marked contrast to the BBC's staid attitude and resistance to change, illegal stations like Radio Caroline adopted a far more adventurous play-list with a healthy proportion of newly released American sounds, including of course, many soul records. In fact, the pirates cleverly made a point of playing records that were ignored by the BBC as it provided a crude but effective listener ratings barometer. The indicator being that if any of the records played on Caroline were successful, it proved that teenagers throughout the country were listening to their broadcasts (although, in reality, a lot of soul records were already popular in the clubs). Sure enough, the hits started coming, including records by emerging stars such as Dionne Warwick, Betty Everett, and in June 1964 Motown's Mary Wells with 'My Guy', which shot to number five in the charts. This was a significant breakthrough for Berry Gordy's fast-growing company, since previous releases had only sold in small amounts to a cognoscenti of soul fans and Mods. The success enjoyed by Mary Wells, however, didn't result in immediate mass recognition for 'The Sound of Young America'. To the record buying public 'My Guy' was just another hit, albeit a catchy one. All this was about to change.

'Ever since his conversion to black American music in the mid '50s, Dave Godin had been pursuing the cause with messianic zeal. Naturally enough, he was a Motown fan right from the company's early days and this led him to setting up a fan club for the Tamla and Motown performers in November 1963. Dave came up with the novel idea of combining two of Gordy's labels to christen his fan-based 'Tamla Motown Appreciation Society'. Berry Gordy was suitably impressed with Godin's efforts – so much so that he sent a three page telegram inviting him to Detroit. Dave duly accepted and arrived in the USA on 15th July 1964. He spent two weeks getting to know the Motown artists and seeing them perform in concert. There was a practical purpose behind Dave Godin's invitation of course, the ever astute Berry Gordy wanted Dave's advice on how to achieve sustained success in the UK. Apart from predicting a big hit for the unreleased 'Where Did Our Love Go' by, the until then hitless, Supremes, Dave suggested that the label should be marketed in Britain as a corporate entity under the Tamla-Motown banner. Sure enough, on his return to the UK, 'Where Did Our Love Go' stormed the charts, quickly followed by 'Baby Love', and the Supremes' made their first UK appearance in October 1964. The following March, the Tamla-Motown label was launched, and the Motown Revue featuring the Supremes, Martha Reeves & the Vandellas, Smokey Robinson & the Miracles, Stevie Wonder and Earl Van Dyke hit the UK. Although the tour wasn't an unqualified success, playing to half-full houses on some dates, it did serve to introduce the Detroit sound to the UK at large, especially after the Revue's memorable TV appearance.

'Tamla-Motown was now firmly fixed in the record-buying public's consciousness, although the hits were slow in coming. Apart from the Supremes' 'Stop In The Name Of Love' (the first release on the new label) which reached the number six position in April 1965, not one Motown record made the UK top twenty until Stevie Wonder's 'Uptight' hit number fourteen in February 1966. Strange as it may seem, household names like the Temptations and the Four Tops were confined to the bottom half of the top fifty, although achieving those positions consistently, which at least proved that there was a regular audience buying their records. That audience was out in the clubs where the unmistakable sound of Motown was all pervasive.

'One might have thought that the new soul crowd at the Whitworth Street Wheel would become disenchanted with Motown as it was no longer their exclusive preserve. In fact, by 1966 it had well and truly gone overground with Temptations and Four Tops records being bought by even the average Joe at his local Co-op. Yet paradoxically, the Wheel crowd's love affair with Motown deepened. Apart from the big name stars, the Soul crowd at Whitworth Street satisfied **143** their thirst for quality black American music by seeking out lesser known records on Motown by the likes of the Elgins, Edwin Starr and Barbara Randolph. Such was the obsession with all things Motown that the search widened to encompass records on other labels that had that 'Detroit sound'. 45s like Darrell Banks' 'Open The Door To Your Heart' and Jamo Thomas' 'I Spy For The FBI' became dance floor classics. The next phase of the Wheel's evolution was just around the corner.'

Twisted Wheel Club Acts first six months of 1967

1967

JANUARY
Saturday 7th – Spellbinders
Sunday 8th – Longstack Humphreys
Saturday 14th – Alvin Cash & the Crawlers
(Backed by UK outfit The Webb)
Sunday 15th – Richard Kent Style
Saturday 21st – Geno Washington & the Ram Jam Band
Sunday 22nd – Ivan's Meads
Saturday 28th – Georgie Fame
Sunday 29th – Victor Brox

FEBRUARY
Saturday 4th – Edwin Starr
Sunday 5th – Haydock's Rockhouse
Saturday 11th – Zoot Money
Sunday 12th – Gin House
Saturday 18th – Geno Washington & the Ram Jam Band
Sunday 19th – The Go-Go's
Saturday 25th – Chris Farlowe & the Thunderbirds
Sunday 26th – Richard Kent Style

MARCH
Saturday 4th – Lee Dorsey
Sunday 5th – Cock-A-Hoops
Saturday 11th – Edwin Starr – 5/-
Sunday 12th – Midnight Train
Saturday 18th – Alan Price Set
Sunday 19th – Victor Brox
Saturday 25th – Easter Saturday – Original Drifters

APRIL
Saturday 1st – Mary Wells
Sunday 2nd – The Puzzle
Saturday 8th – Ben E. King
Sunday 9th – Life 'N' Soul

Saturday 15th – Georgie Fame
Sunday 16th – Midnight Train
Saturday 22nd – Geno Washington & the Ram Jam Band
Sunday 23rd – Milton James Band
Saturday 29th – Original Drifters – Early 6/- Late 20/-
Sunday 30th – Root and Jenny Jackson & the High Timers

MAY
Saturday 6th – Zoot Money & the Big Roll Band
Sunday 7th – Lemon Line
Saturday 13th – The Action
Sunday 14th – Root and Jenny Jackson
Saturday 20th – Tony Merrick Scene
Sunday 21st – Nelson Fletcher Line
Saturday 27th – Lucas and the Mike Cotton Sound
Sunday 28th – Shotgun Package

JUNE
Saturday 3rd – Life and Soul
Sunday 4th – Blue Angels
Saturday 10th – Richard Kent Style 5/-
Sunday 11th – Root and Jenny Jackson
Saturday 17th – Cock-A-Hoops
Sunday 18th – Midnight Train
Saturday 24th – The Epics
Sunday 25th – The Go-Go's

On 7th January 1967, the Jimi Hendrix Experience, supported by the Silver Stone Set, played the New Century Hall. Jimi later went to the Wheel All-Nighter to catch New Jersey soul act the Spellbinders.

145

Mike and Chris Booth

No. 24756

THE TWISTED WHEEL CLUB
6 Whitworth Street, Manchester I
71 Coronation Street, Blackpool

Name ....

Address ....

....

Signature ....

Valid at Both Clubs
until 1st January, 1967

Issued subject to the rules of the Club
NOT TRANSFERABLE

Stewart Bremner

CHAPTER NINE
The Abadi Brothers & Sandburne Enterprises Ltd

THE FIVE ABADI BROTHERS WERE BROUGHT UP IN THE SOUTH OF THE CITY IN THE Barlowmoor Road area, and all went through Burnage Grammar School. The brothers, Ivor, Jack, Phil, Ronald and Richard all aspired to owning their own clubs in the north, and eventually ran the Twisted Wheel, Manchester (Ivor), Guys & Dolls, Manchester (Phil), The 3 Coins, Leeds (Jack) and the Twisted Wheel, Blackpool (Ronald & Richard). The 3 Coins in Leeds never really took off and was also a long way from Manchester, a two hour drive. Although Guys & Dolls was far more successful for Phil, it was the Wheel in Blackpool that was more interesting. The brother's father, David, was now living in Blackpool and they decided to open the sister club in Coronation Street in 1966. An excellent idea as hundreds of regular Wheel members went to either Newquay, Torquay or Blackpool for their holidays.

Sandburne Enterprises Limited was the umbrella name for all of the businesses the brothers ran and shared the same address as the original Twisted Wheel, 26 Brazennose Street, Manchester 2. This aspect of the greater 'Abadi Empire' was run by Ivor and was, amongst other things, an agency, with local acts such as the Blues Giants on its books. It was also a lunchtime café and sandwich delivery service.

The Blackpool Wheel

The Twisted Wheel, Blackpool was a rather short-lived affair as far as being a discotheque was concerned, spanning the summer of '65 to the end of the season in '67 and had its own yellow membership card. Initially set-up as a club to be run by the two youngest Abadi brothers, Ronald and Richard, it was situated at 71 Coronation Street. The ground floor was the café, on the first floor was the dance area, and the second floor being where the stage was, and an overflow on busy nights in the summer season. Ivor suggested that in the summer the club could have one style of music on the first floor and a different type on the top. The regular DJs included Peter and Brian Lunn, Chris Booth, Stuart Bremner, and Pete Von Dort who came up from Manchester. As with the Manchester Wheel, a definitive list of deejays would be impossible; the atmosphere at Blackpool was far more informal and lots of people who worked or helped out at the club would put records on at some point or other. Peter Lunn, a hairdresser by day, testified to the club's own extensive record collection and can still recall the well ordered filing system for various titles; 'Open The Door To Your Heart' 21A, 'Land Of A Thousand Dances' 33B etc. They would be mainly purchased from HMV in Deansgate, Sinafone or Gary Wilde's stall, Blackpool.

A few live acts performed at first, mainly in the season, but they petered out towards the end of '67. They would invariably be British-based acts such as Wheel favourites Jimmy Powell and **147** the Dimensions, Boz People, St Louis Union, the Alan Bown Set and Big City Blues. At first the club held its own on the Mod scene, having a local following independent of the Manchester club. But as it never held All-Nighters, most of its devotees would travel down to Manchester at 11.30pm. Sadly, it suffered from occasional bouts of summer season trouble, especially during Glasgow Fair week. This, and petty drug misuse, attracted considerable police attention. Peter remembers on one occasion when a neighbour of the club, Mr T, complained to the police about the excessive noise and being thumped by a holiday maker who he incorrectly linked with the club. The police arrived and started searching and questioning people with Mr T present. Peter remembered that by pure coincidence the next record played was the Contours' 'It's So Hard Being A Loser', which earned him a slam against the wall by one un-soulful detective.

For various reasons the club never really took off. Brian suggests that the Manchester Wheel was too close, and of course, it had the All-Nighter. He also recalls that the Blackpool Mecca became the place to go for the Blackpool crowd along with Queen's at Clevelys. The most vivid memory of Brian, Peter, and his then girlfriend Virginia, was of Mr Abadi senior and his wife Betty. They seemed to run things on a day-to-day basis in the week, when it was little more than a coffee and snack bar.

Chris and Mike Booth also remember David and Betty with affection. When the record collection at Manchester was stolen, Betty asked Chris to go down there for the Saturday All-Nighter with his records. Chris agreed if he could be allowed to DJ. By all accounts Ivor did as his mother said and Chris got his wish. As the summer season of '67 drew to a close, and both holiday makers and the Blackpool crowd drifted away, the night aspect of the club ended but it did continue as a successful daytime café well into the '70s run by David and Betty.

The Yorkshire crowd at Whitworth Street

Twisted Wheel Club Acts – Second half of 1967

JULY

Saturday 1st – Ivan's Meads

Saturday 8th – Root and Jenny Jackson

The proposed 'final' All-Nighter in 1967 when the Abadis thought that they would finally receive a drinks license from Manchester Corporation. But it was not to be.

Friday 14th – SPECIAL MEMBERS NOTICE

THE LAST ALL-NIGHTER WILL BE

SAT JULY 15TH GENO WASHINGTON

AND THE RAM JAM BAND

ADVANCE TICKETS AVAILABLE

Saturday 15th – Tonight Last All-Night Session

Saturday 21st – Long John Baldry – Bluesology

and the Fix

SPECIAL MEMBERS NOTICE

Due to the fantastic demand the management have

decided that the All-Night sessions will remain open

Every Saturday 11pm – 7.30am Special Summer Price10/-

Saturday 28th – Early – Victor Brox 5/- Late – The Toggery 5 10/-

AUGUST

Saturday 5th – Life 'N' Soul

Saturday 12th – St. Louis Union

Saturday 19th – Powerhouse

Saturday 26th – Alan Bown Set 5/- Late 15/-

Sunday 27th – Soul Set 2/6d

Philip Ryan, Liverpool playwright and actor (credits include Alan Bleasdale's GBH) was a Mod on Merseyside in the '60s and loved soul music.

He went to the local Sink, the Room At The Top Wigan, Birmingham's Whiskey-A-Go-Go, the Mojo, Sheffield and most importantly the Twisted Wheel. Philip wrote a musical based upon the club called In The Midnight Hour.

SEPTEMBER
Saturday 2nd – Chris Farlowe & the Thunderbirds
Saturday 9th – Georgie Fame £1
Saturday 9th – Special Members Notice
The Temptations (comprising of N. Whitfield, E. Holland, C. Grant)
Who Have Recorded – (I Know) I'm Losing You
Are not the same group as are appearing in Salford tonight.
Saturday 15th – Richard Kent Style
Saturday 22nd – The Action
Saturday 30th – Graham Bond 5/-

OCTOBER
Saturday 7th – Ferris Wheel
Saturday 14th – Junior Walker & the All Stars
Saturday 21st – Tuesday's Children
Saturday 28th – Lucas and the Mike Cotton Sound
Saturday 21st October
Whiskey A Go-Go – Salford
All Night Rave
ALL AMERICAN PACKAGE
THE ISLEYS
DUANE EDDY (Backed by Senate from London)
CLYDE McPHATTER (Backed by Soul Survivors)

NOVEMBER
Saturday 4th – Early – Midnight Train –
Late – Ferris Wheel
Saturday 11th – Alan Bown
Saturday 18th – Geno Washington
Saturday 25th – Ben E. King – Amboy Dukes & The Senate

DECEMBER
Saturday 2nd – Ferris Wheel
Saturday 9th – From London The Shell Shock Show
(Joe Tex cancelled)
Saturday 16th – Vibrations (US Soul package) early 7/6 late £1.
Saturday 23rd – Jimmy James & the Vagabonds
Sunday 24th December – Shell Shock Road Show
Tuesday 26th December – Bonanza disc show
Saturday 30th – Alan Bown
Sunday 31st December – Lucas & Mike Cotton Sound

Moe Wright and unknown girl at the Wheel

Phil Saxe behind the decks at Whitworth Street

Heaton Park Reservoir, 1968
Left to right: Ian Alcock, unknown girl, Helen, Derek Howe,
Shirley Hunt, Rick Kintish, Janice Hunt, Rob Mawer,
Sue (Rob's girlfriend), and cropped-off Edmund Ribiki

CHAPTER TEN
The Records...

THAT SACK LOADS OF RARE BLACK AMERICAN 45S WERE BROUGHT INTO THIS COUNTRY BY Liverpool seamen is undoubtedly an urban myth. It is certainly believable that some records arrived via sailors returning to Liverpool or Manchester docks after a trip to the States, but a more realistic explanation could lie elsewhere – the US military base at Burtonwood. Just off the old East Lancs Road between St Helens and Warrington, this was the site of the largest base outside the States and home to thousands of Americans during and after the War.

Off limits to anyone but base personnel, Burtonwood was a totally self-contained American community in England, with its own currency, cinemas, launderettes and shops. No expense was spared in keeping the military and their wives and families happy. Supermarkets at the base were supplied with every conceivable type of goods, shipped directly from the States to make Burtonwood home from home; everything from a pack of American cigarettes to an American refrigerator. The 45 was just another commodity sold over the counter at the PX, and of course, it was inevitable that records would be included amongst their personal belongings.

There has been plenty of discussion about the records spun at Brazennose Street and where they came from. There were many imports played courtesy of Don Robey who, along with a number of other US record company owners, had been persuaded by Roger Eagle to send stuff over. Neil Carter, Rick Green, and the later founders of the Warrington Blues Society, Dave Clarke and Mike Wheeler, were other suppliers of vinyl.

An entire book could be devoted to the many theories as to why there was so much black American music in the north west. After the war, there was an unusually large number of US and Canadian Forces' deserters living in Manchester. The jazz musicians amongst them, along with their records, often being holed up in the cellar of the Band On The Wall Club.

The story, mainly connected to the Beatles and Mersey Beat in general, of seamen returning to Liverpool from the USA and bringing R&B 45s with them is an enduring legend, however Liverpool was in fact on the decline and changing as a port for trans-Atlantic shipping. Along with the new docks such as Tilbury in Essex, Liverpool was becoming a container port and relatively few crew were required. That records came in is undoubtedly true, to what extent and in what quantities is another matter. Brian Rae once asked the Dennisons[1], who at the time were appearing at the Cavern in Liverpool, how they came to record Rufus Thomas's 'Walking The Dog' as early as April '64. They casually replied that the club DJ Billy Butler had been spinning it at the Cavern for weeks. But in our opinion, the PX at Burtonwood and the records taken down to clubs such as the Carlton in Warrington for sale or swap is more credible when it comes to mid '60s soul.

Dave Clarke, initially barman and later deejay at Bill Menvan's Carlton Ballroom, built up a good relationship with several black airmen who frequented the venue. In particular, Alton Witherspoon, Eddie Daniels and Louis Clarke, who wore a mac and pork pie hat, only removing them when he started to dance. Billy Butler was the deejay there at the time, and featured amongst other things, a Duke label spot. Too many people have quoted US airmen and GIs as a major source for records, for them to be ignored. They crop up in London at the Flamingo with records and Rolling Stone Bill Wyman also recalls that they were the most appreciative people in any club audience too.

Those Who Sold Them...

Noah Ancill ran Hyme & Addison's record shop on John Dalton Street, just around the corner from Brazennose Street. This was primarily a jazz shop but increasingly stocked Blues and R&B. It was from here that Roger obtained the now legendary Chuck and Bo LPs that he took to the Wheel that lunchtime in the summer of 1963, when he first attracted the attention of Ivor Abadi. Noah Ancill's son Barry, also opened a shop in 1964 on Blackfriers Street, Barry's Record Rendezvous. At the time, this was the main place in the city to buy records and was certainly the first to stock imports in any quantity. The shop then had individual record booths, where a number of 45s could be taken to listen to in seclusion. Unfortunately, at the end of the decade a small Jewish sweatshop situated above the store caught fire, destroying the record shop below, and Barry moved to the basement of his father's shop for a short while at the start of the '70s, before eventually relocating to new premises. Also on Blackfriers Street was Robinson's Records, which although not a specialist shop was a good source for 45's.

Opposite Barry's on Blackfriers Street, was the Crown. At this pub, meetings of the Northern Blues Appreciation Society took place, having recently moved from the Pack Horse Hotel on Bridge Street. Naturally, Roger Eagle was involved, but the society was actually run by Neil Carter.

Noah's cousin, Ralph Mendelson, also had a record shop on the corner of Corporation Street and Todd Street known as Ralph's Records. A small shop with storage above, it opened in the early '60s and was still doing good business well into the '70s. Ralph's was the first Manchester shop to stock in-demand imports for the fledgling Northern Soul era and Ralph's may well go down in history for being the first retail outlet for Jeff King's notorious Soul Sounds bootleg pressings, which were alleged to have been produced by record company President. (Keith Rylatt recalls Ralph, his sales assistant Doreen and her Glaswegian boyfriend John 'Zan' Sneddon, a face at the Wheel who managed the shop, burning the midnight oil one Friday, chopping the solid centres out of the records to give them a more authentic look. After all they did bear a New York address on the label!) Jeff King had made a couple of low key visits to the Twisted Wheel to hear the big sounds being played, and deejay Phil Saxe recalls there being an unwritten rule among Wheel DJs and serious collectors, not to loan or sell Jeff anything rare as he would invariably press it up. Ralph's brother, Boris also had a record shop at that time, Paul Marsh's in Moss Side, mainly stocking ska, bluebeat and rock steady. In the early '70s, Ralph's stocked plenty of imports but would be quickly brushed aside by Global Records as the interest in US imports increased from a trickle to a flood.

Gary Laine's Spin Inn was another important shop on Cross Street, down a couple of steps at the entrance to the former Bodega Club, Top of the Town. Quite the place to tape the latest imported records in your window for the passing punters. There was also the Top Rank record shop opposite the Mogambo, the Jamboree near the Cathedral and Discotheque on Oxford Road. The Co-op had two branches that stocked deletions, at Deansgate and Stretford. It was from the latter of these that folk like Brian Phillips, Barry Tasker, Rob Bellars and Phil Saxe would buy in-demand stuff, for as little as threepence each. They would take promising items to the Wheel for a spin and gauge the reaction. The Dynatones' 'Fife Piper' was one such purchase, and on being told of its popularity, Phil returned to buy up any remaining copies, which were later sold for as much as twenty five shillings.

Secondhand records could only be found in a few places during the '60s, mainly Tib Street Records, Mazell's on London Road and Johnny Roadhouse's on All Saints. There were also plenty of other excellent shops outside of the city centre, Bowker's in Clayton and Middleton, for instance, were great places, but you had to know your stuff as all of the non-current stock was fastidiously racked up in the back in strict alphabetical order. Bowker's held probably every British released soul 45 at some time or other, being high turnover shops in areas where soul music was popular. Record company reps would love to call and invite them to take a few 'off the wall' releases. Wigan Casino DJ, Richard Searling, recalls asking for Alexander Patton's 'A Li'l Lovin' Sometime'. Old Mr. Bowker, in his usual over deliberate way, made his way to the 'P' rack and to Richard's joy stated 'Ah! Patton, Alexander, Capitol, black. Yes!'

By now, some collectors were starting to send to the States for 45s. Randy's Records on the West Coast regularly advertised in *R&B Scene*, ads were run from Ray Avery's Rare Records, Glendale, California and, a little later, Brian '45' Phillips began regularly importing records from Freeman's in Philadelphia. Serious vinyl addicts also began travelling to America to personally source soul records – though at the time, the price of air tickets to New York was rather prohibitive.

Brian Rae also recalled one guy who knew that the massive Wheel favourite 'I'll Always Love You' by the Detroit Spinners had been quickly deleted in the UK. He was able to buy twenty copies on a visit to the US and on his return he brought them down to the Wheel, it was almost certainly the first time imports had been sold there in any quantity. Even at twenty five shillings each they went in seconds! British records were also beginning to command high prices. Certain records had been deleted and grown in demand; Chubby Checker's '(At The) Discotheque', Bunny Sigler's 'Let The Good Times Roll' and Doris Troy's 'I'll Do Anything (He Wants Me To)' were three early casualties from Cameo-Parkway. If you couldn't get hold of the French import for fifteen shillings, you would probably have to pay twice that amount for a British copy. Brian still recalls having to pay thirty shillings for Tina Britt's 'Real Thing' on London, as he was continually asked for the record.

Martin Koppel, a Yorkshireman originally from Goole, had been on the scene for a long **155**

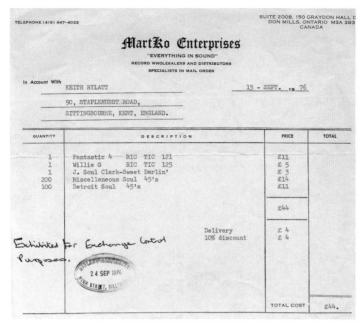

time, either hanging around Hull or Doncaster or driving over to Manchester. Martin went to the States for the first time in 1967, having taken a one year contract in Kitchener, Canada and in the following year brought back records mainly for himself, but also to sell, usually at the Wheel. He recalls the sight of 'Candy' by the Astors on a blue Stax import causing a sensation! One big record that he broke over here was Steve Mancha's 'Sweet Baby' on Groovesville, way ahead of those who claimed to have introduced Detroit imports to the Wheel. In 1971, Martin went back to settle in Canada and trading as Martco, out of Don Mills, became the main overseas supplier of rare, Northern and Detroit 45s, having already imported hundreds of records between 1968–71, either selling them personally or in bulk to Brian Phillips.

John Anderson will definitely go down in history as being the biggest and most influential supplier of soul records since 1968. He was quietly supplying records to the scene long before he moved to England, and a look through back issues of *Record Mirror* from 1968 shows regular ads from John at his Glasgow address, dealing in imports that he had personally picked up in the States. John also dealt in British releases and recalls how he had come across some bulk quantities of unplayed copies of the Tamla/Motown releases on Fontana. He pulled off what at the time he thought was a pretty cool business deal; he bought them for threepence each and sold them on the same day for sixpence each – 100% profit! Plenty of guys visited John from the north of England such as Dick Watt and Detroit expert, Bob Foster – a character who was heavily stocked with Detroit imports by '71, but didn't feel the need to go broadcasting it. John described one of his early customers from suburban London as having the best Detroit collection in the world. There were several collectors from outside of the north seriously into the Motorcity. Anderson's usual method of dealing, however, was mail order and between 1968 and 1970 he certainly despatched a few thousand imports to the north west.

The Soul City shop and label story is well documented elsewhere, but there are still a few snippets of interesting information that should be recorded. Firstly, following the financial flop of their debut disc, 'Don't You Worry' by Don Gardner & Dee Dee Ford, the company decided

to bring forward intended release number five – Gene Chandler's in-demand 'Nothing Can Stop Me' – as their next release. This was a smart move as it made the lower end of the pop charts. They were also very aware of the popularity of the Okeh label and intended to release further Major Lance 45s as well as LPs by both him and Billy Butler. Acetates of the second intended Chris Jackson release, 'Since There's No Doubt' exist but SC120 Larry Williams & Johnny Watson's 'Nobody' never even got that far. They were also about to launch an oldies label called Forget Me

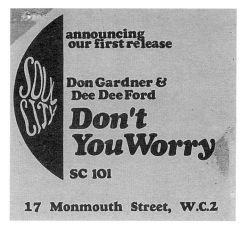

Not, but again this never came to fruition. The first intended release was FS101 James Carr 'That's What I Want To Know'/'You've Got My Mind Messed Up', scheduled for release on 17th October 1969 to be followed by Moses & Joshua Dillard's 'My Elusive Dreams'. The label would also boast an LP with the rather elaborate title of 'Rock & Roll Is Dead…But Won't Lie Down'. Previously called 'Unless You Are Pushing 30', it was proposed to sell the album for 14/6 and would contain sixteen tracks from the 1950s. Their other existing label, Deep Soul, also had a couple of further releases planned. DS9107 Van & Titus 'Cry Baby Cry'/'I Need Your Lovin' on 17th October 1969 and DS9108 Zilla Mayes 'All I Want Is You' on 7th November 1969. Dave's involvement with Okeh firmly ties him in with the discovery of Sandi Sheldon's 'You're Gonna Make Me Love You'.

Graham Stapleton, long time soul aficionado and record dealer from West London, also had a stake in the launch of Sandi Sheldon's Okeh monster via Radio One DJ John Peel. John is reputed to have found the record while doing work for CBS in London and was about to send it to a charity shop in a large bag alongside a hundred or so other discs, when Graham rescued it and sent it north to Wolverhampton. Graham was also behind many other Northern discoveries mainly from his famous stall in Soho's Rupert Street, which became a Mecca for collectors throughout the '70s. The Metro's 'Since I Found My Baby' was one example (bought blind in tribute to the infamous Wakefield club), along with countless others. Dave Godin's angle on the Sandi Sheldon story is that he recalls it being sent to him at Soul City records, hot on the heels of Billy Butler's 'Right Track' and Major Lance's 'The Beat', and he too sent it north. Tony Brown in Cleethorpes was another unsung hero from that era, supplying several up and coming DJs with such stuff as Walter Jackson's 'Where Have All The Flowers Gone' and Moses Smith's 'The Girl Across The Street'.

In the final few of years of the Wheel, F.L. Moore of Leighton Buzzard, Bedfordshire would also start selling imports by mail, and brought over all of the Chess, Checker & Cadet 45s that flooded the scene around '70–71. There were tens of thousands of them, many even turning up in Tesco supermarkets. (Keith Rylatt recalls two soul connoisseurs in the coffee bar of the

Wheel, talking about Marlena Shaw's 'Wade In The Water' that had just been played downstairs. Keith told them that he'd got one through the post from Leighton Buzzard, having no idea that it was rare he'd simply bought the vocal to a great instrumental. F.L. Moore certainly had been selling British releases by post since at least '68. Keith remembers sending off for the by then deleted 'Cool Jerk' by the Capitols. When he received it, he was livid as they had sent the 'wrong' one, by the Three Caps, and in his ignorance he returned the disc without even playing it – unaware that the same recording had been issued twice, once credited to the Three Caps and secondly as the Capitols.)

Torquay's Compass Club is established in '60s soul legend as the place where Mods and soul fans from all over Britain would mix and more importantly, hear each others soul favourites and discoveries. Derek Howe manhandled his entire 45 collection down there one summer! Chris Hill, who rose to fame in the early '70s in Essex and London as a top soul jock, recalls going down to Torquay in '67 and '68 with an already reasonable knowledge and collection of records and being totally blown away when some bloke from 'up north' gave the DJ Bunny Sigler's 'Let The Good Times Roll' to play. He recalls 'the music these guys were bringing down was different, faster, more dynamic'.

Left to right: Derek Fearnley, Eddie Ayrey, Rob Mawer, Sue, Shirley and Janice Hunt, and Derek Howe on holiday Torquay, 1968

1968

Twisted Wheel Club Acts – first six months of 1968

JANUARY
Saturday 6th – Ferris Wheel
Saturday 13th – Lucas & Mike Cotton Sound
Saturday 20th – Geno Washington & Ram Jam Band
Saturday 27th – Edwin Starr

FEBRUARY
Saturday 3rd – Jimmy James & Edwin Starr
Saturday 10th – Richard Kent Style
(James & Bobby Purify postponed, not on tomorrow, Sunday)
Saturday 17th – Robert Parker
Saturday 24th – Amboy Dukes

MARCH
Saturday 2nd – Jimmy James & The Vagabonds
Saturday 9th – Freddie Mack Show
Saturday 16th – Fantastics
Saturday 23rd – Geno Washington
(Impressions on at New Century Hall)
Saturday 30th – Ferris Wheel

APRIL
Saturday 6th – Foundations
Saturday 13th – Ferris Wheel
Saturday 20th – J. J. Jackson
Saturday 27th – Early - Skin Deep
All-Nighter – Ike & Tina Turner Revue

MAY
Saturday 4th – Fantastics
Saturday 11th – Edwin Starr
Saturday 18th – Amboy Dukes
Saturday 25th – James & Bobby Purify

JUNE
Saturday 1st – Oscar Toney Jr.
Saturday 8th – Ferris Wheel
Saturday 15th – Summer All-Nighter
Saturday 22nd – Summer All-Nighter
Saturday 29th – Summer All-Nighter

159

Those Who Bought Them…
John Marriott

John Marriott from Sheffield typifies the calibre of soul fan attracted to the Wheel. John and dozens like him all over the North and Midlands were connoisseurs and soon realised that the only place to go to hear high quality soul was Manchester. John remembers: 'When growing up in Sheffield in the '60s, Saturdays meant two things to me – soul and clothes, with perhaps a little football in between. Violet May's Record Collectors' Corner was one of my haunts. Probably, quite a revolutionary shop title in those days, she was a middle-aged jazz fan who at first ran a secondhand clothes shop with a few records, then a totally secondhand record shop in the South Street area. Then early in 1968, she moved to more modern premises, behind The Moor. The middle shop, which I frequented from 1964, was superb, hundreds of singles all around the 2/- mark, with a couple of special boxes on the counter. One containing full price records, all Island releases, i.e. Sue and ska stuff and another box of 45s that she considered collectable at 3/6 and 4/6, Motown artistes on London, Oriole, Fontana and Stateside. Also, London stuff, such as Bobby Parker, Showmen, Benny Spellman etc. Also rock and roll by Elvis on HMV etc. Soul collectors in Sheffield were few and far between in those days and I could visit the shop in the week after school (and can remember having the piss taken out of my school uniform by a couple of Teds who were always in there and ran the ground breaking *Sun Sound* fanzine from just up the street), decide what I wanted and return on Saturday with no fear of them being bought by anyone else. One memory I have is of her giving me the Sue release poster from behind the counter when the shop moved. Somehow, despite having more stock, the new Moor shop didn't have the same atmosphere and also soul fans from out of the area had by then discovered the shop. All resulting in her eventually stocking Jeff King's Soul Sounds label and upping the price of any danceable soul record she obtained. Other good shops were Bunker & Pratley's electrical shop in the city-centre which, along with regular releases, catered for local West Indians with ska and Sue stuff. Also Ken's Records in the open market which, for about two years, from 1967 to '69 always had a regular supply of UK demos – I picked up the Incredibles, Bobby Sheen, James Carr etc. In fact many of the records that were spun at the Mojo and the Wheel came into stock in one or other of these shops at one time or other.

'Saturday wasn't Saturday without shopping for some clothes as well. Austin's, at Moorhead, was good for Levi's and Lee Riders and for my seventeenth birthday, I was bought a Levi's sand coloured suede jean-jacket, with a brown leather collar, from a great little shop called Male Boutique, on Orchard Street, which was also the first Sheffield shop to stock Ben Shermans. Buying a suit was a major Saturday morning event. We usually went to Jackson's as they had the best selection of mohair, gabardine and tweed cloths and were more responsive to special requests such as longer pocket flaps, hand stitching, more than the usual number of sleeve buttons etc. Funnily enough, looking back, fashions were one of the things that you didn't really get from the Wheel, probably more that you took them.

'After an afternoon watching Sheffield United, it was preparing for the evening. For years, to avoid parental aggro, I always said I was staying overnight with friends. So with my alibi straight, I took the short bus ride to town to meet my girlfriend Mo, to either hang around city centre pubs, the La Favourita coffee bar, the Golden Griddle or Wimpy hamburger cafés or just window shop before catching the train from Victoria station to Manchester. It's hard to convey how such a now common event as visiting a town only 40 miles away was so magical in those days. Sheffield had a reasonable scene and hosted my favourite '60s soul club the Mojo, but Manchester was more exciting, vibrant and glamorous with more than an element of menace – 'Sin City'. On arriving at Piccadilly Station we pretty well picked up from what we had just left in Sheffield – the Dolphin Café or perhaps an early session at the Blue Note before going onto the Wheel itself.

'From my point of view, the attraction was hearing sounds I didn't know or didn't have and these were almost always things that had never been out in the UK – 'Baby Reconsider' by Leon Haywood and Emanuel Lasky's 'I'm A Peace Lovin' Man' always stick in my mind as such great none-UK issued sounds. Sunday morning was again back to the Dolphin, which would be full of people from the Wheel and then back to the station. One particular Sunday morning occasion that sticks in my mind was one after a night of busts and general increased police activity at the Wheel. There were several police officers strung out across Piccadilly Station approach stopping likely Wheel attendees from hanging around the station. After a lengthy total fabrication from my girlfriend Mo, about visiting relatives in Oldham, they let us on the station for a much needed sit down until the train came. The train journey generally took just over an hour, but on that Sunday there was a special service which meant getting off at New Mills station for a half hour bus journey to join another train a few miles further on, for the remainder of the trip. I always remember bartering with someone over some Shorty Long and Kelly Brothers' 45s at a wind swept bus stop in the middle of the Pennines, much to the amusement and amazement of the driver and his passengers. Back in Sheffield, we sometimes went to a free Sunday lunchtime record session at the Bailey's cabaret night spot, which also sometimes featured the week's headline act doing a warm up rehearsal spot. I remember Ronnie Carroll, in full evening dress, performing bland standards, while disinterested Wheelites 'came down' around him.'

Twisted Wheel Club Acts – Summer of 1968

JULY
Saturday 6th – Joe Cocker & Grease Band
Saturday 13th – Summer All-Nighter
Saturday 20th – Summer All-Nighter
Saturday 27th – Summer All-Nighter

AUGUST
Saturday 3rd Summer All-Nighter
Saturday 10th – Summer All-Nighter
Saturday 17th – Summer All-Nighter
Saturday 24th – Ben E. King Late
Saturday 31st – Ferris Wheel Early & Late

SEPTEMBER
Saturday 7th – Ben E. King

Saturday 14th – Clyde McPhatter Early & Late
Saturday 21st – All-Nighter
Saturday 28th – Bruce Channel 5/-

Richard Watt

'I first visited the Wheel in autumn 1967, by which time several Carlisle lads had already been going to the All-Nighters. This would be the first of many visits up to 1970 when I stopped going. Other new venues were attracting my attention, mainly Up The Junction, the Catacombs and the Torch.

'Music was obviously the main reason for going to the Wheel, and in an attempt to keep up with the sounds they were playing, I quickly became an avid record collector. My initial buying was from lists and shops, but I quickly learned that memorising matrix and release numbers was important, as most serious record shops would not allow you to browse through their stock and would only respond to this sort of detailed information.

'Manchester remained the best place to buy records in the North and so it was important to catch the early train from Carlisle on Saturday morning to arrive at Victoria Station by lunchtime. From there it was a very short walk to Ralph's Records on Todd Street where you would meet other like minded collectors and all-nighter goers. Often you had to queue up to get in to view his wondrous stock. The shop was tiny and Ralph was ably assisted by the infamous Zan from Glasgow, and his girl friend Doreen. Typical off-the-shelf items would include Willie Tee 'Thank You John', Darrell Banks 'Open The Door To Your Heart', The Fascinations 'Girls Are Out To Get You' on Sue, or Stateside if you were lucky. Because of the size of the shop there were no booths so you often had to stand around listening to records in the queue before you, which in fact was a great way to hear different stuff. Prices were around 6/- each.

'The next stop would be Gary Laine's Spin Inn, for some reason he always seemed to have more EMI stock than Ralph's – also for ages, multiple copies of Tommy Neal and Bobby Bland on Vocalion and Danny White's 'Keep My Woman Home' on Sue. Spin Inn was even smaller than Ralph's, you had to step down from the street with neatly filed records to the right behind the counter, there were books and lists of stock items, a small central display of LPs and headphones to listen to requests.

'The last stop was Barry's Record Rendezvous on Blackfrier's Street, which was the biggest of the three and had the luxury of listening booths. I recall him having a lot of reissued stock on Direction, Sue etc and although often disregarded by first issue purists there were in fact many first UK airings on them. I don't recall many imports in these shops, certainly in the early part of '68 anyway.

'If time permitted and you could commandeer someone's car, there were some great suburban record shops, Sale Woolworths of all places was excellent, here I bought 'SOS' and 'Headline News' on their first Polydor release for 1/6d each, I also found the Inspirations there too. Disc Stop, 256 Waterloo Road. Manchester 8 is another place I recall.

'When the shops closed and night drew in, the countdown to the Wheel would start in earnest. It was still possible to buy records however, in most of the pre-Wheel haunts or even on the Piccadilly Station concourse. Record dealing in the Wheel did happen, but carrying records around or trips to the cloakroom would only get in the way of dancing, so it was saved for the morning in such places as the Milk Bar before going on to either the Blue Note or the Top 20. Mostly though I went to someone's house or flat to chill out before the train, my thanks go out to Alec Rae, Jim Halliday, Brian Walker and Paul (Digger) Taylor. The trip home inevitably seemed much longer than the trip down but there were always the memories of the last eighteen hours and the next trip to look forward to.

'Throughout 1967–1970, I continued to search high and low for records – all British releases, and had a lot of good strikes in small towns in the North and Scotland. Originally from that side of the border, I used to travel a lot between Carlisle and my dad's place via a place called Galashiels. In November '68, we stopped there, as we often did, and while waiting for him outside of an ice cream parlour I casually browsed in the window of the adjoining music shop. Among the Andy Stewart and Jimmy Shand LPs and guitars and sheet music in the window, I noticed a Chess EP by Fontella Bass. My experience was to check out anything remotely connected with electrical goods, music etc. Inside, I was greeted by a lovely old lady in her sixties, who stood behind a polished glass counter and surrounded by walls of beautiful mahogany racks with sliding doors. The place was compact and spotless. 'I see that you have a Chess EP in the window' I said 'Do you have anything else on Chess?' trying to sound as casual as possible. 'I'll just have a wee look' says Mrs Coull – a lady I was going to get to know well over the next couple of years!

'Out comes a singles cardboard box with CRS on the outside, and inside, full to bursting, are mint gold Chess 45s. They started at 8001 and ran through four boxes, quite possibly there would be every issue here. As there were no other customers, Mrs Coull allowed me to search through all four boxes at my leisure, and Fontella Bass & Bobby McClure's Wheel biggie 'Don't Mess Up A Good Thing' was first out! After browsing through the Chess stuff and realising that courtesy and best behaviour was definitely the name of the game, I slipped in the immortal question: 'Anything on Stateside, Mrs Coull?' 'There's something in there Richard' she replied, pointing to one of the mahogany panels to the right of me. At her invitation I slid the long door sideways to reveal three feet of mint blue Stateside sleeves. All of my matrix and release number memorising went straight out of the window when I opened the next door, a further three feet of blue! My dad's appearance in the shop reminding me that I had been in there for over an hour, brought my first visit to an end. This was the first of many trips there, and despite buying more than one copy of the rarer releases on occasions, Mrs C never increased her prices – 1/- for singles and 1/6 for EPs. When I had exhausted my 'wants' I mentioned the shop to a friend I had made through record collecting from Craigbank, near Glasgow.

'On my next visit to Galashiels, with a few more newly heard 'wants' I called to see how Mrs Coull was, and immediately noticed that nearly all of her stock had gone. I asked why and she casually replied 'Oh a nice young man came in, over six feet tall he was, all the way from Glasgow and he bought the lot. I think he was called John Anderson!'

'The moral of this tale is never give away a 'live lead' – a principal observed by John to this day. I know only of John's very first big US hit in March 1973 at Chester Pike, Darby, Pennsylvania. The rest of them will probably follow him to his grave.

163

'Another friend made through record collecting was Brian Phillips; he used to send me some great lists. I vividly recall on one of his lists from early 1970, he used the expression 'Hi Fellow Groovers' and introduced his first in-depth selection of imports. Other great lists around that time came from Neil Mason in Bury, Geoff Killick in Brighton, Mike Taylor and Richard Selwood from Gloucester. Jeff King's list from Leicester was good, as were those from Dave Hastings and Charlie Gillett in London.

'An amusing epilogue to my story about Mrs Coull concerns my elder brother, Nigel, another avid collector, who always used to beat me to stuff in general. But on this occasion I triumphed, he trained as a Textile Designer from 1961–1964 and lived in digs in of all places…Galashiels. Totally oblivious to the gold mine lying dormant under his nose!'

Twisted Wheel Club Acts – Winter 1968

OCTOBER
Saturday 5th – All-Nighter
Saturday 12th – Edwin Starr
Saturday 17th – All-Nighter
Saturday 26th – All-Nighter

NOVEMBER
Saturday 2nd – Showstoppers
Saturday 9th – Oscar Toney Jr.
Saturday 16th – Oscar Toney Jr.
Saturday 23rd – J. J. Jackson
Saturday 30th – All-Nighter

DECEMBER
7th – Bandwagon
Saturday 14th – Original Drifters
Saturday 21st – All-Nighter
Saturday 28th – Bandwagon Late

Carl Woodroofe

Better known as 'Farmer' Carl Dene, he was one of the most obsessive record collectors who went to the Wheel. Carl reckoned Brian Phillips was his Manchester equivalent! Carl began deejaying at some of the better clubs around Birmingham in the early '60s, La Metro on Livery Street, under the railway arches, probably being the best in those early years. Carl's first visit to the Wheel would be in December 1964. Birmingham's main club for R&B All-Nighters at that time was the Whiskey-A-Go-Go, held at the less romantic sounding venue of the Laura Dixon Dancing School, Navigation Street. After his first visit to Manchester, Carl made the long journey every second week in his van, which was his pride and joy until someone decided to steal it from its Brazennose Street parking spot during the night to get home to Warrington.

There was a hard core of about eight R&B regulars from Birmingham, one being Raymond Chesney ('Ches') who decided to start wearing a mohair suit to the club and started quite a trend with the Brummy lads. Carl would go regularly throughout 1965–66, and its move to Whitworth Street, but like so many others, he recalls that the new Wheel just didn't have the atmosphere of the old one. Carl would take records up to Manchester for Roger to spin and would also buy them there, one of his most treasured transactions was from Roger's own collection; Boot Hog Tefferly & the Loafers' 'I'm Not Going To Work Today' on Sound Stage 7, for thirty shillings – big time money in 1965. His main import supplier at that time was Paul for Music in East London. Most records

however were British releases. He recalls travelling all over England looking for small record shops that hadn't been plundered. This corner of the south Midlands was fast becoming one of the many emerging pockets of soul music in Britain. The Blue Moon club in Cheltenham, painstakingly nurtured by soul DJ Dave Bennett, had grown into the Spa Lounge and was playing rare deletions and imports. The Library Discotheque in Gloucester was doing the same, with guest DJs such as Mike Raven. Richard Selwood was also putting the West of England on the map by selling rare records, firstly as The Rare Record Bureau then as the Wax Machine.

By now, Carl was an established DJ at the Chateau Impney, Droitwich Spa. Doing the 4–7pm slot after returning from Manchester, he would spin many of the records they had heard the night before. In turn, many West Midlands discoveries were taken north, especially in his second flirtation with the Wheel in 1968–69. The Catacombs at Wolverhampton was also unearthing big sounds, one such record being Wheel anthem 'Baby Reconsider' by Leon Haywood, Carl having recently bought it on a trip to F.L. Moore's.

28, Worcester Street, Gloucester. Telephone 26655.

Those Who Played Them – the DJs

In the Wheel's eight-year life span, an undetermined number of people put records on the club's turntables. Ivor was pretty rigid when it came to hiring disc jockeys, and any of them allowing people into the deejay's cage would be dismissed on the spot. Also, he was never very happy about people taking records in for the deejays to play because once records were being passed to and fro it became impossible to keep track of the club's own collection. To try to prevent the pilfering of his records, Ivor used a hole–punch on all of the club's collection. Each record looked rather like the drilled cut-out discs from US warehouses. However, this didn't prevent the whole lot getting stolen some time later.

A definitive list of the club's deejays is almost impossible, because in '60s Britain it wasn't the norm for soul jocks to become well-known. In fact, quite the opposite, it was regarded as being pretty un-cool to do any more than announce the most basic details of the last record. At the Wheel, it was rare to get even that, as the crowd would be expected to know its stuff. Ivor Abadi actively discouraged his deejays from talking too much and told them in no uncertain terms that he paid them to put records on, not to talk. Basically the Wheel jocks were no more or no less important than any other employee; some were hired to serve Fanta, others to play records. With this lack of status in mind, Ivor has little recollection of exactly who did deejay. Thankfully it was after the closure of the Wheel that DJs became 'stars' and could command any following, in the '60s it was simply the club that would have the reputation for good records. Research has been very difficult, guys with small boxes of records would win Ivor's confidence for a few months and then disappear. Conversely one or two prominent personalities who have claimed deejay fame did little more than press their noses against the cage and dream about it. Here, in approximate chronological order, are some of the Twisted Wheel's best disc jockeys:

Geoff Mullin

(January '63, pop sessions, never All-Nighters)
Geoff knew the Abadi brothers from Burnage Grammar. He went to the newly opened club at lunchtimes, while working for the Inland Revenue, and suggested to Ivor that some midday music would go down well, and agreed to take some 45s down the following week. The venture was a success and Geoff graduated to night sessions too. Mullin also suggested live music which was again implemented with the Hellions being the first act. He later went on to manage the group.

(Pete) Bongo Van Dort

(Spring '63, main pop DJ)
Pete Von Dort went out under the name of Bongo Von Dort, and despite the earlier theories about anonymous DJs, Bongo's name went out regularly in the club's publicity for its opening six months. Pete was probably the most versatile of the Wheel DJs, he played pop as well as R&B and was a real Blues enthusiast having an impressive collection of records. He also worked at the Blackpool Wheel playing soul.

Roger Eagle

(September '63 until the closure of Brazennose Street, and Whitworth Street from its opening in Sept '65 until the end of the year)
There are numerous references to Roger throughout the book.

Don Stevens

(Circa '64)
Eagle was adamant that Guy Stevens of Sue Records fame didn't deejay, and simply supplied him with records and advice whenever he visited. But Eddie Barnett, whose memory for detail is unparalleled, is equally as sure that a person called Don Stevens, who had a London accent, crew cut, slender build and slight squint did deejay at some point at Brazennose Street. Sadly, Guy, is now deceased and this description does not fit him anyway. This still leaves open the question of who Don was?

Roger Fairhurst

'What happened to Don Stevens the DJ, the one with the cockney accent?'

EDDIE BARNETT

Neil Carter

('64-65)

Blues and R&B devotee played alternate Saturdays to Roger Eagle at the All-Nighters, certainly from about '64 onwards. Recalls the DJ booth being minuscule, about two decks wide and the width of a door deep. He had to climb in through a hatch because it was so cramped and the twin decks had to stick out into the dance area by about half of their diameter for the same reason. The cartwheels stopped above the decks with a gap of about six inches or so, just enough for enthusiasts in the audience to be able to pass 45s through.

Bobby Derbyshire (Bobby Dee)

('65–66)

Was the next 'main' DJ after Roger left.

Barry Turner

('65–67, Bobby Derbyshire's cousin.)

Brian Walker

(Manchester based, deejayed at Whitworth Street around '67, still involved in the music scene.)

Paul Davis

(1968–close)

Began deejaying in 1968 – stood in for the odd half-hour to give Bobby Dee, and to a lesser extent Barry Turner, a break. Paul began playing regularly on Friday and Saturday evenings after being given the position of resident DJ by Ivor Abadi. (Dee and Turner both not being available one Friday night). Paul progressed to deejaying the early hours of the All-Nighter before handing over to Brian Phillips. He remembers Brian had a terrific record collection. Paul was a big friend of Phil Saxe and Eddie Barnett from the early '60s. Paul coined the phrase 'By Overwhelming Demand And Popular Request' using it to announce the arrival on stage of artists like Junior Walker or Ben E. King. He worked at the Twisted Wheel until its closure and remembers that the last night was very emotional.

He went every Saturday to Barry's Record Rendezvous and bought records on account for the Wheel (and later for the Placemate).

The best acts Paul saw were Junior Walker (Junior's first Wheel visit was also his first UK appearance) and Ike & Tina Turner. Junior Walker was Whitworth Street's biggest attendance and Paul described this first appearance as sensational. He also rated Billy Stewart, Inez & Charlie Foxx, Ben E. King and Jimmy Ruffin. The best white act, in his opinion, was the Spencer Davis Group; 'I thought Stevie Winwood was a special talent. I also liked Georgie Fame and thought John Mayall was way ahead of his time'. In general, Paul considered that black acts sounded like their records, whereas the white bands rarely managed it – Spencer Davis Group being the exception.

As a club member, he started at the old Wheel and vividly remembers watching with admiration Jimmy Reed perform there. He carried on going to the Wheel when it reopened on

Whitworth Street, never having any intention of becoming a deejay, he just loved the music and dancing. He couldn't remember Roger Eagle being at Whitworth Street, but he didn't really take much notice of the deejays in late '65. First and foremost he was a dancer. He occasionally went to Blackpool but never deejayed there. After Roger Eagle, Paul Davis was the Twisted Wheel's next longest serving DJ. He occasionally went to the Oasis but was usually very loyal to the Wheel.

He remembers a gradual shift to more of a rare soul scene in late '68 and early '69, with people asking for more obscure records, 'Brian Phillips had a big part in that'. Paul regularly played Wheel member's own records and recalls that record shops were beginning to stock US imports around 1968. Kids at the Wheel were a great crowd, there were plenty of cliques, though to be more precise, groups dancing at the Wheel from the same area, for instance the North Wales or the Staffordshire crowd. This applied locally too, groups of kids from the same Manchester suburb – the Droylsden gang or the Didsbury crowd. His favourite records were Jackie Wilson's 'I Get the Sweetest Feeling' (import), The Invitations' 'What's Wrong With Me Baby?', Dee Dee Sharp's 'What Kind Of Lady', the Astors' 'Candy' and Alvin Cash's 'Twine Time', all of which he bought as new releases from Barry's. He loved the Drifters, especially Ben E. King and Johnny Moore, the Impressions and Curtis Mayfield and confirms that the last record played was 'Long After Tonight Is All Over' by Jimmy Radcliffe. Like lots of others he didn't

Phil Saxe in the milk bar at Whitworth Street

believe the Wheel would ever close, and never in his wildest dreams did he think that people would be still into it, over thirty years later. Paul got the impression the Abadis were glad to move on, continuing to deejay for the brothers at the Placemate, which opened on the site of the Whitworth Street Wheel.

Brian Rae

('66–68)
Brian was probably the first of the pure soul deejays. Shortly after the club's move to Whitworth Street, and after Roger Eagle had left, the demand for soul became overwhelming and Brian stepped in. (A fuller account appears on pages 187–89.)

Brian Phillips

('69–70)
Brian '45' Phillips confesses to being obsessed by records in the '60s. By day, Brian was a clerk but just as a junkie's life is dictated by drugs, so Brian's was by vinyl. He amassed a huge collection by the late '60s and became a record dealer and DJ. He was responsible for one of the first bootlegs, the Dynatones' 'Hole In The Wall', well before Jeff King visited the club. Brian deejayed at the club from 1969 to its final year. (A fuller account appears on pages 190-92.) **169**

Phil Saxe

('69 to end of '70)

Phil was seventeen when he started to DJ, and modestly claims that if it hadn't have been for the theft of the club's records, he might never have. He and Rob Bellars had good collections and decided to loosely 'amalgamate', which created one of the best collections in the city. In September 1970, Ivor Abadi decided to run Sunday afternoon sessions. This was to compete with the Top 20 in Hollinwood which opened between 11am and 4pm. Phil worked the first half of the Wheel All-nighter from 11.30pm until about 4am before handing over to Les Cokell.

Les Cokell

(Mid '70 to the close)

Les had deejayed a fair amount before he started at the Wheel in 1970. Keith Rylatt certainly remembers him from 1965 at the Bee Gee club in Leeds. He was also the driving force at Harrison's Hoist in Earby a couple of years later. Les began to play rare soul, deletions with plenty of imports. Rob Bellars supplied him with some, but the vast majority of records played by Les were well-known, such as Edwin Starr's 'Back Street' and 'Agent Double-O Soul', which had been established favourites almost since release.

Although Rob Bellars didn't actually put needle to vinyl at the club, he might as well have, as he was one of Manchester's leading authorities on soul records. Rob would regularly bring new and unusual finds down to the Wheel for the deejays to spin.

Twisted Wheel Club Acts – Early 1969

JANUARY
Saturday 4th – Early and Late – Selofane
Saturday 11th – Billy Stewart
Saturday 18th – Sixth Anniversary Year – Junior Walker & The All Stars
Saturday 25th – Early – Free/Late – Ferris Wheel

FEBRUARY
Saturday 1st – Root & Jenny Jackson
Saturday 8th – Johnny Johnson and the Bandwagon
Saturday 15th – New Vibrations
Saturday 22nd – US Flat-top Road Show

MARCH
Saturday 1st – Ben E. King
Saturday 8th – Ferris Wheel
Saturday 15th – Marv Johnson
Saturday 22nd – G Clefs – 8 Piece All American Soul Show
Saturday 29th – Ben E. King
Return Visit By Demand

1969

CHAPTER ELEVEN
By Overwhelming Demand And Popular Request
January 1969 – Saturday 9.45pm
Manchester City Centre
Phil Scott

THE EXPRESS BUS FROM GLOSSOP, THE NUMBER SIX, HAD DROPPED MY BROTHER BOB AND I ON the corner of Piccadilly and Oldham Street. Although there had been a light snowfall during the afternoon, the temperature in town that night was just above freezing. A chill in the air warned me though, that a very cold welcome was in store for us, sometime early on Sunday morning, when we stepped out of the furnace of the All-Nighter and faced the bitter cold of the deserted Manchester streets.

Neon lights brightly lit a crowded Piccadilly. Hurrying along onto London Road, swinging our overnight holdalls, collars turned up against the night, we passed the Blue Dolphin. It was empty apart from a couple of old guys sat huddled over a cup of steaming tea. Tomorrow it would be full of young people waiting for the first train home, talking about the All-Nighter, and coming down.

The smell of beer hit us as we moved on past the Brunswick. It was packed with noisy Saturday night drinkers. I smiled to myself, in less than thirty minutes the bell for 'Last Orders' would ring, signalling the end of their night, and the start of ours. We hit the station at Piccadilly minutes later, and walked briskly up the approach just in time to hear the announcement of the arrival of a train from Wolverhampton. There was a sudden roar as hundreds of football fans thundered past, returning to Piccadilly on a special from London.

The station was busy, and passengers streamed from the platforms to catch taxis on the rank. In the far corner of the booking hall, I noticed a group of familiar faces. 'Faces' from the Wheel. They too had travelled to Manchester on that cold night, arriving by train from cities all over the country. Some I knew by nickname, but usually I called them by their first name, followed by the town from where they had come from. They were standing with friends who had arrived at the station to meet them. Billy from Sheffield shaking hands with Tony from Burnley, Judy from Stafford talking to Barry from Salford.

We mooched around the station for about an hour. More soul fans came onto the station off the streets, and arrived on last minute trains. Everyone was carrying holdalls, people were meeting and greeting like long lost brothers. Everyone seemed to know each other, and if they were newcomers to the scene, they were quickly introduced and greeted like old friends with 'Soul shakes' and beaming smiles.

Everything was Right On, everyone was cool…I could feel the buzz, sense the atmosphere. **171**

In With The 'In' Crowd

The 'in' crowd' was dressed and ready for business, in smart mohair suits, full length suede or leather coats, or faded Levi's. With their short, neatly cropped hair, Ben Shermans and shiny Oxford brogues, they stood out a mile from the normal jerks on the station. I was talking to a guy from Wolverhampton called Mick when I recognised a fawn coloured mohair rapidly moving towards me. It had a centre vent that was so long it looked as though the jacket would split in half, it was Mafia Dave from Farnworth. His polaroids reflected the glare from the overhead lights of the station as he grabbed my hand and shook it vigorously. I looked over my shoulder and the All-Nighter crowd had already began to make a move from the relative warmth of the station. It was time to head down the approach into the dark Manchester night, to a street called Whitworth Street…and to a queue for a different world.

11.30pm The Queue

We tagged onto the end of the queue at the corner of Whitworth Street and London Road. The queue must have started well before the early session had ended. Hands deep in pockets, I shuffled my feet in an attempt to keep warm as the queue moved forward. In the distance, I could here the muted sounds of a Discotron, and then a voice asking for membership cards to be ready. It was big Jack, the bouncer, making his way from the red glow at the club's entrance, along the queue, checking the numbers of the crowd.

At last we approached the doorway of the Wheel. Bright red and orange lights from behind the distinctive Twisted Wheel Club sign at the front of the club entrance illuminated the people in front of me. In turn I entered the Wheel and went left, instinctively reaching into the back of my Wranglers for my crumpled Wheel card. It was warm inside the small corridor that led to the cash desk. On the wall were large posters, one was advertising a forthcoming Ben E. King All-Nighter. I moved forward until I reached a waist high black cartwheel behind which sat Elaine on the till. Above her head the red bars of a wall-mounted electric heater glowed. I smiled, paid her my thirty shillings and stuffed the card back into my jeans.

Midnight

A sudden rush of adrenalin hit me as I entered the club. I was welcomed by the sweet smell of freshly percolated coffee, and the pulsating rhythm of Willie Mitchell's 'Driving Beat', it immediately sent a shiver rattling down my spine…'And When You Hear That Driving Beat, You Know That Everything's Gonna Be Alright…Alright…Alright'!

I forced my way past the busy cloakroom queue, to the front of an already crowded drinks bar after getting rid of my holdall, and ordered a drink from the girl behind the counter. She was reaching into a large Kelvinator chest-type fridge pulling Cokes out three at a time. A guy next to me, with long sideburns and a blue check Ben Sherman button-down, slowly stirred the coffee in his plastic cup as he waited for friends to come in from the queue outside. He moved and swayed to the sound of Leon Haywood's 'Baby Reconsider' which was belting out of the upstairs speakers.

The upstairs area of the Wheel was crowded. Soft amber and orange light spilled out onto the stone floor from behind abstract patterns of black, wrought iron wheels. Suddenly there was the sound of a thumping bass and the snap of brass as another slab of soul bounced from wall

THE TWISTED WHEEL CLUB
6 WHITWORTH STREET, MANCHESTER 1
Tel. CENtral 1179
presents
SATURDAY - Forthcoming Attractions

APRIL
6th   **THE FOUNDATIONS**
13th   **SPECIAL ATTRACTION**
20th   **J. J. JACKSON**
27th   **THE IKE & TINA TURNER REVUE**
     ALL AMERICAN SHOW
     (LATE SESSION ONLY)

MAY
4th   **Ex FABULOUS TEMPTATIONS**
     THE FANTASTICS
11th   **EDWIN STARR**
18th   **AMBOY DUKES**
25th   **JAMES & BOBBY PURIFY**

Advance Tickets Now Available
or
PAY AT THE DOOR

No Parking on Whitworth Street, or Minshull
Street South PLEASE
CORPORATION CAR PARK AVAILABLE
Aytoun Street, Every Night (No Charge)

THE TWISTED WHEEL CLUB
6 WHITWORTH STREET, MANCHESTER 1
Tel. CENtral 1179
presents
SATURDAY - Forthcoming Attraction

JUNE
1st   **OSCAR TONEY JUNIOR**
8th   **THE FERRIS WHEEL**
15th   **THE GASS**
22nd   **J. B. ROAD SHOW**
29th   **The Greatest Show on Earth, with OSSIE LAYNE**

JULY
6th   **JOE COCKER**
     & THE GREASE BAND
13th   **RIVERS INVITATION**
20th   **O'HARA'S PLAYBOYS**
27th   **WHISKY MAC**

Advance Tickets Now Available
or
PAY AT THE DOOR

No Parking on Whitworth Street, or Minshull
Street South PLEASE
CORPORATION CAR PARK AVAILABLE
Aytoun Street, Every Night (No Charge)

THE TWISTED WHEEL CLUB
6 WHITWORTH STREET, MANCHESTER 1
Tel. CENtral 1179

By Popular Request . . .
Sat. August 17th, 1968
DIRECT FROM AMERICA
The Return Visit of the
IKE & TINA TURNER
Review
STARRING
IKE & TINA TURNER
★
THE IKETES
★
10 Pcs. ALL AMERICAN
ORCHESTRA
★
Don't Miss This Great Attraction
LATE SESSION 11 p.m. - 7-30 a.m.
ADVANCE TICKETS NOW AVAILABLE . . 25/-
POSTAL BOOKINGS ACCEPTABLE (S.A.E.)

THE TWISTED WHEEL CLUB
6 WHITWORTH STREET, MANCHESTER 1
Tel. CENtral 1179
presents

By Overwhelming Demand and
Popular Request . . .
Sat. Sept. 7th, 1968
DIRECT FROM AMERICA
YET AGAIN
The Return Visit of
BEN-E-KING
Plus! Plus! Plus!
THE COUNTS

Don't Miss This Great Attraction
LATE SESSION 11 p.m. - 7-30 a.m.
ADVANCE TICKETS NOW AVAILABLE . . . 25/-
POSTAL BOOKINGS ACCEPTABLE (S.A.E.)

THE TWISTED WHEEL CLUB
6 WHITWORTH STREET, MANCHESTER 1
Tel. CENtral 1179
presents

By Popular Request
Overwhelming Demand . . .
Sat. November 16th, 1968
DIRECT FROM AMERICA
The Return Visit of
OSCAR
TONEY
JUNIOR

LATE SESSION 11 p.m. - 7-30 a.m.
ADVANCE TICKETS NOW AVAILABLE £1
or
PAY AT THE DOOR
POSTAL BOOKINGS ACCEPTABLE (S.A.E.)
Don't Miss This Great Attraction

THE TWISTED WHEEL
MANCHESTER

SATURDAY DECEMBER 7TH

bandwagon

THE TWISTED WHEEL CLUB
6 WHITWORTH STREET, ANCHESTER 1
Tel. CENtral 1179

SATURDAY - Forthcoming Attraction

NOVEMBER
2nd   **THE SHOW STOPPERS**
9th   **OSCAR TONEY JUNIOR**
16th   **SPECIAL ATTRACTION**
23rd   **J. J. JACKSON**
30th   **SPECIAL ATTRACTION**

DECEMBER
7th   **THE BAND WAGON**
14th   **THE SHOW STOPPERS**
21st   **THE FERRIS WHEEL**
28th   **THE BAND WAGON**

Advance Tickets Now Available
or
PAY AT THE DOOR

No Parking on Whitworth Street, or
Minshull Street South PLEASE
CORPORATION CAR PARK AVAILABLE
Aytoun Street, Every Night (No Charge)

THE TWISTED WHEEL CLUB
6 WHITWORTH STREET, MANCHESTER 1
Tel. CENtral 1179

Owing to the postponement of the
ISLEY BROTHERS Tour of England,
we have managed to book on
Saturday, Dec. 14th
THE
ORIGINAL
DRIFTERS

LATE SESSION 11 p.m. - 7-30 a.m.
ADVANCE TICKETS NOW AVAILABLE £1
or
PAY AT THE DOOR
POSTAL BOOKINGS ACCEPTABLE (S.A.E.)
Don't Miss This Great Attraction

No Parking on Whitworth Street, or
Minshull Street South PLEASE
CORPORATION CAR PARK AVAILABLE
Aytoun Street, Every Night (No Charge)

THE TWISTED WHEEL CLUB
6 WHITWORTH STREET, MANCHESTER 1
Tel. CENtral 1179

SATURDAY - Forthcoming Attraction
NOVEMBER
16th   **OSCAR TONEY JUNIOR**
23rd   **J. J. JACKSON**
30th   **SPECIAL ATTRACTION**
DECEMBER
7th   **THE BAND WAGON**
14th   **THE SHOW STOPPERS**
21st   **THE FERRIS WHEEL**
28th   **THE BAND WAGON**

Saturday, January 18th, 1969
JUNIOR WALKER
& THE ALL STARS

Advance Tickets Now Available
or
PAY AT THE DOOR

No Parking on Whitworth Street, or
Minshull Street South PLEASE
CORPORATION CAR PARK AVAILABLE
Aytoun Street, Every Night (No Charge)

THE TWISTED WHEEL CLUB
6 WHITWORTH STREET, MANCHESTER 1
Tel. CENtral 1179

SATURDAY – Forthcoming Attraction

(Christmas Eve, Christmas Day, Boxing Day and New Year's Eve)
CLUB CLOSED

DECEMBER
28th THE BAND WAGON
JANUARY
4th TOP AMERICAN ATTRACTION
11th BILLY STEWART

Jan 18th **JUNIOR WALKER** AND THE ALL STARS

25th TOP AMERICAN ATTRACTION
FEBRUARY
1st WILLIAM BELL & JUDY CLAY
8th JOE TEX & HIS ORCHESTRA

No Parking on Whitworth Street, or Minshull Street South PLEASE
CORPORATION CAR PARK AVAILABLE
Aytoun Street, Every Night (No Charge)

THE TWISTED WHEEL CLUB
6 WHITWORTH STREET, MANCHESTER 1
Tel. CENtral 1179

THIRD TIME LUCKY!!!
Sat. Jan. 18th 1969
DIRECT FROM AMERICA
The Return Visit of

JUNIOR WALKER and the All Stars

Late Session Only 11 p.m. – 7-30 a.m.
ADVANCE TICKETS NOW AVAILABLE . . . 30/-
POSTAL BOOKINGS ACCEPTABLE (S.A.E.)
Don't Miss This Great Attraction

THE TWISTED WHEEL CLUB
6 WHITWORTH STREET, MANCHESTER 1
Tel. CENtral 1179

SATURDAY – Forthcoming Attraction

FEBRUARY
1st ROOT 'N' JENNY JACKSON
8th THE BAND WAGON
15th SPECIAL AMERICAN ATTRACTION
22nd SPECIAL AMERICAN ATTRACTION
MARCH
1st BEN - E - KING
8th THE FERRIS WHEEL
15th VERY SPECIAL AMERICAN ATTRACTION
22nd SPECIAL AMERICAN ATTRACTION
29th SPECIAL AMERICAN ATTRACTION

No Parking on Whitworth Street, or Minshull Street South PLEASE
CORPORATION CAR PARK AVAILABLE
Aytoun Street, Every Night (No Charge)

THE TWISTED WHEEL CLUB
6 WHITWORTH STREET, MANCHESTER 1
Tel. CENtral 1179

SATURDAY – Forthcoming Attraction

JANUARY
18th JUNIOR WALKER and The All Stars
25th BILLY STEWART
THE FERRIS WHEEL
FEBRUARY
1st EDWIN STARR
8th CARLA THOMAS
15th TOP AMERICAN ATTRACTION
22nd TOP AMERICAN ATTRACTION
MARCH
1st BEN - E - KING
8th THE FERRIS WHEEL

No Parking on Whitworth Street, or Minshull Street South PLEASE
CORPORATION CAR PARK AVAILABLE
Aytoun Street, Every Night (No Charge)

28th THE BAND WAGON

THE TWISTED WHEEL CLUB
6 WHITWORTH STREET, MANCHESTER 1
Tel. CENtral 1179

presents
Very Special American Attraction
Sat. March 15th, 1969
TOP TEN RECORDING ARTIST
"I'LL PICK A ROSE FOR MY ROSE"

MARV JOHNSON

LATE SESSION 11 p.m. – 7-30 a.m.
Advance Tickets Now Available £1
or
PAY AT THE DOOR

THE TWISTED WHEEL CLUB
6 WHITWORTH STREET, MANCHESTER 1
Tel. CENtral 1179

SATURDAY – Forthcoming Attraction

MARCH
29th BEN - E - KING
APRIL
5th THE RONETTES
12th J. J. JACKSON
19th THE BANDWAGON
26th OSCAR TONEY JUNIOR
MAY
3rd THE DRIFTERS
10th THE PLATTERS
17th INNEZ & CHARLIE FOXX
24th SPECIAL AMERICAN ATTRACTION
31st THE FERRIS WHEEL

No Parking on Whitworth Street, or Minshull Street South PLEASE
CORPORATION CAR PARK AVAILABLE
Aytoun Street, Every Night (No Charge)

THE TWISTED WHEEL CLUB
6 WHITWORTH STREET, MANCHESTER 1
Tel. CENtral 1179

presents
BY POPULAR REQUEST
Sat. March 29th, 1969
RETURN VISIT OF

BEN -E- KING

LATE SESSION 11 p.m. – 7-30 a.m.
Advance Tickets Now Available 25/-
or
PAY AT THE DOOR

THE TWISTED WHEEL CLUB
6 WHITWORTH STREET, MANCHESTER 1
Tel. CENtral 1179

SATURDAY – Forthcoming Attraction

MAY
3rd THE DRIFTERS
10th OSCAR TONEY JUNIOR
17th INNEZ & CHARLIE FOXX
24th BOB & EARL
31st THE FERRIS WHEEL
JUNE
7th Special American Attraction
14th Special American Attraction
21st THE VIBRATIONS
28th JAMO THOMAS 'I SPY FOR THE F.B.I.'

No Parking on Whitworth Street, or Minshull Street South PLEASE
CORPORATION CAR PARK AVAILABLE
Aytoun Street, Every Night (No Charge)

THE TWISTED WHEEL **MANCHESTER**

SAT. MAY 17TH

INEZ & CHARLIE FOXX

THE TWISTED WHEEL CLUB
6 WHITWORTH STREET, MANCHESTER 1
Tel. CENtral 1179

SATURDAY – Forthcoming Attraction

JUNE
7th THE PLATTERS
14th AMBOY DUKES
21st ROOT 'N' JENNY JACKSON
28th JAMO THOMAS 'I SPY FOR THE F.B.I.'
JULY
5th JIMMY RUFFIN
12th JAMES CARR (FREEDOM TRAIN)
19th THE RONNETTES
26th THE CRYSTALS

No Parking on Whitworth Street, or Minshull Street South PLEASE
CORPORATION CAR PARK AVAILABLE
Aytoun Street, Every Night (No Charge)

THE TWISTED WHEEL **MANCHESTER**

JIMMY RUFFIN
'WHAT BECOMES OF THE BROKEN HEARTED'

SATURDAY, 5th JULY

THE TWISTED WHEEL CLUB
6 WHITWORTH STREET, MANCHESTER 1
Tel. CENtral 1179

SATURDAY – Forthcoming Attraction

JUNE
28th JAMO THOMAS 'I SPY FOR THE F.B.I.'
JULY
5th JIMMY RUFFIN
12th THE TRIFLE
19th THE CRYSTALS
26th THE STATE EXPRESS
AUGUST
2nd THE TOYS / KINGSIZE KEEN SHOW
9th THE RONNETTES FLAMINGOES
16th CRAZY ELEPHANT / THE ▮▮▮▮▮
23rd THE HOGLINE
30th JAMES & BOBBY PURIFY

No Parking on Whitworth Street, or Minshull Street South PLEASE
CORPORATION CAR PARK AVAILABLE
Aytoun Street, Every Night (No Charge)

1st WILLIAM BELL & JUDY CLAY
8th JOE TEX & HIS ORCHESTRA

to wall. With perfect timing, dancers jumped high in the air and landed face down on all fours before leaping acrobatically back to their feet without missing a beat.

1.30am

I walked down the steep stairs that led to the cellar part of the club, chandeliers of old chrome cycle wheels hanging above my head. The intro to Bobby Bland's 'Call On Me' echoed up from below: 'Love and affection…A heart so true…'. At the bottom of the stairs, I turned left into the small corridor of the cellar. Through the curved brickwork archway to my right was the large room that housed the stage. It was packed. The crowd were dancing up a storm to Chuck Jackson's 'Chains Of Love'. I turned left and went through another walled arch into the other part of the cellar.

Lights from behind large black wooden wheels softly illuminated the walls of the room. Condensation made the red Victorian brickwork shine. It ran from the curve of the ceiling, down the smooth walls of the cavernous cellar, to form pools of water on the black stone floor. All available floor space was full.

Lithe young dancers performed fast and intricate dance-steps, oblivious to the slippery floor. I dodged the endless spins, kicks and backdrops, and made my way to the large cage at the back of the room, made from a welded frame of bicycle wheels. Through the spokes I could see Paul Davis, one of the Wheel deejays, busy thumbing his way through the mass of 45s stacked behind him.

On the right, running the full length of the room was a tunnel formed by the walled archways of the cellar. Through a large wooded wheel set in the wall dividing the tunnel from the room I recognised faces that I had seen on the station.

The cellar was as hot as a furnace. Sweat ran down the faces of the dances. Mohair jackets had long been stored away. A guy stripped to the waist in just braces and jeans gulped water from a re-filled coke bottle. The driving beat went on and on. 'Hey Baby I'm Back'…then the beat of a drum, a chugging rhythm from Chicago: Alvin Cash's' 'Philly Freeze' stoked up the dancers. They were in a frenzy, dancing non-stop and pausing only for a split second to strip and change into a fresh shirt, grabbed quickly from a hold-all…the sounds kept coming.

Dry mouths rapidly chewed gum and 'popping eyes' stared all around. The smell of Brut, mixed with cigarette smoke and the smell of sweat. I felt a sudden buzz and a shiver run down my spine as I heard the tinkling of a piano intro, the Contours' 'Just A Little Misunderstanding'. There was a loud 'crack' as the brothers and sisters clapped, right on time, as one. The record faded and the deejay followed on with the sweet harmonies of the Poets' 'She Blew A Good Thing'.

On and on the music flowed. Alexander Patton's 'A L'il Lovin' Sometime' faded out as the Sharpees' 'Tired Of Being Lonely' faded in. I walked back to the corridor at the bottom of the stairs, and through the archway into the room where the stage was. The whole scene was jumping. The sound of James Carr waded in, a thumping bass, 'I Wanna Know'…gyrating dancers, in total harmony with each other and their surroundings, weaved their magic around the floor, in perfect time to the furious beat. It was dazzling to watch the acrobats work their spell on the dancefloor. A backdrop and flick of the body, a leap high in the air. A spin and a twist, a jerk and a whip, the blur of skating legs.

2.20am

The crowd swelled as people from every other part of the club converged on the stage room. Dancers were forced to quit as valuable floor space in front of the stage was taken up by more and more people. Behind me, people were stood on the bench seats that ran along the walls of the raised area at the back of the room. The deejay was playing Bobby Freeman's 'Duck'. More of the crowd stood in the archway, unable to get into the room. Hundreds of faces, all looking forward…hundreds of people in 'soul wonderland'.

There was activity on the stage. The music stopped and the voice of the deejay came over the speakers…'By Overwhelming Demand And Popular Request, The Twisted Wheel Proudly Presents… Right Now… Live On Stage… JUNIOR WALKER and the ALL STARS!'

Bright lights flooded the stage. The All Stars kicked straight into a 'Twistlackawanna' instrumental with amazing style, whipping up an already frantic crowd into a frenzy. A sea of arms, raised high in the air, clapped to the beat.

Behind me there was movement. From the back of the room I could see the smiling face of Junior Walker being escorted through the crowd. Above the tight and raunchy rhythm of the All Stars, a chant rang out… 'JUNIOR, JUNIOR, JUNIOR!'. Eventually, Junior Walker, a white towel draped over his shoulder, broke free from the crowd and leapt onto the stage. It was hot and the crowd was high. Black leather fists punched the air… 'JUNIOR, JUNIOR, JUNIOR!'

The All Stars responded, the drummer changed the beat with a fierce burst on the snare. A rapid fire intro…a rhythm from Detroit… 'JUNIOR, JUNIOR, JUNIOR!'

The wailing screech from Junior's tenor sax cut in, drowning the cries of the crowd. Junior grabbed the mike… 'I said SHOTGUN'… raw emotion… 'SHOOT BEFORE YOU RUN NOW'…The shuddering organ replied to the chant… 'DO THE JERK, BABY, DO THE JERK NOW'. The beat from the All Stars was relentless. A swirling organ and teasing guitar, that haunting tenor sax. Into 'Roadrunner', then 'Shoot Your Shot' and non-stop into 'Shake And Fingerpop'. The whole place shook to that fresh Motown sound. The Wheel's brick cellars provided perfect acoustics, the sound of Detroit rang out in the night. It bounced off the walls and reverberated around the cavernous stage room. The pace never let up…the beat never let go. 'Pucker Up Buttercup' and 'Cleo's Mood' were followed by the smoother edged vocals of 'Come See About Me' and Marvin Gaye's 'How Sweet It Is'. 'COME SEE ABOUT JUNIOR' the crowed screamed.

For more than an hour, Junior Walker and the All Stars held the crowd in a trance. Encore followed encore until the crowd finally let them go…'JUNIOR, JUNIOR, JUNIOR!'…the chant rang out, long after Junior and the brilliant All Stars had forced their way from the stage.

Long After The Night Was All Over

The haunting sound of Dee Dee Sharp's 'What Kind of Lady' filled the air. The audience slowly drifted away and dancers quickly reclaimed their spot at the front of the stage. The whole place was buzzing. The deejay played Bud Harper's 'Mr. Soul' and then Tommy Neal's 'Going To A Happening', the Impressions' 'I Love You (Yeah)' and Jackie Wilson's 'Whispers'. I wandered off and walked from room to room in search of cooler air. Upstairs to the drinks bar for a coke, back down again to the tunnel next to the deejay's cage. I danced with friends that I hadn't seen for weeks. On and on through the night we danced. 'Sweet Thing' and 'Fingerpoppin', 'One Way Street' and 'Gonna Fix You Good'.

It seemed like only five minutes, but when I looked at my watch, for the first time that night, it was already six in the morning. All too soon it was time to go.

I grabbed my holdall from the cloakroom, changed out of my sweat-soaked shirt and to the strains of Jimmy Radcliffe, headed for the door. I stepped out into the crisp Manchester morning, the pavements glistened with frost as patches of daylight started to appear as dawn broke. I quickly caught up with some friends who had already left the furnace. The city was still asleep and it felt as if it belonged just to us, as we walked the deserted streets towards Piccadilly Gardens. The sounds of the All-Nighter and the beat of the Wheel were still spinning around in my head long after the night was all over.

Twisted Wheel Club Acts – Early Months of 1970

JANUARY

Saturday 3rd – Root and Jenny Jackson

Saturday 10th – Red River Band

Saturday 17th – Showstoppers

Saturday 24th – Edwin Starr

Saturday 31st – Jimmy Ruffin

FEBRUARY

Saturday 7th – Fantastics

Saturday 14th – Oscar Toney Junior

Saturday 21st – Edwin Starr

Saturday 28th – Johnny Johnson and the Bandwagon

MARCH

Saturday 7th – Herbie Goins

Saturday 14th – Jimmy Ruffin – 20/-

Saturday 21st – Junior Walker – Doors Open at 10.15

Saturday 28th – Lucas and the Soul Sounds

1970

The Soul Clan

There seemed to be certain areas of England that kept a tighter grip on the '60s soul scene than others, mainly in the north, but not exclusively. Some towns seemed to progress with contemporary soul music while others preferred the rare oldies scene. Bradford, Gloucester, Manchester and North Wales were good examples.

John Massen, a big Bradford devotee, made many journeys to the Wheel. He began going by bus along with the rest of the Bradford crowd: Sue Bushby, Donna Jowett, (later Dent), Ann Greeno, Mick Aherne, Paul Rees, Steve Ridealgh, Edwina Buckley, Ian Richards and others. John remembers: 'Ian got himself a mini van which we began to use, and on one memorable visit to Manchester we arrived outside of the Dolphin where he had arranged to meet Ann Greeno, who'd travelled by bus. Earlier in the day I had borrowed 10/- from Ann and had **177** planned to give it back to her as soon as we met in Manchester. I was slightly uneasy about passing money outside of the Dolphin, but she insisted and the money was handed over. The next thing I knew, was that a couple of coppers in plain clothes were arresting us! Ann Greeno, Ian Richards and myself spent the next couple of hours in Whitworth Street police station. We were all searched but obviously had nothing. On this occasion the squad had moved far too quickly. While inside the station, I recall a radio playing in the background and one record, not the norm for pop radio then, came blasting over the air-waves – 'Heatwave' by Martha & the Vandellas. Needless to say, it just served to put us in the mood for the night ahead.' Other folk who travelled from Bradford included Bob Nelson, Steve Marsden and Ronnie Townsley.

If Bradford seemed to have an unusually big Wheel following, then the same could be said of the Cheltenham area. Graham 'Docker' White was one of the Wheel regulars from nearby Gloucester.

'When I first started to go to the Wheel, sometime in 1968, we would call in at Stourport-on-Severn and pick up two friends who we had got to know at the Chateau Impney, and they had often scored during the week from sources in either Birmingham or Wolverhampton. When we got there we would go to the White Hart on the corner of Whitworth Street for a few pints before going into the Wheel. When the lads from Stourport stopped going, I started to go with a couple of lads from Cheltenham whom I had known for some years, going back to the Blue Moon Club in '66. On the way to the Wheel, they would score from a bloke in Sale, and on the rare occasions that they couldn't get anything there, we would go on a tour of his Manchester suppliers to see what they could pick up. I was later told by a reliable source that most of the lads from the Cheltenham, Gloucester, and Worcester areas who went to Manchester, were listed by the local police as likely drug users!

'Although myself and the Cheltenham lads were fussy about our clothes (as many ex-Mods were), I don't recall the Wheel being too fashion conscious, Ben Sherman shirts and Levi's or Lee Riders being the norm. But when it came to records, we would travel all over the country in search of them. Imports were hard to get outside of London, although F.L. Moore in Leighton Buzzard was a good source. We visited most major towns in the south of England in the hope of finding old stocks of deleted records. Usually these trips were fruitless but one goldmine was a shop called Record Collectors and Accessories, in Picton Street, Bristol. I'm not sure who first discovered it, it may have been 'Froggy' Taylor. The shop's policy was to order one copy of every record released. Can you imagine finding a shop with every Stateside, Chess, Motown and Sue release in stock?

'It was kept a closely guarded secret amongst a few collectors, but luckily I was the one with a car so they couldn't get there without me. Record Corner in Balham was also a good source. My record collection reached about six hundred, but I was very selective and didn't want every issue on Stax or Atlantic etc. All of the close friends that I made at the Wheel were record collectors too – Brian Phillips, Rob Bellars, Les Cokell etc. In fact, I spent most of the night talking records. A top ten would need some serious thought but my favourite would have to be the Flamingos' 'Boogaloo Party'. After the All-Nighter we would sometimes go to a coffee bar in town or on to the Top 20 but that had a bad reputation for trouble and so we didn't go that often.'

Sandra Tunstall (now Longmire) was from Worcester and her long journey was typical of the effort to which people went to, to get to the Wheel each weekend.

THE TWISTED WHEEL
MANCHESTER

ARTHUR CONLEY

29th November 1969

THE TWISTED WHEEL
MANCHESTER

PERCY SLEDGE December 20th 1969

THE TWISTED WHEEL
MANCHESTER

RETURN VISIT BY DEMAND
EDWIN STARR
Saturday February 21st 1970

ADVANCE TICKETS AVAILABLE S.A.E. AND AT THE CLUB
FROM 9 pm ON SATURDAY FEBRUARY 21st OR PAY AT THE DOOR

THE TWISTED WHEEL
MANCHESTER

JUNIOR WALKER
AND THE ALL STARS
on Saturday 21st March

THE TWISTED WHEEL CLUB
6 WHITWORTH STREET, MANCHESTER 1
Tel. CENtral 1179

'SPOT DRAW'
MEMBERS NOTICE

From April 4th, 1970 we have held a 'SPOT DRAW' Cash Prize Competition Every Saturday.

The Prize is now £30
Listed below are names of Members who would have won had they been present on the night.

April 4th Membership No. 1078
 Mr. R. BEARDSLEY, Ilkeston, Derby ..£10
April 11th Membership No. 431
 Mr. R. LENRINSHIRE, Edwinstowe, Notts £15
April 18th Membership No. 1182
 Mr. D. ROBINSON, Marple £20
April 25th Membership No. 513
 Mr. P. BROWN, Barnsley £25

Every members' number goes into the draw each week. The winning member must be present at the time of the draw (approx. 2 a.m.). If the prize is not won it increases by £5 each Saturday until it is won.

REMEMBER — someone must win sometime — why not you?

THE TWISTED WHEEL CLUB
6 WHITWORTH STREET, MANCHESTER 1
Tel. CENtral 1179

MEMBERS NOTICE
SPECIAL SUMMER
ALL NIGHTER PRICE
Every Saturday
[FROM 9th MAY, 1970]

15/-
ONLY
15/-

THE TWISTED WHEEL CLUB
6 WHITWORTH STREET, MANCHESTER 1
Tel. CENtral 1179

SPECIAL ATTRACTION
FROM AMERICA
SATURDAY, AUG. 8th

MAJOR
LANCE

All Pay at the Door
Admission 15/-

THE TWISTED WHEEL CLUB
6 WHITWORTH STREET, MANCHESTER 1
Tel. CENtral 1179

Sunday
Afternoon
Sessions
11 a.m. till 4-30 p.m.

From
6th SEPTEMBER, 1970

4/- ONLY 4/-
EVERY SUNDAY

THE TWISTED WHEEL CLUB
6 WHITWORTH STREET, MANCHESTER 1
Tel. CENtral 1179

BOXING DAY
Saturday, 26th December, 1970
11 p.m. to 7-30 a.m.

Johnny
Johnson
and his BANDWAGON

Advance Tickets Now Available at the Club
and also on Saturday, December 26th, 1970
from 8-30 p.m. or Pay at the Door.

Doors Open 11 p.m.

'I originally joined the Blackpool Wheel while on a week's holiday and enjoyed the music and atmosphere so much, I made the long journey up north to join the Manchester club. Mary Hopkins (now Knowles) and I were about sixteen at the time and it all seemed quite an adventure – we were really hooked on the music, Motown and Soul. It was great getting back home and telling our friends about the latest music and fashions – Manchester was really ahead of its time.

'Unfortunately, I also have an unhappy memory of the Wheel – I had my handbag stolen from beneath my feet. I must have dozed off! I never got anything back, I didn't have much money in it but at that stage I used to carry loads of letters and photos around with me that could never be replaced. I always felt it was my punishment for telling my mum I was staying with friends. She didn't approve of All-Nighters. I think I always told the truth from then on! We sometimes went to Victoria Station afterwards for a coffee. I remember yellow shirts being fashionable, which looked great in the club, but next morning, with a matching face – no! Quite a few of us travelled up on New Year's Eve 1966 to see the Alan Bown Set, as we knew them – Jess Roden was from Kidderminster.

'We also used to go to the Chateau Impney, which was great for All-Nighters and not so far for us to travel. I also think that as we got older we realised that it was easier to go somewhere close rather than a five or six hour coach journey to a place where, after all, we didn't really know anyone. As time went by, more and more discotheques were opening and a similar sound and atmosphere was being created. Other like-minded friends at the time were Bernie Challis, Andy McCorrigan, Phillip 'Pippy' Goodhead and Richard Oakley who has since sadly passed away.

'I must add that we had a day out in Manchester recently as my son is in University there, and we walked the full length of Whitworth Street and couldn't find anything resembling the Wheel as I remember it, perhaps thirty years on I was being too optimistic!'[1]

Harry Thomas from Prestatyn was typical of the dozens that faithfully travelled the considerable distance from North Wales to Manchester for the All-Nighters.

'I wouldn't say that time flies but it certainly doesn't crawl like it used to. It's hard to believe that it was 1968, over thirty years ago, that I took the train, with my friend Tony Smith, from Prestatyn station every Saturday night for three years to where the heart of soul music was located in Britain – the Twisted Wheel in Manchester. Tony is no longer with us, and I would like my short account of those great times to be dedicated to his memory.

'On the train, we would meet up with friends from Anglesey, Bangor, Llandudno, Colwyn Bay and Rhyl, all people I had met through going to the Wheel – Dave Price, Jeff Dodd, John Ivor, Keith Parry, Dougie Goodall, Little Ian, Postie, 'Big' Pete, Que, Merv, Alan Evans, Mike and Marlene Adams, Pat 'Pill', Keith Horrocks, Dennis Jones, Arthur Standling, Keith Waite, Anthony Hamilton, Barbara and Sherry, Les Church and Poly.

'From 12 midnight on Saturday until 8 o'clock on Sunday morning I would be among the friendliest crowd of familiar faces, all listening to the most emotional, passionate and addictive music on planet earth. If there was a higher cloud than cloud nine, I was on it! The intimate and exhilarating atmosphere at the Wheel was as thick as London fog, the air was filled with the smell of Brut after-shave, everyone wore it in those days, even the girls. Having passed

180 through the coffee bar and handing in your coat and bag you went down stairs, which were steep and narrow to the cellar like rooms below. Everyone's breath smelled of mint, as we all chewed gum and many wore sunglasses, I wonder why? The brick walls echoed to the sounds being relayed from the DJ's cage – Marvin Smith, the Astors, Gene Chandler, Danny White, Jackie Edwards, Bobby Sheen, the list was endless. This is now all in the past, taken away by the powers that be in Manchester. But one thing they couldn't take away were our memories.'

Manchester of course provided at least fifty per cent of the membership but there certainly wasn't any 'our territory' rubbish, and Ivor Abadi recalls only half a dozen fights in over eight years. Dave Hall came from West Gorton, Manchester and travelled to the Wheel with Mike Curtis.

'We all met up at the Dolphin Café – Ian Dunning, Gilly, John Barlow and Alan Shultz. Normally we travelled on the thirty five bus from Cheetham Hill; as the bus came from Bury, John and Alan would already be on it. We would leave the Dolphin and tramp around to Chorlton Street Bus Station or Piccadilly Station to meet up with other lads that we knew. Very few people had cars in those days. I started going to the Wheel in May '69 until it closed in '71, after which Mike C joined the French Foreign Legion – he lasted about two weeks before coming back home. He then joined the British Army. He tracked me down in 1977, but I haven't seen him since. Actually, it was Gary Laine from Spin Inn who put us on to the Wheel, when we went in to buy records. He would call us Little Richard and Chubby Checker. He always had loads of records out the back and despite mithering him to look through, he never let us. One unusual place we did get records from however was a club on Oxford Road called Takis, where the DJ was Paul Pender. He used to sell us records for the price of a Coke.

'In the Wheel I recall everyone's names carved on the toilet walls. Also the sound system was the worst you've ever heard, piping the music round to all areas. We used to hang around the tunnel, the row of archways near the DJ's room, talking records, gear and nothing in general. Clapping, spins and back-drops were the order of the night. True record collectors preferred the music on the decks rather than the live artist on stage. I always remember at about 4am when people were sitting on the stone floor, getting a bit down, suddenly '6 x 6' would come on and bring the whole place back to life, as if by magic. On the last night, one or two of us tried to remove the wooden cart-wheels from the wall by kicking seven shades of shit out of them, but alas they were there forever. Even though the place was a bit of a dump, everybody was hand clappin' and foot stompin'. Enjoying every minute of the time they spent there.'

Ian Dunning, then from Stretford, was another Manchester regular.

'We used to meet in the Dolphin or the Queen's Hotel opposite. We would then walk down to Victoria Station to meet friends off of the train such as Eugene French from Middlesborough and Mike Kay from Darlington, then wander down to Piccadilly to meet Little Frankie from Worcester or Frankie from Ormskirk. Loads of people just had nick-names: Blob, Flash, Batman, Billy Whizz, Gilly, Booper, Docker, Dicko, Mafia Dave and Nai (me!) Other people I recall were: Dennis the Mac, Paul Donovan, Gordon Thompson, Dave Price, Tony Wallwork, Mike Curtis, Dave Hall, Alan Shultz, John Barlow, Tony Davidson, the Naylor brothers, American Jack (draft dodging), Curtis from Oldham, John Behan, Joe Dooley, Joey Hodligan, Scotch Joe, Rob Bellars, Phil Saxe, Moe, Brent Irons, Trevor De Lacy (Smith), Tommy Walsh, Dave Valencia, John 'Zan' Sneddon, Iain Sneddon, Kim Dent, Kenny Massall, Phil Morgan and Jimmy Moran. Of the girls I remember; Sharon Baldwin, Liz Priv (Przywitowski), Sue **181**

Bushby, Lynn Garritty, Barbara Sweeny, Venessa Stafford, Joan McCarthy and two girls known as 'the Black Widows' who used to only dress in black from head to toe, I think they were from Stoke. Then there were two girls from Blackpool who only dressed in white and were called the 'White Angels.' Afterwards we would go to one of the all night coffee bars, usually Snack Time on Newton Street, then at lunchtime to the White Hart, before returning to the Wheel for the Sunday Afternoon sessions.'

Twisted Wheel Club Acts – Spring 1970

APRIL
Saturday 4th – Fontella Bass
Saturday 11th – Bob & Marcia
Saturday 18th – Harry J and the All Stars
Saturday 25th – Showstoppers

MAY
Saturday 2nd – Ben E. King
Saturday 9th – All-Nighter
Saturday 16th – All-Nighter
Saturday 23rd – Ben E. King
Saturday 30th – Unknown

JUNE
Saturday 6th – Marv Johnson
Saturday 13th – All-Nighter
Saturday 20th – Jimmy Ruffin
Saturday 27th – All-Nighter 10/-

Scots On Swingers

David Meikle was an absolute devotee and regularly made trips down from Scotland at the end of the sixties to hear his beloved music and related the following story.

'In December 1967, Glasgow was in the midst of a massive Mod scene and clubs such as the legendary Maryland, reverberated to the sounds of Motown, Stax and Atlantic. I was sixteen-years-old at the time and already showing signs of vinyl dependency, but it was of the Jimi Hendrix type, not the Four Tops or the Temptations. This was of course a problem in macho Glasgow, where if you weren't 'in' you were most definitely 'out'.

'A fellow work-mate took me aside one day and thrust a copy of the Miracles 'Going To A Go Go' LP into my hand. After several plays it began to click, and I recall thinking that there was something magical in this LP, great vocals and great lyrics – it wasn't long before I had my own copy. The Detroit Spinners and the Isley Brothers followed. I was hooked on the Motown Sound. A couple of months later, I discovered *Blues & Soul*, which at that time was in its more compact format. John Abbey's reviews were impeccable and my first decade as a collector hinged on his every word. It was also in this magazine that I first came across the Twisted Wheel Club and its amazing array of American artists. Another Motown artist came to my notice via Radio Luxembourg – Edwin Starr. His 'I Am The Man For You Baby' was played on various shows for many weeks, and Edwin's unique vocals complemented, what I still regard, a most underrated tune. The 'Soul Master' album followed, and for me Edwin was already a legend.

'In 1969, I was offered a deejay spot in Glasgow's La Caverna and on Mondays and Thursdays was able to play the sounds of soul in one of the few bars allowed to play black music in the city at that time. Sadly the Mod scene was over and the trendies had moved on to the 'music of the long hairs'. The bar was still busy however and about a dozen soul fans helped to generate some great nights. Among those was John Anderson who was already known in soul circles in England via his mail-order service.

'An advert in *Blues & Soul* in January 1970, caught my notice when Edwin Starr was listed as appearing at the Wheel on January 24th. My mate and I had met Mancunians in Torquay at the magical Compass Club the previous year, and they told us a visit to the Wheel would be a night to remember. Over the next twelve months, most of us would make it to Manchester and I personally managed ten visits, mainly due to the free travel facilities offered by my employer, British Rail. Thursday nights at La Caverna were always special before heading south on the Saturday morning, the sense of anticipation was amazing.

'An early train would take us from Glasgow Central to Manchester Victoria in time for a weigh-in, a couple of cheap LPs in W.H. Smith on the station platform, and on to Barry's Record Rendezvous in Blackfriars Street for some serious purchases from the singles racks. From Barry's it was back to the left luggage to lock away our new finds. During the football **183** season, we would head to Maine Road or Old Trafford to watch Francis Lee, George Best and company. At five o'clock we would return to the city centre to watch the Scottish results in a TV shop in Piccadilly. The Indian restaurant across from Piccadilly Station usually got a visit after that. The weekend was just beginning!

'Like all industrial cities, in winter, Manchester had a cold, dank, murky feel about it, but I will always recall the special atmosphere in the city centre as the night life began – it truly was the place to be in 1970. There were of course many concerts in the city at that time and I was privileged to see Sam & Dave, Joe Tex, Arthur Conley, Jimmy Ruffin and Booker T & the MGs in other venues, such as the Odeon in Oxford Street or the Free Trade Hall. If there were no soul acts on however, it was back to Rowntrees Sound in Corporation Street and a great evening of popular soul music in the downstairs lounge. Many Wheel fans from other parts of the country used this as a starting point for the evening.

'From there we would head to the White Hart on Whitworth Street, which was of course next door to the Twisted Wheel, for a final drink before the All-Nighter. I can vividly recall a record dealer in the pub with copies of the then newly released Invictus singles. They caused tremendous excitement but I doubt if anybody could have anticipated their future success. It was in this pub however that the atmosphere began to build and there were dozens of people milling around, talking records and soul music. For us this was completely unique and the buzz was incredible, totally electric.

'There always seemed to be a large queue outside the club and Ivor Abadi was usually at the main door asking newcomers to complete membership forms. From there it was pay as you go, and into the top level of the club where the coffee bar and the cloakroom were. In the caverns below hundreds of people were already dancing, formed in circles or in long lines, this was truly a club with a difference. It was also new for us to meet so many females who were into the music. I had been a collector for several years by then, but the sounds being played were all new to me. Big beaty numbers with loads of saxophone, girl choruses and happy-go-lucky lyrics, just made for people who could dance – and could they dance.

'Dave Godin rightly proclaimed them as the greatest dancers he'd seen outside of America. Some were as good as a poor man's Gene Kelly. It had to be seen to be believed. One dancer in particular always caught my eye and that was 'Booper'. He could be seen spinning from room to room to the incredibly weird and difficult 'Scratchy' by Travis Wammack – we all looked on in amazement.

'Ben Sherman's and Levi's were the norm at the Wheel and most people brought a change of clothing. Black driving gloves were prevalent too, a possible acknowledgement of the Black Power movement in the States. When stirring numbers came on, such as Major Lance's 'Everybody Loves A Good Time', the gloves could be seen punching the air and clapping in perfect time to the beat – creating the most fantastic atmosphere. The disc jockeys were of a high calibre too and in particular Les Cokell.

'Surprisingly, most of the music played was on UK issue, imports were always in the minority. However one import that did catch my eye, however, was Edwin Starr's 'Back Street'. I already had all his Motown and Polydor releases but nothing on the original US label. I will never forget the first time that I heard this fantastic record and it remains an all time favourite.

'Charles Hatcher's (Edwin Starr) lyrics, could have been made for The Twisted Wheel Club.

I've been along Main Street where society is the thing,
People that live on Main Street, they don't know how to swing.
But the people on the backstreet, they swing all night long.
Although I live on the Main Street, the Back Street is where I belong.
Back Street…Show me the Back Street'.

'We were underground in Manchester's Back Streets creating a scene which lasts to this day. A scene which applauds every aspect of Sixties soul music – the artists, producers, arrangers, songwriters, label owners, studios and all. Today, Edwin is still hailed for his stage act, but in 1970 he was awesome. I had the privilege of seeing him three times at the Wheel and will never forget being on the small stage with him, belting out 'Time', which had just been released.

'My only regret is never seeing Major Lance at the club. I had enquired by mail to Ivor about the possibility of his appearance to which he kindly responded with a hopeful message. We travelled down on August 8th, but sadly Lance never appeared.

'Looking back, it is surprising how contemporary the sounds were. Many of the records were already ultra rare, such as Leon Haywood's 'Baby Reconsider', but they were no more than four or five years old. I must also admit that several artists sounded fantastic in this arena too, in particular 'You're Ready Now' by Frankie Valli and 'Break Out' by Mitch Ryder and the Detroit Wheels – their contribution to the scene must be acknowledged. I can recall somebody in one of the rooms with a large suitcase full of rare records. They were a joy to behold and their price tags whetted the appetite for the music even further. There seemed to be an endless list of unknown artists emerging, with fantastic names like Hoagy Lands, Richard Temple, Mamie Galore, Rose Batiste. Who were these people? Where did they come from? Amazingly they were only the tip of the iceberg.

'Of course, there was always a down side to the evening, and that was when we entered the last half hour. Every record was cherished until the dreaded fire exit opened at 8am, and everybody descended the few stairs that took us into the yard behind the club and on to Piccadilly Square. Even then the music wasn't over, as invariably someone would have a Discotron playing some more unknown tunes – the appetite was enormous. Some even went on to the Top 20 in Hollinwood or returned to the Wheel's afternoon sessions, which began later that year. For the travellers from Glasgow though, it was back to Victoria Station for the long trip north. Final move was to get on the scales and see how much weight we had lost in the last twenty four hours – it was always amazing! There was always time on the train for singing lines from the most memorable songs – for example 'Discotheque', 'A Li'l Lovin' Sometimes', 'That's Enough' or 'A Quitter Never Wins' – they all had fantastic punch lines. You could never get the melodies out of your head. Luckily the train was usually empty!

'Strangely, when the club closed in 1971 it was the beginning of another era. The word about the rare soul scene was spreading and Northern Soul had emerged as its logo. I later attended Up The Junction, Blackpool Mecca, the Torch and Catacombs, but there was always a belief in soul music circles that the original was always the best and there is no doubt that the Twisted Wheel was the best. Every time I'm in Manchester I go down to Whitworth Street just to get the feeling of it again – it had such an impact on me.

'In December 1998, I visited Detroit, where of course much of our wonderful music was   **185** created. First port of call was the Golden World Studio on West Davison – bought out by Motown in 1967. A fading 'Motown Studio B' sign, hangs proudly on the side of this otherwise insignificant building. From there to United Sound Studios, on Second Avenue. The structure is very similar to Hitsville but on a much grander scale. Tragically the premises were due for demolition at the beginning of 1999, a victim of the Edsel Freeway. Finally I visited the Motown Museum which spoke for itself – a wonderful tribute to the unbelievable achievements of Berry Gordy Jr. and his array of stars.

'As I stood outside these Meccas, I thought of the Twisted Wheel Club and of the great times I had there. I also remembered, however, the contribution made by the citizens of Northern Soul's greatest cities – Detroit, Chicago, New York, Philadelphia and Los Angeles. Without them the Wheel would have been just another club.'

Twisted Wheel Club Acts – Summer of 1970

JULY

Saturday 4th – All-Nighter 10/-

Saturday 11th – The Drifters

Saturday 18th – All-Nighter – Next Week Major Lance

Saturday 25th – Major Lance Unable To Appear – Tonight Drifters 15/-

AUGUST

Saturday 1st – 10/- Summer All-Nighter

Saturday 8th – 10/- Summer All-Nighter

Saturday 15th – 10/- Summer All-Nighter

Saturday 22nd – 10/- Summer All-Nighter

Saturday 29th – 10/- Summer All-Nighter

SEPTEMBER

Saturday 5th – Horatio Soul and the Pavements 15/-

Saturday 12th – Top 10 Recording Artists – Sweet Inspirations

Johnny Johnson and the Bandwagon

'Nothing to do on Sunday afternoons?

Then why not come along

To our Sunday afternoon sessions?

Every Sunday 11.00 – 4.30pm 4/-

Saturday 19th – Root and Jenny Jackson

Saturday 26th – Fantastics

CHAPTER TWELVE
Those Who Bought Them And Played Them

Brian Rae

IN THE EARLY '60S BRIAN LEFT HIS WARRINGTON HOME FOR COLLEGE IN LONDON. HE WOULD also go to that other place of learning, the university of life, in Brian's case, the Flamingo, Marquee and Scene clubs to name but a few. Before moving south, Brian had already visited Liverpool's Cavern and various Manchester clubs and was fairly up on pop music. On leaving college in London in mid '64 Brian took his first job and soon got in with a young mod who also worked at John Lines in Tottenham Court Road. Brian was quickly introduced to the London club scene, and recalls one particular Friday all-nighter at the Cellar Club, High Street, Kingston, which stayed open round the clock until Sunday night, this visit coinciding with the release of the Small Faces' 'Whatcha Gonna Do About It?'. The massive impact that the record had on the audience never left him and little did he know that the same hysteria would later be repeated in Manchester when he would be the first Wheel DJ to spin Arthur Conley's 'Sweet Soul Music'. (Seven times on the Saturday of release, Brian recalls!)

His taste moved quickly towards R&B after meeting another work colleague, Chris Lorimer, from Leeds, heavily into the music and who would later work for United Artists. Brian now began a long career of collecting and playing soul music at a serious level. Chris introduced him to Dave Godin who was regarded as the London scene's kingpin for all matters R&B. Brian and Dave quickly became acquainted and one of the first ventures he got roped into was the now infamous *Ready, Steady, Go! - James Brown Special*. Dave collected Brian from his flat in his Ford Pilot and sped off to Heathrow to meet the James Brown entourage. Sadly the plane yielded not one of them; they hadn't even boarded in the USA, (eventually to arrive one week later). Brian recalls Dave's despondency soon turned to delight however when one Miss Irma Thomas walked down the steps instead and so an impromptu welcome party and press reception was quickly arranged.

Brian visited the Scene club and heard both Guy Stevens and James Hamilton deejaying. James was influential, not only as a DJ, but more importantly as a record reviewer in *Record Mirror*. James (and Norman Jopling) would review the records a week prior to release and provide invaluable catalogue numbers so Brian could order them ready for playing on the weekend of release. Brian had no particular favourite record shops in London but recalls buying most of them in the Portobello Road and Ladbrook Grove area.

Tarren, his girl friend at the time, sent a letter describing a great new club that all the Manchester Mods were attending called the Twisted Wheel. Although Rae was still in the south, he visited the Wheel and continued to do so in preference to the more fashion-led clubs in the capital.

Brian returned to Warrington and took a job in a firm with a printing section where two girls worked and listened to Radio Caroline continually. They would tip Brian off to all of the popular records that were getting action. One such disc was Darrell Banks' 'Open The Door To Your Heart'. Upon hearing it, Brian immediately placed an advance order quoting the London-American catalogue number as given in *Record Mirror*. The shop assistant told him that he was one of about a dozen people to do the same that week. Friday came with no record arriving at the shop, and Brian was told that there was a delay, and of course the rest is history (the rights to the disc were transferred to EMI, and the few London promotional copies that were pressed on London-American are now sought after collectors' items). Brian took delivery of his Stateside copy about three weeks later, by which time, interest and intrigue had hyped the record into outer space!

Brian had a standing order with one Miss Morgan at Warrington Electric record shop for any discs that were to be released with particular catalogue prefixes, for example TMG, SS, CRS, or AT. One revered catalogue was that of Sue and Island, yet outside of the London area these were notoriously difficult to obtain. He recalls Lufton's Records in Tottenham Court Road (famous for appearing on the cover of the first Sue Story LP) were big stockists. But in Warrington, Brian had to rely upon Birmingham record distributor H. R. Taylor, who would stock up their van with records and then gradually off load them as they drove north. Needless to say stocks dwindled by the time the van rolled into Warrington and so Rae had to make do with what was left. These and other Saturday purchases were quickly taken round to the back room of a pub where they would be played on a Discatron, and organised into a rudimentary play list for his spot at the Co-op Ballroom on Sunday night. This spot was heavily influenced by the Wheel All-Nighter, by the records spun, the clothes worn, and generally how people were hanging out.

Brian's first visit to the Wheel saw the 'King of Rock & Soul' on stage, the great Solomon Burke, complete with cloak and crown. Having moved back north, Brian became a regular and decided to audition as a DJ one Tuesday night. Ivor and Phil would certainly have their say but 'Ugly' Ray Teret decided that Brian was the man. Brian's early impressions inside the cage were of the modest pair of Garrard decks and the 30-watt amp that fed the numerous but notoriously poor speakers. Brian was paid thirty shillings for his spot, but this did include sweeping up the DJ booth and along the row of arches.

Certain nights stand out, probably the finest being the visit of the Ike & Tina Turner Revue. One problem however was how to fit them all in! Apart from Ike & Tina there were the Ikettes, as well as the entire Ike Turner Band. Little space remained in the stage room, kids would have to stand on the steps or in the raised area opposite to see them. On the night when Jimmy James and the Vagabonds appeared, Brian vividly recalls Jimmy beckoning to a black guy in the crowd to get up on stage introducing him as Tony Clarke.

Another great night was when Alvin Cash appeared. Brian had gone over to Sheffield to support them as DJ in an early evening show, and then returned to Manchester with them to play the Wheel. Alvin was touring with his brothers, the Crawlers, and while Alvin handled the vocals the dance troupe would perform a selection of the big current dances in the USA. Brian recalls them being the first to do back drops in the club.

Another notable event happened one Sunday morning in 1967 after the All-Nighter. **188** Normally Brian would go to Piccadilly toilets to wash and change before going on to the morning session at the Stax Club where he was a DJ, and then on to Rowntrees Sound for the afternoon session, before finally catching the train back to Warrington. This particular morning found Brian and a couple of girls sitting on Central station financially embarrassed. He didn't even have enough for the bus fair at the other end. A tramp who had been sleeping on the bench next to them had obviously been listening because he fumbled a bit inside his sock and handed them a five pound note, a lot of money then, and stipulated that it was not to be used for food (funnily enough they didn't have much of an appetite anyway). One week later, Brian recalled reading in the stop press of the *Manchester Evening News* that a tramp had been found dead with over £5,000 on him.

Shortly after would be Brian's final night at the Wheel when J.J. Jackson was the live act. The Supremes had played the Free Trade Hall the same evening.

Twisted Wheel Club Acts – Late 1969

APRIL
Saturday 5th - Ronettes
Saturday 12th - J. J. Jackson
Saturday 19th - From America - The Bandwagon
Saturday 26th - Platters

MAY
Saturday 3rd - Early and Late - Drifters and
the Freddie Mack Sound
Saturday 10th - Oscar Tony Junior
Saturday 17th - Inez and Charlie Foxx
Saturday 24th - Bob and Earl
    Bob and Earl
    Bob and Earl
    Bob and Earl
Top Ten Recording Artists 'Harlem Shuffle'
Saturday 31st - By Overwhelming Demand
The Return Visit Of Inez and Charlie Foxx

JUNE
Saturday 7th - Platters
Saturday 14th - 10/- All-Nighter
Saturday 21st - Root and Jenny Jackson 10/-
Saturday 28th - Jamo Thomas - 12/6d

Brian '45' Phillips

Brian was brought up in a tough part of north Manchester called Langley, and his older brother's musical tastes were a big influence. He introduced to the twelve-year-old Brian, the likes of Sonny Boy Williams and Little Richard. Phillips recalls that 'his' school uniform was a shirt with Sonny Boy's name on the back. As a teenager, Brian did the usual round of Manchester's clubs until he discovered the Wheel, becoming a regular thereafter. He was also dabbling with deejaying at such places as the Kontiki in Middleton for ten shillings a session.

Brian was building up a sizeable record collection and becoming obsessed with buying and collecting vinyl. Brian was totally consumed by it, any available cash being ploughed into his passion, even to the point of 'borrowing' his dad's weekly repayments to Burton's that he would volunteer to take down town to pay for him. To hear Brian talk of those days confirms the expression 'vinyl junkie', with every waking hour centred around obtaining records.

A typical day as a clerk at the city's Corn Exchange, would run something like this: get to work, do a bit when ever the boss was looking, but meanwhile be writing out a record sales list for one of the company secretaries to type up. In the coffee break shoot into town doing as many small shops as possible, looking for any new arrivals. Go back to work, and eat lunch without the boss noticing. As soon as lunchtime arrived, get straight down to Mazell's, look through a large pile of 45s, need to buy forty of them but only have money for twenty, plead with them to hold the others until 5pm when you would be able to get back. Return to work, get a sub from the wages girl, let the boss see your face before he made his weekly visit to Liverpool, and as soon as his car door closed get straight on the bus to Prestwich to clean a few windows. Wednesday was always Mr Davidson's for three pounds. He had a big house and they were special new plastic ones that needed doing inside and out! Get back to town to pay off Mazell's and drop by Johnny Roadhouse.

Friday was the day to get your pay packet as early as possible, and get down to the Co-op on Deansgate to buy up deletions – especially good on Statesides – maybe bump into Phil Saxe or Rob Bellars at the same game. Go home get changed, get back into town with the intention of going to a record session, sometimes the Wheel but get distracted in the Dolphin, and end up buying three nice 45s and be left with no money to go to the club, let alone the bus fare back. Walk home.

Saturday would be a day return to any major city for record hunting, Brian's favourite being London. Get round as many places as possible: Dobell's, Moondog's but Soul City in Deptford was always a must. Get home, changed and then because all of the money had gone on *[handwritten annotations]* →*Dickie* *thanks for writing* *great to hear from you.* *as you will read it is an Auction* *So I cant tell you prices at moment* *Manchester J.WALKER* *21.3-1970* *ext* ⊗ *see you at* ⊗ *sometime Bri*

BRIAN '45' PHILLIPS,
5 GILPIN WALK,
LANGLEY EST.,
MIDDLETON,
MANCHESTER.

Hi Fellow groovers,

Glad youve sent for a list - enclosed is the advertised l st of about 800 collectors items.

This is an Auction which the closing date is March 28th Saturday 1970, by then all bids shall be in. There is no mimum bids but bid sensibly and don't be affraid to bid its never to much trouble to obtain a record you want. Please enclose an S.A.E. with all bids and you will be notified on how they went on successful or not.

The major point of this front note is that if you bid for any record on a British label which is say worth about £1.10.0. please also enclose how much you would bid for it on import. As by the end of March I will have about fifty or more imports I've already listed on British for Sale. Such records include e.g. Sweet thing, Boy from New York City, Wahed ashore, Youre feady now, Thats enough etc. So when bidding for rarer British in brackets state bid on import.

Anyway hope youre gonna be lucky - Just like to thank the Twisted Wheel Manchester for this is where I first heard all these records.

Packing and Post will be charged extra according to successes. Also in future I will be starting a regular import system of all these rareties, so if you want to be put on the list please enclose two stamp addressed envelopes instead of one when bidding., list will be prepared at regular intervals. If you require information on bidding please stae in bids.

Yours faithully,

Brian '45' Phillips

P.S. if you require any records not on these lists please send me a list of them and I'll try and import them for the future, with maximum price. *P.S. i'm D.J at Wheel regular these*

records, go to chip shop and trade a Marvin Gaye for pie and chips. Get into town, go to the Mogambo or Blue Dolphin to sell a few more for entry to the Wheel All-Nighter.

Brian started to supply both collectors and DJs with deleted, rare and imported 45s. One particular deal involved a batch of Sue singles for sale on a small stall in town at one shilling each. Then deleted, Sue records were highly prized, and a town centre record shop owner and night club DJ was very keen to get hold of some. He bumped into Phillips who, hearing his plea, told him that a very influential contact he had in London was in town the following day, and that Brian would 'phone him to bring up some of the rarer and more esoteric Sue releases. The following day, Brian went round to request some cash up front, after all they were going to be London prices, at 10/- each! The guy refused but Brian was able to talk him round when he returned with his mates Vespa as a 'deposit'. Brian then shot straight around to Shude Hill to buy up the stock of records, even managing to get a discount on the one shilling asking price. He returned to Cross Street to finish the business. Brian recalls that when the 'deal' was

Above: Brian '45' Phillips' sale list from early 1970, sent to Carlisle collector Dick Watt. Brian suggested that they meet up at the Twisted Wheel for the Junior Walker show on 21st March.
Left: In November 2000, Brian and Dick eventually make the date at the Wheel, over thirty years later. 191

eventually sussed some weeks later, the DJ never spoke to him again. Brian's habit could also be expensive, he recalls buying Bobby Bland's 'Call On Me' for fifty shillings in 1968.

The Sue deal was atypical however, Brian's overwhelming love of the music and otherwise fair dealing earned him a solid reputation throughout Britain, and in an age of few cheque books and telephones most folk would happily send him cash. This mail order business was the first UK operation to specialise in rare and deleted sounds. Another first for Phillips was his use of EMIdiscs, to record sounds that were unobtainable, such as the Dynatones 'Hold On I'm Comin', taken from their rare album. These entrepreneurial skills would eventually make him a rich man!

His break as a DJ came shortly after the Wheel's record collection was stolen. Paul Davis recommended to Ivor, that Brian should have an audition. Ivor was reluctant as Brian was a 'punter', but agreed to him initially taking on a job serving drinks for four shillings, which he did for several weeks reluctantly. Phillips knew the records being played weren't a patch on what he had in his own collection and the only decent ones that were being played were bought from him anyway! He eventually got behind the decks and became the first DJ to start playing rarer stuff, obscure deletions, small label items and imports. The first ones that he played down there were Johnnie Taylor's 'Changes', Mitch Ryder's 'You Get Your Kicks' and the Sharpees 'Do The 45' for which he became famous.

Brian deejayed from April '69 to the end of the summer of 1970. He was a keen footballer and getting up on Sunday for a game was becoming more and more difficult. And deejays such as Les Cokell playing newer import releases was not Brian's idea of a soul music policy.

Twisted Wheel Club Acts – Summer of 1969

JULY
Saturday 5th - Jimmy Ruffin
Saturday 12th - All-Nighter 10/-
Saturday 19th - Crystals
Saturday 26th - All-Nighter 10/-

AUGUST
Saturday 2nd - Jamo Thomas
Saturday 9th - Crystals
Saturday 16th - Root and Jenny Jackson
Saturday 23rd - Ronettes
Saturday 30th - Eden Rock

SEPTEMBER
Saturday 6th - Root and Jenny Jackson
Saturday 13th – State Express
Saturday 20th - Drifters
Saturday 27th - Hit Recording Artists of 'Poison Ivy'
and 'Yakety Yak' - The Coasters - 11.00–7.30.

Those Who Stole Them...

In the summer of 1968 the hallowed Wheel record collection was stolen. This act of near sacrilege caused initial mayhem, upset and the near closure of the Wheel, but it is arguable, that as a result the club embarked upon a new musical era with different style records being brought in from club members far and wide.

The theft took place mid week when somebody used a sledgehammer to smash their way in through the fire door, and helped themselves to every 45 on the shelves in the deejay booth. The records soon began to appear around Manchester, some in secondhand shops in All Saint's or Tib Street, and some openly sold or swapped amongst collectors. They were distinctive enough, whether British demos, issues or imports as they all had a large plain sticker with a silver star on top, and many having a small hole punched in the label. The culprits became known, and although the Abadi brothers took the matter to the police it was difficult to prove.

The next Saturday All-Nighter was only a few days away, and as many discs as possible had been purchased from around town. Barry's, where the club had an account, was particularly helpful and as many friends, members and deejays as could be contacted brought in 45s. Rumours spread like wild fire that the Wheel would surely have to close, now that the unique record collection – its life blood – was no more. But in true soul brotherhood fashion, club members came to the rescue, donating or lending the club scores of precious 45s. As mentioned earlier, Chris Booth, DJ at the Blackpool Wheel was summoned with his collection (Phil Scott donated the Wheel's anthem of the time, Chubby Checker's 'At The Discotheque' on Cameo-Parkway).

The theft of the collection came with a silver lining, and the new sounds brought to the club, particularly from

Charlie & Inez Foxx

Wolverhampton, only improved the calibre of the music heard at the Wheel. There was also a spate of thefts shortly after the new premises opened. Cash was being systematically taken from the club's petty cash tin. The Abadi brothers began to eliminate the various employees who had access to the funds, but the cash kept disappearing. Totally baffled, Phil Abadi deduced that the mysterious thief was somehow breaking in at night, as no damage was ever caused. As the three brothers were the only key holders to both the outer doors and the office, Phil decided to spend the night in the club right next to the cash. Dawn broke without any sign of the night intruder.

Mystified Phil began to prepare for the day ahead, when suddenly he heard a key turn in the outer door. He was then amazed to see a small figure, wrestle open the office fanlight and drop through, making straight for the desk. Phil steeled himself to confront the desperado, and turning on the light, was amazed to see the intruder was none other than the builder who had been employed by the Black Cat landlords to build the famous boundary wall a few months earlier. The Abadi brothers had in fact been suitably impressed with the bricklayer's workmanship and instead of taking police action it was decided to 'employ' him to do various alterations in the new club!

Twisted Wheel Club Acts – Autumn 1969

OCTOBER
Saturday 4th October – Clarence 'Frogman' Henry
Saturday 11th - Marv Johnson
Saturday 18th - Ben E. King
Saturday 25th - Lee Dorsey

NOVEMBER
Saturday 1st - Shirelles
Saturday 8th - Inez and Charlie Foxx
Saturday 15th - Platters
Saturday 22nd - Fontella Bass
Saturday 29th - Arthur Conley

DECEMBER
Saturday 6th - Ronettes
Saturday 13th - James and Bobby Purify
Saturday 20th - Percy Sledge
Saturday 27th - Eden Rock

CHAPTER THIRTEEN
'That's What I Want To Know'

Many questionnaires were sent out during the research for this book, and the following reply from Trevor Bridge was typical.

What town did you travel from to get to the Wheel?
Burscough, Near Ormskirk. S.W. Lancashire.

Where did you meet?
Usually at the bottom of Piccadilly Station approach. There were always lots of people assembling and meeting there before walking down to the club.

Who did you meet up with?
Friends from home (Ormskirk and Kirkby areas) who had travelled separately.

How did you travel to Manchester?
We normally got to Manchester by hitchhiking along the East Lancs Road (A580). Blokes would travel in groups of two, or there would be a guy/girl together – couples would not necessarily be in a relationship, just part of a big local gang whose lives revolved around going to the Wheel. During the winter months, I watched football games at Preston North End and would either hitch from there afterwards or travel by train from Preston station to Manchester Victoria.

Where would you guess people scored their gear?
In Ormskirk, for about a year (1966), supply was obtained from a huge American car, which was parked on Saturday afternoons in the middle of the town centre car park. Very subtle! Later, a number of the more criminally-minded people obtained supplies from either burgled chemist shops or, so it was rumoured, from the Smith, Kline and French factory in Liverpool. There was certainly never a shortage (or so I was told!)

What was the date of your first and last visit to the club?
1966 to 1969.

Do you recall any people travelling great distances?
I remember a large contingent from Dumfrieshire and another from Wellington, Shropshire. **195**

There were a lot of people from Liverpool and I recall, amongst many others, people from Holmfirth, Yorkshire.

Famous personalities?

I remember someone purporting to be a Radio One deejay, sitting behind the spokes with Paul Davis. It was shortly after the Wheel's records were stolen and I had lent about a hundred of mine to Paul (as I regularly did at that time). The so-called deejay (whose name eludes me at the moment) stole my copy of 'So Much In Love' by The Tymes on Cameo-Parkway.

What about the clothes?

Fashion was fairly important, although when Mods progressed to 'Soul Boys', I don't think clothes were quite as important. We still dressed in our own style, but gone were the Mohair suits. I wore the same shirt virtually every week for an inordinate length of time – it was dark green, made out of a strange lightweight, almost bobbly material, had a collar and three buttons and was similar to a modern day polo shirt. I was very fond of it! We used to always take a change of clothes, making use of the Wheel cloakroom and toilets. Ben Sherman shirts were still popular.

Where did you buy your records?

I used to spend most of my spare time trawling through record shops throughout Lancashire (Preston, Blackburn, Burnley, Wigan etc), and the Liverpool and Manchester areas, armed with my list of issue numbers of deletions. There were still many independent shops around at the time with large stocks – with a bit of effort rare records could be found fairly regularly and bought at retail prices. Due to the underground nature of the scene, the shops were pretty much unaware of the value of these records, which was brilliant. During this period, I never paid more than shop price for any record, and still managed to accumulate a large collection. Whilst I was originally collecting (up until 1969, when my collection was stolen), I cannot remember seeing many US imports. I also used to write down the details of new records I heard at the Wheel and purchased them from my local shop in Ormskirk, or from a shop in Preston where I was at school.

I particularly remember buying 'Everbody's Goin' To The Love-In' by Bob Brady & the Conchords from a certain Mr. Bob Brady's record shop in Preston one Saturday morning!

Did you go anywhere before the All-Nighter or afterwards?

Not usually. We would travel to Manchester just to for the All-Nighter and travel straight back. We did use the Blue Dolphin coffee bar on London Road quite regularly and went for the occasional under-age drink at the Dive Bar at Piccadilly.

Did you personally witness any Drug Squad activity inside the club?

The DS were always in the club to my recollection, and it was obvious who they were. I just remember them wandering about or standing next to the cloakroom entrance, I don't recall seeing them bothering anyone unduly. Away from the club, they used to try and mingle with Wheel kids at the bottom of Piccadilly Station approach. I particularly remember one occasion when they were questioning someone there – a girl dropped some pills onto the pavement causing them to rush over. The girl nonchalantly let them scrabble about on the floor picking up the pills, and when they had collected them all up announced rather disdainfully that they were iron tablets. It was purely a diversionary tactic of course – by this time the person originally being questioned had disappeared into the night.

On another evening at the same location, I was carrying three small envelopes, one for myself, and the others for two of my friends. The DS suddenly appeared, panicking me into swallowing all three, contents and all. I had an exceptionally good night, and on the Sunday did my paper round in record time, almost wearing out the tyres on my bike! I can't remember my friends being disappointed, so they presumably must have scored again.

I was once waiting for a girl on Preston Railway Station – I'd been to a football game and she was travelling from Ormskirk to meet me, so that we could hitchhike together. I realised I was on the wrong platform as the train was pulling in and ran up a flight of steps and across the footbridge. I was running along the adjacent platform when I realised that I was being chased by a gang of men, shouting at me. This made me run faster, until I realised that there was no escape and gave up. When they caught up with me they produced warrant cards and asked why I was running. I explained that I was meeting someone and had been on the wrong platform. They accused me of trying to get on a train without paying, which was ridiculous and I told them so. They took me to the station's police room and made me empty my pockets. When they saw my Wheel membership card they got very excited and strip-searched me. I thought this was a bit extreme, but as I was 'clean', I wasn't too bothered, especially as I didn't want them to find the girl I was meeting since she had earlier visited the Ormskirk car park I mentioned earlier. I hadn't seen her on the station but was hoping that she'd seen what had happened and had made herself scarce.

The police were extremely naive:

DETECTIVE ONE	Do you take drugs?
ME	No.
DETECTIVE TWO	Are you sure?
ME	Yes.
DETECTIVE THREE	Does anyone ever ask you to carry anything?
ME	What do you mean?
DETECTIVE TWO	You know what we mean. We all know about the Twisted Wheel Club. Now does anyone ever ask you to carry any packages?
ME	Oh! *(feigning surprise)* You mean drugs.
DETECTIVE FOUR	Yes, drugs.
ME	No. I'm not that stupid. I'm studying for my A Levels because I want to go to University. I wouldn't be so stupid as to get mixed up with drugs.
DETECTIVE TWO	Do your parents know that you go to the Twisted Wheel?
ME	No they don't, but I'm sixteen, so I can do what I want and you can't tell them.

DETECTIVE TWO	You're a clever one are you?
	(Aggressive good cop, bad cop routine begins)
DETECTIVE THREE	Who were you meeting? You can't remember can you?
ME	No.
	(Thinking to myself – thank you, if you'd let the bad cop carry on I might have told you more)

They carried on for a while longer but by then, even at my tender age, I had realised that they were pretty inept and wouldn't have got anything out of me even if they had kept me there all night. At first I was very nervous, and if they had been good at their job they might well have tricked me into telling them something useful. After all – I was just a young working class kid from the sticks! Sorry to digress, but it was a true Wheel related event. Looking back it still causes me much amusement. Incidentally, our local village police sergeant later told me much later that he had been informed of the event.

After the closure of the Wheel did you continue going to clubs?
No.

How old where you when you first went?
Fifteen-years-old. (Or perhaps just turned sixteen).

Do you remember any of the people there?
Friends from home that I can still remember (Ormskirk and Kirkby areas): Geoff Cheetham, Bobby Derbyshire, Keith and Carol Breakall, Sue Costello, Pete Simpson and his brother, Gordon McRae and Steve Pennington.

Can you describe what your feelings were about going to the All-Night sessions at the Wheel? Perhaps give some of your recollections about going to the Wheel?
As with many, many others, going to the Wheel was the most important thing in my life, and still, thirty years later, sometimes sends a shiver down my spine when I think about it. From Sunday morning to the following Saturday, my mind was consumed with looking forward to the next session. I was totally obsessed.

I will always remember in vivid detail, the first time I went to the Wheel, which was in 1966. There were five of us, three regulars and two, including myself, first-timers. I recollect walking down London Road, on the opposite side to the railway station approach, towards Whitworth Street, and Gordon passed me a pill and told me to swallow it. At the time I only had a vague idea what it was, but it wasn't very long before I found out! Later it took more than one, but that first experience was unforgettable. In the meantime, we rounded the corner into Whitworth Street to be faced, for me, the first sight of the long queue of people I instantly recognised as being the type I belonged to, or thought I did. After all, I had for a long time been a Mod and had a collection of Tamla-Motown and Atlantic singles. We shuffled our way to the head of the queue where I paid for my first wheel-shaped membership card, and stepped inside.

198   The coffee bar was the first place encountered, and I remember this strange but wonderful sounding music – it was certainly not the Four Tops or Otis Redding. Mind you the speakers in that part of the club were never of a high quality! We then made our way down into the labyrinth of small rooms where people were engaged in the most incredible dance routines.

I was amazed. I had never even dreamt of such things. Without exception, people were very friendly, wanting to know your name, where you were from, and talking, talking, talking. I was completely hooked, and from then on could not be kept away from the place.

I soon became interested in the music played at the club and wanted to find out the names of the records so that I could start collecting them. The best way was to hang around the DJ room, which was where the most knowledgeable people frequented. They would happily give you the information required, or of course the DJ would help out. I would spend a great deal of my time in this way, and gradually built up a good collection. To my parents' great delight, these records were played relentlessly night after night at home.

At the time when the Wheel's records were stolen, I would take my collection along and deposit it with Paul Davis behind the famous wall of spokes. I could not comprehend how anyone could even contemplate stealing what to me was sacrosanct, let alone actually carry out such an act. It did my ego some good though when my records were used, especially when Paul would play a great pile of them one after the other, and then the final buzz – he would thank me by name over the most sacred sound system in the world. Heaven!

I had a comprehensive Major Lance collection, mainly picked up at less than half price and unplayed on Wigan Market. I knew of him through 'Um, Um, Um, Um, Um, Um' and 'Ain't No Soul (Left In These Old Shoes)', but until I got them home, did not know the other titles. Up until the time of the record robbery, Major Lance was not featured very heavily in the Wheel's play-list, but then Paul Davis started to regularly play my copies and I like to think that I had at least some influence on his records becoming as popular as they did. That's the way I remember it anyway!

I was always far more interested in records than the live acts, and would watch even world famous stars only for a token few minutes in the stage room before returning to the DJ room or another part of the club. Of course records were still being played in the rest of the club whilst the acts were actually performing.

Did you go to any other soul or night clubs in the '60s and early '70s?

I went to local clubs in the Ormskirk area where soul music was very popular. I was a deejay at the time playing at such venues as Ormskirk Catholic Club.

Were you a Mod? How did you dress? Did you have a scooter?

Yes, I was definitely a Mod! Earlier on I wore mohair suits with a very long centre rear vent and six buttons per sleeve. Ben Sherman shirts. I didn't have a scooter. In Ormskirk very few of us were interested in them, but at school in Preston they were very popular although none of the so-called 'Mods' there went to the Wheel.

Where did you buy your clothes at the time?

Places like Harry Fenton's and a few small independent shops in Preston who had cashed in on the Mod scene.

Did you go to any of the Sunday morning soul sessions after the Wheel All Nighter?

No. We normally went to a café.

What acts did you see at the Wheel?

Junior Walker & the All Stars, Ferris Wheel, Inez & Charlie Foxx and many others – I was mainly interested in records though and would only watch acts for a short time before going back into the other room where they played records while the acts were on.

Do you remember any of the deejays at the Wheel?

Quite a few, but I can only recall Paul Davis by name.

Twisted Wheel Acts – late Autumn 1970

OCTOBER

Saturday 3rd - Hightimers

Sunday afternoon sessions

Every Sunday 11.00 - 4.30pm 4/-

Saturday 10th - Johnny Johnson & the Bandwagon

Saturday 17th - Joyce Bond Review

Saturday 24th - Root and Jenny Jackson

Saturday 31st - Jimmy Ruffin

NOVEMBER

Saturday 7th - All-Nighter

Saturday 14th - Ben E. King

Saturday 21st - All-Nighter

Saturday 28th - All-Nighter

DECEMBER

Saturday 5th - Lucas & Soul Sound

Saturday 12th - Root & Jenny Jackson

Saturday 19th - All-Nighter

Saturday 26th - Johnny Johnson & Bandwagon

CHAPTER FOURTEEN
Last Night

BACK IN 1966, IVOR, PHIL & JACK ABADI APPLIED FOR A DRINKS LICENSE TO MANCHESTER Corporation and received the first of several refusals. It isn't clear why, as one of the main points of the Manchester Corporation Act was to encourage such applications to enable the authorities to maintain closer control over the previously unregulated coffee dance clubs. In the summer of 1967, the brothers made another application and were confident of success. They even went to the extent of announcing that the forthcoming All-Nighter on Saturday 15th July, featuring Geno Washington & the Ram Jam Band, would be the last. Typically at the eleventh hour, the application was refused and the closure cancelled. Not surprisingly, the following week's advertisement read: 'Long John Baldry, Bluesology and the Fix. SPECIAL MEMBERS NOTICE. Due to the fantastic demand the management have decided that All-Night sessions will remain open – Every Saturday 11–7.30am. Special Summer Price 10/-'.

But the real thing happened in 1970, when the corporation, backed by the police, decided to put pressure on the Abadi brothers and the Twisted Wheel. Although the drug squad had no evidence of drug dealing within the club, a decision was made to close the club in the summer of '70. Autumn saw the various appeal hearings, and 31st January 1971 was the final time soul music was heard at an all-nighter in the club. There were a few odd sessions after this date, but these were certainly not All-Nighters.

Police sources agree that the Brazennose Street Wheel had caused them problems. Theft of amphetamines from chemists, break-ins and people caught in possession as far afield as Bradford, often had all-nighter connections. Raids, surveillance and pressure were fairly constant then. However, when the club moved to Whitworth Street, a reluctant acceptance seemed to evolve, that at least most of the known drug activity was taking place under one roof, opposite one of their own stations. And the last thing that the Abadi brothers wanted was any connection with the misuse of drugs.

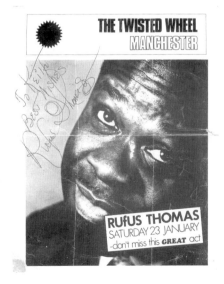

At the start of the new decade, the authorities decided to act. One theory as to why this particular bout of pressure would be the one to close the club, is the feeling that the Abadis might not resist as much as they had in the past. After all, despite what one might be led to think by Northern Soul historians, attendances at these 'hole in

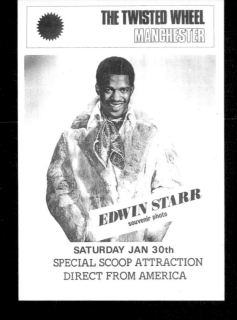

THE TWISTED WHEEL
MANCHESTER

EDWIN STARR
souvenir photo

SATURDAY JAN 30th
SPECIAL SCOOP ATTRACTION
DIRECT FROM AMERICA

'Funny, but it didn't feel like the last night. It was as exciting and as much fun as the first time I played there.'

EDWIN STARR

the wall' soul clubs was gradually dropping. The sixties was over, and there were now other distractions. New places to go, fresh music to listen to, and different fashions to follow – more than one ex-Wheel member had followed Roger Eagle down to the Magic Village in Crompton Court. Ivor Abadi admits that if they had fought the closure tooth and nail they could have won, but who could blame him for not bothering. The rest of Manchester's clubland had moved on to scampi and chips, 'chicken in a basket', drinks licenses and cabaret for the sophisticated twenty-somethings. One other local club that had taken this step was making more in one night than the Wheel would in one month. There were various stages to the closure procedure, with Ivor appealing at each one, with loyal members attending the hearings.

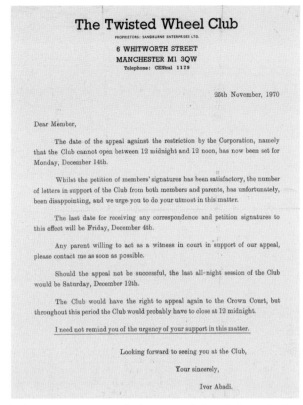

Abadi even gave various interested parties, including parents, guided tours of the club with the All-Nighters in full swing. We recall thinking what a bold move this was; sunken faced dancers, with their clothes drenched in perspiration, eyes like golf balls dancing the night away! These various postponements gave rise to several 'last nights' but after losing the final appeal, Ivor decided to declare when the final session would be, and Edwin Starr, a favourite at the Wheel, was booked for what was bound to be a very emotional session.

The imminent closure brought different reactions; older faces returned, folk who obviously hadn't been to the club for a good few years. Not surprisingly, their Wheel uniforms of shiny three-button mohair suits looked a little dated. Other veteran members turned up, in kaftans with tinted specs and long hair. Some in more contemporary dress, but still with the Mod ideal of being up-to-date, hip, and looking expensive. There were some making their first ever visit to the Wheel.

That January in 1971 saw the biggest attendances at the club for years. The Wheel crowd was now fairly diverse in its appearance, basically anything went but there was still a certain something that kept them apart and above the rest of humanity. There was also a healthy age range, some of the younger element being smart skinheads and the more senior, looking quite respectable. All however had one thing in common, they were experiencing the hallowed temple of R&B for the last time, and all with their own special memories of good times.

Many commented how much they thought it had changed, particularly the dress and records. Also how young the newer members looked, a bit like the 'how young policemen seem nowadays' syndrome. One such guy bought a copy of Percy Sledge's 'Baby Help Me' from a record box, and when he saw that it was a French picture sleeve, he seemed a little disappointed that it wasn't the familiar red label that he recalled from years before.

203

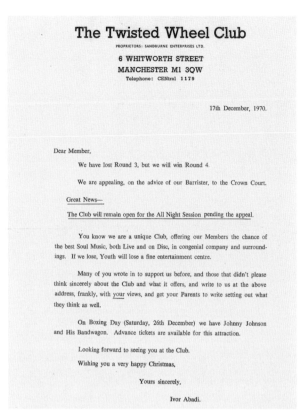

The Twisted Wheel Club

PROPRIETORS: SANDBURNE ENTERPRISES LTD.

**6 WHITWORTH STREET
MANCHESTER M1 3QW**
Telephone: CENtral 1179

17th December, 1970.

Dear Member,

We have lost Round 3, but we will win Round 4.

We are appealing, on the advice of our Barrister, to the Crown Court.

Great News—

The Club will remain open for the All Night Session pending the appeal.

You know we are a unique Club, offering our Members the chance of the best Soul Music, both Live and on Disc, in congenial company and surroundings. If we lose, Youth will lose a fine entertainment centre.

Many of you wrote in to support us before, and those that didn't please think sincerely about the Club and what it offers, and write to us at the above address, frankly, with your views, and get your Parents to write setting out what they think as well.

On Boxing Day (Saturday, 26th December) we have Johnny Johnson and His Bandwagon. Advance tickets are available for this attraction.

Looking forward to seeing you at the Club.

Wishing you a very happy Christmas,

Yours sincerely,

Ivor Abadi.

The final week of the month saw handbills in Manchester record shops for Edwin Starr's appearance on the Saturday, it had to be all-ticket as it seemed like folk from all over the North and Midlands were planning on being there. The build up to the weekend began on Thursday with letters and phone calls flying all over the place. Arrangements were being made for old friends to meet in the usual time honoured places; Piccadilly Station, Victoria Station, the Dolphin, Lower Moseley Street bus station, the White Hart and any one of a dozen coffee bars. And when the evening of Saturday 30th January finally arrived, it was all rather bizarre. People gathering in Manchester from all over the place, making nostalgic visits to Ralph's, mingling with the new Northern Soul crowd as well as those who had never left the scene, and were still hanging out at these locations as if they were their second home.

The queue outside the Wheel was understandably long and started to form well before midnight, stretching way beyond the derelict café down Whitworth Street. It was a particularly cold night too, the well-wrapped queue quietly moved forward, with a notable lack of merriment more evident in times gone by. Once inside however, the old magic of the Wheel's atmosphere instantly took over, and any feeling of a wake was instantly forgotten. In fact by 1.30am, the sense of excitement made the hairs stand-up, on even the most conservative of necks. The speakers boomed out club oldics as well as the new favourites on import – 'Show Time', 'Darkest Days', 'Shotgun And The Duck' … Old friends shook hands, meeting up after many years, youngsters, on their debut, stared totally awe struck at the acrobatic feats from even the most ordinary dancers and most unusually people were already beginning to gather in the stage room to see their hero from Detroit, Agent-00 Soul, Edwin Starr. In the coffee bar, all the tables were occupied, Fanta and Coke bottles everywhere, people were even sitting in the dreaded 'cold room' at the rear.

Then at about 2.30am, despite the ageing speaker system, the unmistakable sound of Paul Davis' voice uttered the immortal words: 'Ladies and Gentlemen, by overwhelming demand and popular request, for the last time at the Twisted Wheel, Manchester…Edwin Starr'. The backing band received an unusually ecstatic welcome as the stage lights went up and they launched into their first warm-up number. Then, dramatically, amidst the jostling and jockeying for a good position in the lower part of the stage room, a cable attached to a large speaker cabinet was caught by a waving hand. The result was disastrous, the whole thing crashing down onto some poor guy's head. He looked very young and his head began to bleed quite badly. As he was led off by his girl friend, a few folk must have thought about the reception he would get in casualty, whether he had taken any gear, and how he would explain things to his mother if he was 'stopping at a friends'.

The band played on and after one more number the man himself jumped on to the stage as if from nowhere. The place went berserk. It was obvious that Edwin had intended to launch straight into his first number, but as he couldn't even hear himself think it all seemed a bit pointless. After what seemed an age, some sort of order was reached and the air was filled with the deafening but millisecond-precise sound of the famous Twisted Wheel hand clap and Edwin was then able to embark upon surely the greatest soul finale ever staged on this planet. He had obviously been carefully briefed because that night Edwin covered every one of his records that had graced the Wheel's turntables: 'My Weakness Is You', 'Back Street', 'Agent-00 Soul', 'Stop Her On Sight', 'Headine News' – even 'War' seemed like an old favourite.

After two encores Edwin disappeared, the lights went back down and the soul sounds once again regained the attention of the sweat-drenched crowd. Those terrible speakers that couldn't cope with the higher notes, did in fact add a distinctive Wheel character to certain records, usually those with a vibe led introduction. 'Secret Agent' and 'Baby Do the Philly Dog' never sounded the same again, especially when squeaky clean stereo CDs got there high tech hands on them.

It was now nearing dawn, and for some weird reason the solemnity of the occasion gradually seemed to make itself felt. People were beginning to put on their coats, hands were being shaken, but not like aloof Englishmen, more like ghetto soul brothers leaving a club in Philadelphia. Hugs, kisses and a few tears were shed, people half knew that they may never see these old friends again. Where else could people from all social classes and backgrounds meet? Friends from Gloucester, Scotland, Yorkshire, Wales, Stoke… Before we knew it, the sunrise of the 31st was lighting up the city's horizon, visible through the ventilation fans in the stage room wall. Jimmy Radcliffe's sad lament soon filled the air as the house lights went up, and dozens of sombre soul fans, well wrapped up in anticipation of the icy Mancunian morning quietly filed out, under the stage out into the cobbled backyard of the Wheel. Those rusty steel doors finally and quietly closed for the last time at 8am Sunday January 31st 1971. Little did anyone dream that this was such an historic moment, or that the legend would live well into the next century, heralding the start of the biggest underground phenomenon ever, Northern Soul.

Final Days At The Twisted Wheel 1971

JANUARY
Saturday 2nd - Tonight All-Nighter 11.00–7.30am
All Pay At The Door
Saturday 9th - Tonight All-Nighter 11.00–7.30am
All Pay At The Door
Saturday 16th - Blakes Bang Bang Show
Next Saturday - Rufus Thomas

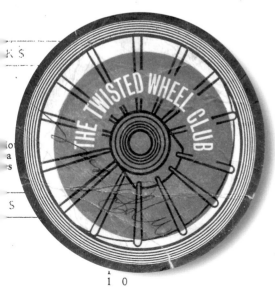

TWISTED WHEEL

MENU

SAVOUFIES

Egg on Toast	2	0
(Scrambled, Poached, Fried)		
Welsh Rarebit	2	0
Beans on Toast	2	0
Spaghetti on Toast	2	0
Tomatoes on Toast	2	0
Mushrooms on Toast	3	0
Buck Rarebit	3	0
Corn-on-Cob	2	6
Spaghetti Bolognaise	4	0

ENTREES

(The following served with French Fried or
Creamed Potatoes and Choice of Vegetables)

Fried Egg	2	6
Plain Omelette	3	6

THE TWISTED WHEEL CLUB
6 WHITWORTH STREET, MANCHESTER 1
Tel. CENtral 1179

MEMBERS NOTICE

**SPECIAL SUMMER
ALL NIGHTER PRICE**
Every Saturday

10/-
ONLY

10/-

LONDON
AMERICAN RECORDINGS

MADE IN ENGLAND
THE DECCA RECORD CO. LTD

45 R.P.M

Ⓟ 1965

Recorded by
HI,
NEW YORK

Burlington
Music

K/T

HLU
10004
S

MSCL.7374

EVERYTHING IS GONNA BE ALRIGHT
(Mitchell)
WILLIE MITCHELL

Friday 22nd - Twisted Wheel
MEMBERS NOTICE
Appeal Date now set for next Monday, Jan 25
This Saturday will be last All Night Session if we lose the Appeal
TOMORROW SATURDAY
ALL-NIGHTER
RUFUS THOMAS

Saturday 23rd - Twisted Wheel
MEMBERS NOTICE
Appeal Date now set for Tuesday, February 2
Next Saturday, January 30 with Edwin Starr will be the last
All Night Session if we lose the Appeal
Tonight 11–7.30
RUFUS THOMAS
RUFUS THOMAS
RUFUS THOMAS
Tickets available at Club
Tonight from 9pm or pay at the door

Friday 29th - Twisted Wheel
MEMBERS NOTICE
Appeal Date now set for Tuesday, February 2
This Saturday will be the last All Night Session if we lose the Appeal
THIS SATURDAY
ALL NIGHTER
EDWIN STARR
EDWIN STARR
EDWIN STARR
Advance tickets available at Club from 9 pm Saturday or pay at the Door

Saturday 30th - Twisted Wheel
MEMBERS NOTICE
Appeal Date now set for Tuesday, February 2
Tonight will be the last All Night session if we lose the Appeal
TONIGHT
ALL NIGHTER
EDWIN STARR
EDWIN STARR
EDWIN STARR
Advance tickets available at
Club from 9 pm Saturday or pay at the Door

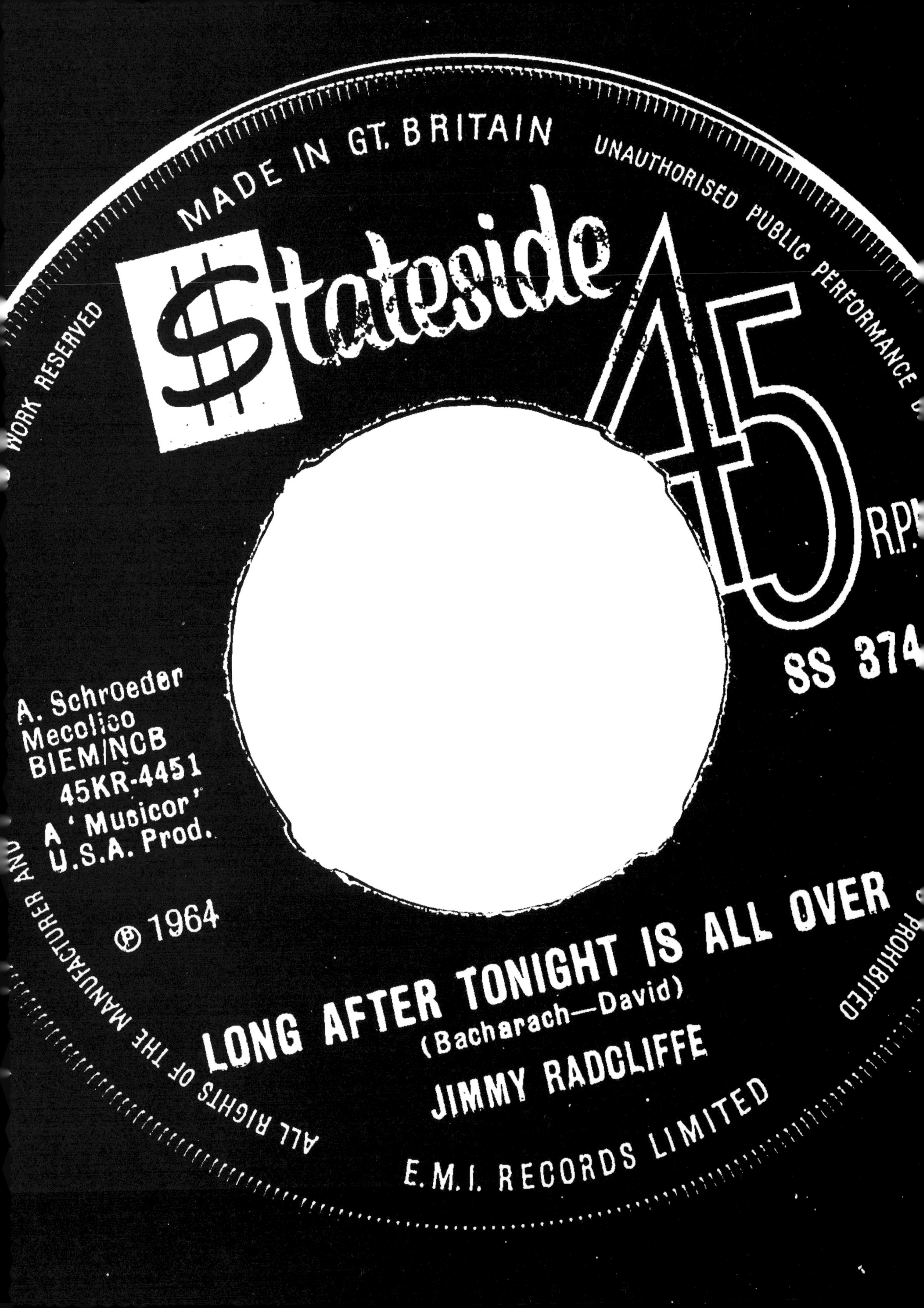

MADE IN GT. BRITAIN
UNAUTHORISED PUBLIC PERFORMANCE
Stateside
45
SS 374
A. Schroeder
Mecolico
BIEM/NCB
45KR-4451
A 'Musicor'
U.S.A. Prod.
℗ 1964
LONG AFTER TONIGHT IS ALL OVER
(Bacharach—David)
JIMMY RADCLIFFE
E.M.I. RECORDS LIMITED
ALL RIGHTS OF THE MANUFACTURER AND
WORK RESERVED
PROHIBITED

CHAPTER FIFTEEN
Long After Tonight Is All Over

THE RECORDS WILL SHOW THAT THE LAST ALL-NIGHTER AT THE WHEEL WAS ON THE 30TH January 1971. Although this is true, it was not as legend has it, the closure of the club. After all, the court action was simply to stop the All-Night sessions. The club continued to hold one more regular session but, as you can imagine, it didn't last long and one week later on 6th February the Twisted Wheel officially closed.

By now other venues were beginning to emerge; Manchester' Pendulum, the Mecca at Blackpool, the Catacombs in Wolverhampton, Va-Va's in Bolton, the Wakefield Metro, Crewe's Up The Junction, and the Golden Torch at Tunstall. All playing an extension of what the Wheel had evolved into, certainly in its twilight months anyway: a mixture of rare deleted oldies that had once gained British release or newly-discovered oldies on US import.

Most ex-Wheel members moved with this trend, and became fully immersed in the new and exciting Northern scene. Derek Howe simply did what he had always done – bought current releases from such places as One Stop on Piccadilly Station approach. Others, such as DJ Les Cokell, would use their start behind the decks at the Wheel to build reputations at places such as the Blackpool Mecca. Established jocks like Brian Rae would spread the new word all over the north west. Brian Phillips would expand his hobby from selling records to friends to becoming the north's most influential dealer. Rob Bellars would amass an impressive collection.

Of course some people, often those in their mid twenties and older, left the scene totally. Mick Taylor from Doncaster was one such person. He saw the closure of the Wheel as the end of an era, which of course it was, and can even pinpoint the actual time and place where it ended for him.

'A mate of mine from Doncaster, called Tom Sligh, played me a record on his Discotron, that he had just heard called 'Wear It On Our Face' by the Dells. My usual practice was to order the LP of the single, if there was one, from Record Corner or direct from the States. I therefore ordered the Dells' album, 'There Is', from London, but by the time the six weeks delivery time was up the soul and Mod thing was gone, I'm not sure if I could have carried on anyway, to be honest we'd had enough. I never did get round to picking the LP up from Record Corner even though I'd paid for it!'

It was the end of the swinging sixties, by the time the Wigan Casino All-nighter opened in September '73, even the clothes aspect of the scene had gone to the wall. No more £150 handmade suits and shoes, high collared button downs were gone and suede and leather was definitely frowned upon. Mick emigrated to Canada, soon to meet up with Martin Koppel.

Wheel regular Graham 'Docker' White from Gloucester: 'I went to the last all-nighter, **209** which I recall as being quite sombre. I did visit a few other clubs after, one in Bradford and one in Crewe, but the magic had gone for me, so I got married and settled down. I think that most of us realised on that last night, things weren't going to be the same anywhere else. My most vivid memory of that last visit was of Les Cokell begging to borrow my copy of 'The Drifter' by Ray Pollard, which I lent him but never got back! I never saw him again until very sadly hearing of his death.'

Following our chat, Graham dropped us a note containing a few missing details. He then ended it in a humble, yet typical way that encapsulated the love and emotion of every story from every ex-Wheel member we had spoken to: 'Thanks for your interest, it was a special place and a special time in my life. Please ring me if you think I can be of any further help – Graham'.

> 1971
> February
> Saturday 6th – Tonight Early Session
> 8pm to 12 Midnight
> BLAKE'S BANG BANG SHOW
> 5/- ONLY 5/-
> THERE WILL BE NO MORE ALL-NIGHT SESSIONS AT THE CLUB

Come And Get These Memories

Margaret Unwin (now Bowden) formerly from Gorton, used to buy her clothes for the night at Crowther's Boutique, King Street. She got her records from the shop next to the Top Ten Club with her friend Diane Hulse (now McIntyre) before meeting the crowd from Queensferry – Michael, Peter and Ian McQuillan and Dave Kay from Liverpool. Then on to the Wheel and the Blue Note or Top 20 the morning after.

Norma Barratt from Whitefield was a young fourteen-year-old when she started attending the Wheel and has fond memories of John Mayall and Spencer Davis in particular, who gave her his coke bottle as a memento.

John Bollen, long standing soul fan on the scene, paid his dues at Harrison's Hoist, the Golden Disc, the Birdtrap and Burnley Mecca before going to the Wheel. His time at Hornsey Art College meant rather a long trip north towards the end. Friends Denis Blackburn, George Boocock, Julian Bentley and Tim Newbould all helped keep the Yorkshire soul scene going in the '60s.

Bill Ball, originally from Blackpool and then Rochdale was a total Wheel devotee. 'Never missed a week apart from my holiday!' Would meet the Wheel gang at the Masque Coffee Bar or the Chambers: Dave Fleming, Kathy Brown, Carl Hill, Debbie & Sharon Garlick, Janet Reeves, Kath Whicker, Chris Shine, Paddy Higgins and Pete Dunn. They would get the 24 bus to Stevenson Square to meet up with Johnny Keane, J.C., Zac Mills, Les Miller, Dave Allen, Kathy Burgess, Val (Snowy), Joan McCarthy, Jonah, Dennis Shannon, Brian Warner, Joey Hardy and Gordon Thomson, to name but a few, at either the Dolphin or in the Wheel itself. They also went to the Chance, the Blue Note and the Top 20.

John Behan, from Whitefield, was one of the top Manchester Wheel guys, referred to by many as the bloke to know.

Sue Bushby, from Bradford, would travel over by bus with friends Donna, Edwina and Andy and would meet up with Frank Licurci, Allen Pilkington and Elaine Cummins. After some great nights at the Wheel, they would go to the Top 20 before the trip back to Bradford. Thank you for the loan of your photos Sue.

Dave Clarke, from Warrington, was a blues and R&B enthusiast, who went to the Brazennose Street Wheel with the likes of Rick Green, Neil Carter and Bob Groom. They were experts on the music and certainly kept the visiting artists on their toes when it came to probing questions about obscure 78rpm recordings. Dave has gone on to become one of the country's leading R&B authorities and has provided this book with masses of invaluable information. Thanks Dave!

Liverpool's Larry Clarke, was another Wheel regular, who used to meet Dennis Hawe, Nick Cowan and Kevin Murray at Livingstone's before going to Manchester. Steve Thomas and Ray Faulkner were other Liverpool regulars. Larry's dad's record shop in Bridge Road, Litherland was handy, and helped him amass a collection of over five hundred 45s.

Graham Coates travelled an awful long way from Lincoln to be at the Wheel. Graham was, and still is, a leading authority on British released soul 45s. Thanks for your help Graham.

Trev & Tina Dunn from Bolton, who look far too young to have gone to Brazennose Street – but they did!

Robbie Dunn from Liverpool, would go to the Room At The Top in Wigan beforehand and recalls Tony Hawthorne playing some good records there too. Robbie nominates 'Booper' as being the best dancer he saw at the Wheel, and one night in particular when he turned up wearing a clown's suit, complete with ruff. He would go over to Manchester with a couple of girls from Southport, Yvonne and Michelle

Stan Evans from Liverpool, Wheel regular and still heavily into the scene, had info on the elusive book *Just Ask The Lonely* by Vivien Terry; the story of Mods and soul fans in a northern city and All-Nighters at the Wheel. Stan would meet Mick Jones, Tony Dean, Ray Faulkner, Alan Graham, Tommy Audley, Dennis Jones, Rose McGuire and Sylvia Hart outside of C&A on Church Street, before travelling to Manchester. Sometimes they would attend the Floral Hall in Southport first. When they got there they would make their way to Piccadilly Station to meet Pete Smith, Tony Smith, Tony Creech and the Kirby gang. Stan told us that the kids who used to take gear from Liverpool allegedly had contacts who worked for Evan's Medical in Speke, Halewood. The best place for records back then was Edward's secondhand shop in Kensington, Liverpool 6. Stan recalls some quite hairy moments: Joe Dooley winning the spot draw prize of £85 and being too scared to leave the club, and drug dealers fighting things out either in the Black Cat or in Minshull Street car park. Other faces he recalls from those days were Arnie Clark, Pete Ogden, Rob Meadows and of course Frank 'Booper' New.

Dave Evison, from Stoke, would meet up with Andy Myatt, Phil Morgan, Tombo, Chat and Sparky outside of the Bluenote. They would then seek out Nev Piers from Darlington, Charlie and Roy from Ashbourne and John and Mick Harris from Sandbach before going to the All-nighter. Dave bought some great records from Cath Jones' Shack in Sandbach and Sherwin's in Hanley.

Graham Ellwood, originally from Nottingham, would meet in the Bell Inn with folk like Eric Lambert and Dave Bowren before getting the bus to Manchester.

SOUTH BANK CLUB, DIAL SQUARE
GRIMSBY

ALL NIGHT DANCE

Saturday 23rd May, 11 p.m.

to

Sunday 24th May, 7 Am.

with the best in Rhythm & Blues, Soul and Rock

Starring Special Guest D.J. from Manchester's Famous

Twisted Wheel Club

Brian "45" Phillips

supported by Scunthorpe's Top R & B Man Himself

Fred Benson

plus Go Go Dancers and Light Show

Admission 7/6   Girls admitted free before 11.30 p.m.

FREE MEMBERSHIP THIS WEEK ONLY

Kenny Floyd was from Grimsby, and would gather with Tony Brown, Keith Thompson, Mick Tartelin, Terry Tyler, and the infamous Fred Benson in the Lifeboat Hotel, prior to their long drive to Manchester.

Frank Gierak, from Derby, on his first visit to the Wheel, saw Jimmy Ruffin performing 'It's Wonderful To Be Loved By You' for the first time in Britain. Recalls Frank 'Booper' and Walter Willis as being great dancers. Borrowed the large 'What's On' poster, on his way out one Sunday morning.

Jay Keyver, originally from Selby, Yorkshire and now Uxbridge, Canada, via Paderborn, Germany! Jay was one of the original Mods that travelled to Manchester and the old Wheel. Jay had a well paid job and could dress well, buy records and get around on an LI150. From Hull to Liverpool, catching big attractions such as the Stax Show at the Queen's Hall, Leeds. Jay now runs his own Tae Kwon-Do school in Ontario.

Colin Metcalfe, originally from Stalybridge, used to see his girlfriend onto her last bus at Chorlton Street Bus Station, telling her he too was then going home. But of course, he was heading down to Whitworth Street. On one occasion a car pulled up next to him and the driver asked if he knew where the Twisted Wheel was. Colin told them he was on his way there and so was invited to jump into the back. His fellow passenger was one Arthur Conley.

John Milne from the Wirral, lived in Wallasey, and would meet up with friend Phil Malloy in Liscard and go to Manchester via either Liverpool or Chester. His first visit was at the end of 1965, and he continued going up to 1970. He would also travel down to the Chateau Impney and would meet the crowd from Worcester in Manchester. He would sometimes go to the Sink in Liverpool first, but more likely the Blue Note.

Fran O'Brien, another long-standing soul fan from Skipton, Yorkshire, served the same soul apprenticeship as friend Johnny Bollen in the clubs of West Yorks. Fran persuaded Dave Godin to travel north to visit the Wheel. After a time away from the scene, Fran is now a regular at the better quality soul events. As well-dressed as always with sister Pauline. Fran, like so many others generously gave us precious photographs but more importantly, time.

Nick Parkin, one of Keith Rylatt's teenage friends from Wakefield. 'Our first visit to the Wheel was with John Hannan. I have vague recollections of us strutting around Leeds in mohair suits, sun-glasses and large cigars prior to getting on the last train to Manchester. We were the second generation of Wheel goers from Wakefield. There was a crowd who were a few years older than us, led by Dave Carney who had started going in '65. Dave was a very smart dresser and I always remember an old leather motorbike jacket he used to go to work in with a large wheel on the back and the words 'THE TWISTED WHEEL'. Others who went were

Phil Wilsher, Alex Hurdus, Kev Stakes, Ron Holiday, Paul Harrison, Dave Colley, Ronnie O'Toole, Paul Bagnall and Brian Leek. The crowd who were our age, would meet at Victoria Station, they were Dick & Julie Pointon, Rob Lemoine, Steve Welcer, John Nicholson and Stan Spencer. Stan had been to Manchester a few times, either as a guest of Ivor Abadi or Her Majesty, and certainly burnt the candle at both ends and has since sadly passed away. Stan was one of the characters that went over from Yorkshire, and on one occasion we found ourselves stranded on the last diesel train from Leeds to Manchester, somewhere on the top of the Pennines. The driver could not get the train started and had resorted to lifting the floor panel up in our carriage to get to the root of the trouble. Time however was passing by, and as the midnight hour approached, Stan, who had already been taunting the conductor about his wig, approached the driver, and came out with the immortal line: 'If tha' can get it goin' afore midneet, I'll give thee these green n' clears!'

Bob Scott, younger brother of Phil Scott, started attending the club under the wing of his brother. His first recollections are of hearing Barbara Acklin's 'Am I The Same Girl' while signing his first membership application form, and Barbara Randolph's 'I Get A Feeling' as he descended the stairs to the dance floors. Bob has been a constant source of information, inspiration and encouragement, thanks.

Dave Slater from Hyde, who spent many nights at the Wheel and has an astonishingly accurate memory, is still an active record collector, promoter and venue attender. His knowledge of records is impressive. Dave is involved in the Twisted Wheel revival nights around Hyde and Dukinfield.

Phil Stables from Doncaster, was the catalyst for this project. He had intended writing an article about his adventures at the Wheel for Keith Rylatt's fanzine *Come And Get These Memories*. This then grew into a special issue, which graduated to this! Phil was a Mod and soul fan in his hometown of Doncaster, and soon graduated to such places as Sheffield and the 'King' Mojo. When the Mojo closed down he and plenty of other devotees then began to travel to Manchester and the Twisted Wheel. Phil became one of the main faces at the club and would certainly pay his dues, often attending the Blue Orchid All-nighter on Friday prior to the Wheel. As well as having a good collection of records, Phil also had a reputation as a sharp dresser. When the Wheel closed Phil moved with the scene and attended all of the main All-Nighters well into the '70s.

Mick 'Popeye' Taylor was from Doncaster and would either catch the train or hitch over Snake Pass to get to the All-Nighters. Along with Dek Wynn, he was a Wheel regular for several years after the various venues on his side of the Pennines had gradually closed down – the King Mojo, the Nite Owl, the Dungeon and Beachcomber, the String O' Beads and the Tin Chicken. Once before the Wheel, they made an ill-fated visit to the Majestic club and were subsequently relieved of their spare cash. Mick now deejays in Canada and is still into the music. He boasts the car license plate SKF 10 (Smith, Kline & French!).

Barry Tasker must go down in history as one of the main soul music stalwarts in Manchester. Barry's first Wheel visit to Brazennose Street was in '64 and he was hooked, later becoming a Whitworth Street regular. Travelling into the city centre from Longsite he would meet up with mates from both home and Stockport. They would mainly congregate at the Mogambo or Blackbird coffee bars and later on at the Cona in Tib Lane, the Town Hall Tavern, the Rising Sun and eventually, towards the end the White Hart, the Globe Bar on Piccadilly Station or the Bull's Head, Fairfield Street. Barry was one of the main faces at the Wheel and had deejayed before in Manchester. It wasn't therefore surprising that he became the DJ at the next big club in the city, the Pendulum. Barry has been a good friend to us both, particularly Phil, and has kept this project going on the many occasions when we have felt like throwing in the towel.

Derek Watmough from Bolton also started his days at the old Wheel, and recalls seeing such acts as Chris Farlow down there. Before going to Manchester he would often go to La Camber club in Bolton, which had modelled its layout and decor along the lines of the Wheel. Derek is still very much into the scene and a regular at the better soul events.

At its closure, the Wheel membership ran into tens of thousands, and it is clearly impossible to acknowledge everybody. However Phil Scott would like to mention the following: Jack Harrison of Droylsden, who never missed an All-nighter at Whitworth Street and to this day is one of the club's greatest devotees. His brothers Stuart and Bob, Stevie Moores, Col Metcalfe, Slim Jim, John Edwards, Roy Hooton and the Droylsden crowd of '67. Also Phil Ashton, Neil Silcocks, Mick Wykes, Judith Dooley and all the great kids from Ashton-under-Lyne, and last but not least two top boys from Beswick, Stevie Allan and Dave Lilley. God bless you all.

Going underground

■ ARCHAEOLOGISTS have been getting very excited in recent weeks about the uncovering of a crucial piece of Manchester history from Roman times in Castlefield. But ageing hippies have also been chortling to themselves over the temporary re-emergence of another landmark in the city's rich heritage.

Part of Lincoln Square, that grandly-named but unprepossessing open space in the city centre's Brazennose Street, collapsed into a former basement beneath its concrete paving which had to be re-filled.

The subterranean space beneath Abe's larger-than-life statue, inscribed with the politically correct version of his letter to the Men of Manchester and the miserable fountain dedicated to Charles and Diana, was once the legendary Twisted Wheel Club.

Here, in the mid-sixties, to the blues hollers of Howlin' Wolf, Sonny Boy Williamson and Muddy Waters, Manchester's taste for distinctive rock music, amphetamines and marijuana, was born. Buried in Brazennose Street are memories of a generation which was as "mad for it" as the current one. Heady days. There should be a blue (or a purple heart-shaped) plaque.

Manchester Evening News, 3rd March 1997

We Thank You

IAN BLACKBURN, for allowing Keith to use his Prestwich home like a hotel on countless visits to Manchester. TREVOR BRIDGE, for lengthy and invaluable stories.

TIM BROWN at Anglo-American and Beatin' Rhythm for publicity. PATRICK CAMPBELL, for assistance with editing. ANDREW CLARK from Blackpool, for record information and contacts.

DAVE CLEGG for supplying the Twisted Wheel architect's plans.

ADY CROASDELL, Kent Records, for contacts at the 100 Club, London.

CATHERINE from Fleetwood, for stories of the Cove and the Lancaster crowd.

PETE COGLEY, for contacts and information on the Widnes scene. BOB DICKINSON, publicity.

BILL DRUMMOND at *The Guardian*. Plugs. IAN DUNNING for great stories and tattoo!

BOB FOSTER, Llandudno – a thirty year friendship and the '60s expert bar none.

ED FOTHERGILL, information. PETER GIBBON at Ace/Kent Records for great tales of curry with Inez & Charlie Foxx. PAUL GOATHAM for frequent technical help and advice. Paul has rescued many a lost file, often being dragged out of bed or the pub when things went wrong on the PC. LES HARE, King Bee Records, Chorlton, for numerous contacts and help.

TOM HODGKINSON, *The Idler*. Plugs. IAN JONES, Norwich. Advice and archive material.

DEITER KAPALLA, Germany. For helping rescue the Brazennose Street footage from obscurity.

DENIS KILCOMMONS, *Huddersfield Examiner*. Contacts. RAY KING, *Manchester Evening News* for use of their archive material. DAVE LANGLEY, Runcorn. Great stories.

JOHN LESTER, Motown and Golden World information. IAN LEVINE. Contacts, photographs and publicity. MANCHESTER PUBLIC LIBRARY for archive material. MARY NOLAN at Chris Rea's office for arranging the interview with Chris. SEAN O'BRIEN, Newquay. Archive material. MARTIN PEEL, Colwyn Bay. Brazennose Street information. STEVE PILKINGTON for Motown information. JOHN REED, at Castle Music, for help with British R&B and beat group information. STEVE RICHARDS, for the Ben E. King photographs.

MIKE RITSON and STUART RUSSELL for production help and advice. KEV ROBERTS, publicity.

PETE ROBERTS, Failsworth, for publicity. MICK SVEIKUTIS, Biddulph. Archive material on the Torch. TOM SMITH at Manchester's Beatin' Rythmn for encouragement and publicity.

BOB STEPHENSON, Grimsargh. Great stories. AL TAYLOR, Doncaster. Archive material.

GINGER TAYLOR, Stories and contacts ANGELA WELSH, Manuscript typing.

PETE WINGFIELD, London for *Soul Beat* information. PAUL WELSBY, the Hideaway, Manchester and *New Breed* magazine, publicity.

Background photograph shows Whitwork Street Wheel in 1997. (Keith Rylatt)

Twisted Wheel Whitworth Street Records – Just A Few Of The Many

It would be impossible to list every record that was played at the club – you could probably fill a book with just the Motown and Atlantic 45s played.

AD-LIBS 'The Boy From New York City' (US-Blue Cat/UK-Red Bird)
ROLANDO ALPHONSO (WITH THE SOUL BROTHERS) 'Phoenix City' (UK-Doctor Bird)
AMERICAN POETS 'She Blew A Good Thing'(US-Symbol/UK-London)
ANGELS 'My Boyfriend's Back' (US-Smash/UK-Mercury)
ARTISTICS 'I'm Gonna Miss You' (US-Brunswick/UK-Coral)
ASTORS 'Candy' (US-Stax/UK-Atlantic)
DARRELL BANKS 'Open the Door To Your Heart' (US-Revilot/UK-London & Stateside)
HOMER BANKS 'A Lot Of Love' (US-Minit/UK-Liberty)
HOMER BANKS '60 Minutes Of Your Love' (US-Minit/UK-Liberty)
BAR-KAYS 'Soul Finger' (US-Volt/UK-Stax)
FONTELLA BASS & BOBBY McCLURE 'Don't Mess Up A Good Thing'
    (US-Checker/UK-Chess)
BOBBY BLAND 'Call On Me' (US-Duke)
BOB & EARL 'Harlem Shuffle' (US-Marc/UK-Island)
JAMES BOOKER 'Gonzo' (US-Peacock/UK-Vogue)
BOB BRADY & THE CONCHORDS 'Everybody's Going To The Love-In'
    (US-Chariot/UK-Bell)
AL 'TNT' BRAGGS 'Earthquake' (US-Peacock/UK-Vocalion)
JAMES BROWN & THE FAMOUS FLAMES 'Papa's Got A Brand New Bag Pt 1'
    (US-King/UK-London)
BILLY BUTLER 'The Right Track' (US-OKeh/UK-Soul City)
JAMES CARR 'That's What I Wanna Know' (US-Goldwax/UK-Stateside)
ALVIN CASH & THE CRAWLERS 'Twine Time' (US-Mar-V-Lus/UK-Stateside)
GENE CHANDLER & BARBARA ACKLIN 'From The Teacher To The Preacher'
    (US-Brunswick)
GENE CHANDLER 'Nothing Can Stop Me' (UK-Constellation/UK-Stateside)
CHUBBY CHECKER '(At The) Discotheque' (US-Parkway/UK-Cameo-Parkway)
TONY CLARKE 'Ain't Love Good, Ain't Love Proud' (US Chess & UK-Pye International)
TONY CLARKE 'The Entertainer' (US & UK-Chess)
ARTHUR CONLEY 'Sweet Soul Music' (US-Atco/UK-Atlantic)
CONTOURS 'Determination'/'Just A Little Misunderstanding'
    (US-Gordy/UK-Tamla-Motown)
CONTOURS 'First I Look At The Purse' (US-Gordy)
SAM COOKE 'It's Got The Whole World Shaking' (US & US-RCA)
DON COVAY 'See Saw' (US & UK-Atlantic)
DON COVAY 'Sookie Sookie' (US & UK-Atlantic)
DELLS 'Wear It On Our Face' (US-Cadet/UK-Chess)
MOSES & JOSHUA DILLARD 'My Elusive Dreams' (US-Mala/UK-Stateside)
216 MOSES & JOSHUA DILLARD 'Get Out of My Heart' (US-Mala/UK-Bell)

FATS DOMINO 'It Keeps Rainin' '
   (US-Imperial/UK-London)
DYNATONES The Fife Piper
   (US-St Clair & HIB/UK-Pye International)
ESQUIRES 'Get On Up' (US-Bunky/UK-Stateside)
ESQUIRES 'And Get Away' (US-Bunky/UK-Stateside)
FANATICS 'Dancing To The Shotgun' (US-Backbeat)
FANTASTIC JOHNNY C 'Boogaloo Down Broadway'
   (US-Phil-LA of Soul/UK-London)
FASCINATIONS 'Girls Are Out To Get You'
   (US-Mayfield/UK-Stateside)
FLAMINGOS 'Boogaloo Party' (US & UK-Philips)
DARROW FLETCHER 'The Pain Gets a Little Deeper'
   (US-Groovy/UK-London)
FOLKS BROTHERS 'Carolina' (UK-Blue Beat)
INEZ & CHARLIE FOXX 'Tightrope' (US-Dynamo/UK-Stateside)
ART FREEMAN 'Slippin' Around' (US-Fame/UK-Atlantic)
BOBBY FREEMAN 'The Duck' (US-Autumn/UK-Pye International)
BOBBY FREEMAN 'C'mon And Swim' (US-Autumn/UK-Pye International)
REX GARVIN & THE MIGHTY CRAVERS 'Sock It To 'Em JB' (US-Like/UK-Atlantic)
BUD HARPER 'Mr. Soul' (US-Peacock/UK-Vocalion)
SLIM HARPO 'Baby Scratch My Back' (US-Excello/UK-Stateside)
LEON HAYWOOD 'Baby Reconsider' (US-Fatfish)
JIMMY HOLIDAY & CLYDIE KING 'Ready Willing And Able' (US-Minit/UK-Liberty)
HUMAN BEINZ 'Nobody But Me' (US & UK-Capitol)
IMPRESSIONS 'I Love You (Yeah)' (US-ABC-Paramount/UK-HMV)
IMPRESSIONS 'You've Been Cheatin' (US-ABC-Paramount/UK-HMV)
IMPRESSIONS 'Can't Satisfy' (US-ABC/UK-HMV)
INVITATIONS 'What's Wrong With Me Baby?' (US-DynoVoice/UK-Stateside)
CHRIS (MARKE) JACKSON 'I'll Never Forget You' (US-Jamie/UK-Soul City
CHUCK JACKSON 'Chains Of Love' (US-Wand/UK-Pye International)
CHUCK JACKSON 'Good Things Come To Those Who Wait' (US-Wand)
DEON JACKSON 'Love Makes The World Go Round' (US-Carla/UK-Atlantic)
DEON JACKSON 'Ooh Baby' (US-Carla/UK-Atlantic)
LOU JOHNSON 'Reach Out For Me' (US-Big Top/UK-London)
MARV JOHNSON 'You've Got The Love I Love' (US-Gordy/UK-Tamla-Motown)
KING CURTIS 'Memphis Soul Stew' (US-Atco/UK-Atlantic)
MAJOR LANCE 'Hey Little Girl' (US-OKeh/UK-Columbia)
MAJOR LANCE 'The Matador' (US-OKeh/UK-Columbia)
MICKEY LEE LANE Hey Sah-Lo-Ney (US-Swan/UK-Stateside)
LARKS 'The Jerk' (US-Money/UK-Pye International)
JACKIE LEE 'Darkest Days' (US-ABC)
RAMSEY LEWIS 'Wade In The Water' (US-Cadet/UK-Chess)

LITTLE ANTHONY & THE IMPERIALS 'Gonna Fix You Good'
   (US-Veep/UK-United Artists)
LITTLE ANTHONY & THE IMPERIALS 'Going Out Of My Head'
   (US-Veep/UK-United Artists)
LITTLE HANK 'Mr. Bang Bang Man' (US-Sound Stage 7/UK-London & Monument)
LITTLE MILTON 'Grits Ain't Groceries (All Around The World)' (US-Checker/UK-Chess)
LOS CANARIOS 'Get On Your Knees' (UK-Major Minor)
MARVELETTES 'Don't Mess With Bill' (US-Tamla/UK-Tamla-Motown)
MIGHTY SAM 'Papa True Love' (US-Amy/UK-Soul City)
RONNIE MILSAP 'Ain't No Soul' (US-Scepter/UK-Pye International)
WILLIE MITCHELL 'Everything's Gonna Be Alright' (US-Hi/UK-London)
WILLIE MITCHELL 'That Drivin' Beat' (US-Hi/UK-London)
TOMMY NEAL 'Going To A Happening' (US-PaMeLine & Palmer/UK-Vocalion)
O'JAYS 'I Dig Your Act' (US-/UK-Stateside)
O'JAYS 'Working On Your Case' (US-
OLYMPICS 'Secret Agents' (US-Mirwood/UK-Fontana)
OLYMPICS 'Baby, Do The Philly Dog' (US-Mirwood/UK-Fontana)
PACKERS 'Hole In The Wall'
   (US-Pure Soul/UK-Pye International)
ALEXANDER PATTON 'A L'il Lovin' Sometime'
   (UK & US-Capitol)
BILLY PRESTON 'Billy's Bag' (US & UK-Sue)
JAMES & BOBBY PURIFY 'Shake A Tail Feather'
   (US-Bell/UK-Stateside)
JIMMY RADCLIFFE 'Long After Tonight Is All Over'
   (US-Musicor/UK-Stateside)
RADIANTS 'Hold On' (UK & US-Chess)
BARBARA RANDOLPH 'I Got A Feeling'
   (US-Soul/UK-Tamla-Motown)
ROSCO ROBINSON 'That's Enough' (US-Wand/UK-Pye International)
ROUND ROBIN 'Kick That Little Foot Sally' (US-Domain/UK-London)
MITCH RYDER & THE DETROIT WHEELS 'You Get Your Kicks' (US-New Voice)
SHADES OF BLUE 'Oh! How Happy' (US-Impact/UK-Sue)
DEE DEE SHARP 'What Kind of Lady' (US-Gamble/UK-Action)
SHARPEES 'Tired Of Being Lonely' (US- /UK-Stateside)
SHARPEES 'Do The 45' (US-One-Derful!)
MARLENA SHAW 'Let's Wade In The Water' (US-Cadet)
BOBBY SHEEN 'Dr. Love' (US & UK-Capitol)
SANDI SHELDON You're Gonna Make Me Love You' (US-Okeh)
SKATALITES 'Guns Of Navarone'(
MARVIN SMITH 'Have More Time' (US-Brunswick/UK-Coral)
SOUL BROTHERS SIX 'She's Some Kind Of Wonderful'

(US-Lyndell & Atlantic/UK-Atlantic)

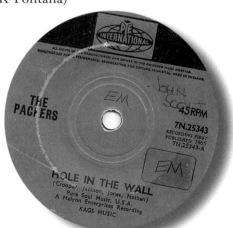

SPELLBINDERS 'Help Me (Get Myself Together Again)' (US-Columbia/UK-CBS)

SPELLBINDERS 'Chain Reaction' (US-Columbia/UK-CBS)

SPINNERS 'I'll Always Love You' (US-Motown/UK-Tamla-Motown)

SPINNERS 'Sweet Thing' (US-Motown/UK-Tamla-Motown)

TAMS 'Hey Girl Don't Bother Me'
    (US-ABC-Paramount/UK-HMV)

JOHNNIE TAYLOR 'Changes' (US-Stax)

WILLIE TEE 'Walking Up A One Way Street'
    (US-Nola & Atlantic/UK-Atlantic)

JOE TEX 'Show Me' (US-Dial/UK-Atlantic)

JAMO THOMAS & HIS PARTY SOUL BROTHERS
    'I Spy For The FBI' (US-Thomas/UK-Polydor)

GEORGE TORRENCE & THE NATURALS
    '(Mama Come Quick, And Bring Your) Lickin' Stick'
    (US-Shout/UK-London)

FRANKIE VALLI 'You're Ready Now' (US-Smash/UK-Philips)

EARL VAN DYKE & THE SOUL BROTHERS
    'All For You' US-Soul/UK-Tamla-Motown)

EARL VAN DYKE & THE SOUL BROTHERS '6 x 6' (US-Soul/UK-Tamla-Motown)

JUNIOR WALKER & THE ALL STARS 'Cleo's Mood'
    (US-Harvey & Soul/UK-Tamla-Motown)

JUNIOR WALKER & THE ALL STARS 'Shotgun' (US-Soul/UK-Tamla-Motown)

JUNIOR WALKER & THE ALL STARS '(I'm A) Road Runner'
    (US-Soul/UK-Tamla-Motown)

JUNIOR WALKER & THE ALL STARS 'How Sweet It Is (To Be Loved By You)'
    (US-Soul/UK-Tamla-Motown)

DEE DEE WARWICK 'We're Doing Fine' (US-Blue Rock/UK-Mercury))

LARRY WILLIAMS & JOHNNY 'GUITAR' WATSON 'A Quitter Never Wins'
    (US-OKeh/UK-Columbia)

JACKIE WILSON 'Whispers (Gettin' Louder)' (US-Brunswick/UK-Coral)

JACKIE WILSON 'Since You Showed Me How to Be Happy' (US-Brunswick/UK-Coral)

'On The Right Track Baby'

Scores of lesser known British beat and R&B groups played at the *Twisted Wheel* in the first half of its eight-year existence.

If you would like to explore these artists further, the following list gives 1960s recording information on all UK-based acts that performed at the club.

NAME OF ACT	TOWN OF ORIGIN	No OF 45s	No OF RELEASES & RECORD COMPANIES					
Action	London	5	Parlophone					
Addicts	Widnes	1	Decca					
Alan Bown Set	London	10	5 Pye	2 MGM	1 Music-Fact	2 Deram		
Alan Price Set	Newcastle	10	9 Decca	1 Deram				
Alex Harvey & Soul Band	Glasgow	8	3 Polydor	3 Fontana				
(First three with Soul Band, rest, various line-ups)			2 Decca					
Alexis Korner's Blues Inc.	London	6	1 Tempo	2 Parlophone	1 King	2 Fontana		
Amboy Dukes	Notts	7	6 Polydor	1 Fontana				
Animals	Newcastle	9	7 Columbia	2 Decca				
Applejacks	Birmingham	8	7 Decca	1 CBS				
Artwoods	London	6	5 Decca	1 Parlophone				
Avalons	Liverpool	1	Island					
Beat Boys	Sheffield	1	Decca					
Big 3	Liverpool	4	Decca					
Blues Council	–	1	Parlophone					
Bluesology	Middlesex	2	Fontana					
Boz (People)	London	6	Columbia					
Brian Auger Trinity	London	6	3 Columbia	3 Marmalade				
Bry Martin & Marauders	Birmingham	4	3 Decca	1 Fontana				
Buddy Britten & Regents	Liverpool	2	1 Columbia	1 Oriole				
Cheynes	London	3	Columbia					
Chris Farlow & Thunderbirds	London	19	6 Columbia	1 Decca	12 Immediate			
Clayton Squares	Liverpool	2	Decca					
Cops'n'Robbers	Watford	3	1 Decca	2 Pye				
Country Gentlemen	Manchester	1	Decca					
Cyclones	Bristol / L'pool	1	Oriole					
Cymerons	Manchester	2	1 Decca	1 Polydor				
Cyril Davis All Stars with Long John Baldry	London	3	Pye Int.					
David John & the Mood	Preston	3	1 Vocalion	2 Parlophone				
Downliners Sect	London	9	Columbia					

Artist	City	Count			
Duffy Powell & Sorrows	Coventry	7	Piccadilly		
Escorts	Liverpool	6	5 Fontana	1 Columbia	
Excheckers	Liverpool	1	Decca		
Ferris Wheel	Bradford	4	3 Pye	1 Polydor	
Fairies	Colchester	3	1 Decca	2 HMV	
Falling Leaves	Oxford	2	1 Parlophone	1 Decca	
Five Embers	Edinburgh	2	Decca		
Four Just Men	Liverpool	1	Parlophone		
Four Most	Liverpool	11	8 Parlophone	3 CBS	
Four Pennies	Blackburn	9	Philips		
Frank Kelly & Hunters	Glasgow	4	Fontana		
Freddie Starr	Liverpool	1	Decca		
Freddie Starr & Midnighters	Liverpool	2	Decca		
Geno Washington & Ram Jam Band	London	10	6 Piccadilly	4 Pye	
Georgie Fame & Blue Flames	London	16	10 Columbia	6 CBS	
(First 7 with Blue Flames, remainder solo)					
Gogos	Newcastle	1	Oriole		
Graham Bond Organisation	London	6	1 Decca	4 Columbia	1 Page One
Groundhogs (John Lee's...)	London	2	Liberty		
Haydock's Rockhouse	Manchester	2	Columbia		
Herbie Goins & Nitetimers	London	2	Parlophone		
Helene & Kinsmen	Northampton	2	Decca		
Hellions	Birmingham	3	Piccadilly		
Herd	London	9	3 Parlophone	6 Fontana	
Herman's Hermits	Manchester	18	Columbia		
Hipster Image	Sheffield	1	Decca		
Hollies	Manchester	20	Parlophone		
Ian Crawford & Boomerangs	Manchester	2	Fontana		
Incas	Birmingham	1	Parlophone		
Ivan('s) Mead	Manchester	2	Parlophone		
Jackie Lynton	Liverpool	12	8 Piccadilly	1 Decca	3 Columbia

Jackie Lynton & Teenbeats also Jackie Lynton & Cutters

All records cut solo

Artist	Location	Count	Labels
Jeanie & Statesides	Chester	3	Columbia
Jeannie	Chester	1	Parlophone
Jeannie & the Big Guys	Chester	1	Decca
Jimmy Cliff & Sounds System also with Explosive Sound	London	7	1 Stateside, 1 Fontana, 4 Island, 1 Trojan
Jimmy James & Vagabonds	London	7	1 Columbia, 5 Piccadilly, 1 Pye
Jimmy Powell	Birmingham	3	Decca
Jimmy Powell & 5 Dimensions	Birmingham	2	Pye
Jimmy Powell & Dimensions	Birmingham	6	1 Strike, 3 Decca, 2 Youngblood
Joe Cocker Big Blues / Grease Band	Sheffield	4	1 Decca, 3 Regal Zonophone
John Mayall's Blues Breakers	London	12	11 Decca, 1 Polydor
Johnny Peters & JPs	Manchester	1	Decca
Kinks	London	22	Pye
Lance Harvey & King Pins	Manchester	1	Pye
Lance Harvey & Statesmen	Manchester	2	1 Decca, 1 Fontana
Life 'n' Soul	Manchester	2	Decca
Listen	Birmingham	1	CBS
Long John Baldry	London	13	6 United Artists, 7 Pye
Lorraine Gray & Chapperrones	Rochdale	2	Fontana
Lucas & Mike Cotton Sound	US / UK	3	1 Pye, 2 MGM
Malc Clarke & Cresters	Leeds	2	HMV
Manfred Mann	London	21	11 HMV, 10 Fontana
Mark Leeman 5	London	4	Columbia
Me & Them	-	3	Pye
Mighty Avengers	Rugby	4	Decca
Mike Cotton Sound	London	9	8 Columbia, 1 Polydor
Millie	London	10	Fontana
Mojos	Liverpool	7	6 Decca, 1 Liberty
Outer Limits	Leeds	2	1 Deram, 1 Instant
Paramounts	Southend	6	Parlophone
Paul Ryan & Crescents	Neath	2	Columbia

Name	Location	No.			
Powerhouse 6	Manchester	2	Decca			
Pretty Things	London	13	10 Fontana	3 Columbia		
R&B Incorporated	Southport	1	Fontana			
Ram Jam Band	London	1	Columbia			
Rats (two groups with same name)	Hull	2	1 Oriole	1 CBS		
Rats	Lancs	3	2 Columbia	1 Oak		
Red Caps	Walsall	3	Decca			
Renegades	Birmingham	4	Parlophone	President	Columbia	Polydor
Rey Anton	Bournemouth	2	Oriole			
Rey Anton & Batons	Bournemouth	1	Oriole			
Rey Anton & Peppermint Men	Bournemouth	5	Parlophone			
Rey Anton & Pro Form {ula}	Bournemouth	3	Parlophone			
Richard Kent Style	Manchester	5	3 Columbia	1 MCA	1 Mercury	
Rockin' Berries	Birmingham	16	2 Decca	10 Piccadilly	4 Pye	
Rod Stewart & Soul Agents	London	4	1 Decca	2 Columbia	1 Immediate	
Root & Jenny Jackson	Leeds	2	Beacon			
Score	London	1	Decca			
Senate	Scotland	1	Columbia			
Sheffields	Sheffields	3	Pye			
Shotgun Express	London	2	Columbia			
Small Faces	London	14	8 Decca	6 Immediate		
Soul Agents	London	3	Pye			
Spencer Davis	Birmingham	13	10 Fontana	3 United Arts		
Stevie Darbishire	S. Africa/London	5	Decca			
T-Bones	London	2	Columbia			
Toggery 5	Manchester	2	Parlophone			
Tony Dee & Shake Outs	-	1	Piccadilly			
Tony Merrick Scene	Salford	2	Columbia			
Tony Sheridan & Bobby Patrick Big 6	Cheltenham/Liverpool	2	Decca			
Trend Setters	Leighton Buzzard	1	Silver Phoenix			
Tuesday's Children	Essex	6	2 Columbia	2 Pye	1 King	1 Mercury

Unit 4 + 2	Herts.	14	9 Decca	5 Fontana	
Victor Brox (With Annette Reis)	Manchester	1	Fontana		
VIPs	Carlisle	4	1 RCA	1 CBS	2 Island
Voids	Somerset	1	Polydor		
Wayne Fontana	Manchester	13	Fontana		
Web(b) (backing Alvin Cash)	London	3	Deram		
Whirlwinds	Manchester	1	H.M.V.		
Who	London	16	6 Brunswick	4 Reaction	6 Track
Wynder K Frog	London / Lancs	5	Island		
Yardbirds	London	10	Columbia		
Young Ones	Liverpool	1	Decca		
Zombies	St Albans	14	11 Decca	3 CBS	
Zoot Money's Big Roll Band	London	9	8 Columbia	1 Decca	

Regarding the names of groups

Many changed their names slightly as they evolved or as personnel changed e.g. Jimmy Powell & the Dimensions appears with three entries because he, and they, recorded under different guises, but, essentially it was the same band that appeared regularly at the club. Things can also get complicated as this band would later have connections with the Score who, in turn, are connected to the Paramounts, later Procol Harum.

Places of origin

Again not always straight forward e.g. Georgie Fame & The Blue Flames. Georgie, born in Leigh, Lancashire, began life backing Billy Fury in Liverpool, but then moved to London and joined the capital-based Blue Flames, so we have described them as being from London.

Notes

CHAPTER ONE

1. In 1949, Jesse Blayton was the first black to own a radio station, WERD in Atlanta. By 1960 that number had only reached four, and by 1970 just fourteen.

2. Not least amongst the legion of black performers that Presley admired was ex-Beale Streeter Johnny Ace. Ace was a black God at the time and would have five R&B number ones before Presley cut his first record. As fate would have it, Ace's last and biggest hit 'Pledging My Love' (released only days after his tragic death playing Russian roulette) would also be the flip side of Presley's final record for RCA years later, 'Way Down', recorded just before Presley died.

3. Alan Freed spent his life in controversy. He was villified by R&B purists as an exploiter of black music (although there were plenty of others doing that – black and white), he was hounded by white extremists and protest groups, and chased by the IRS for non-payment of taxes. To his credit, he caused uproar by insisting that a US television station film black and white teenagers dancing together and banned white cover versions of black music whilst working for New York radio station WINS. But don't think that Freed was sympathetic to the cause of promoting black music or the black entertainer. Like others, Freed managed to manipulate record companies into paying for discs to be played and insisted on being named as joint songwriter to share in any royalty payments. Once the writer of the song had agreed to this, Freed would then promote the song. An example of this was the Moonglows' massive hit 'Sincerely'. By being allowed to change just one word, he landed joint credit for writing what was to become a million seller, ripping off the song's true composer Harvey Fuqua. The 1958 US Government inquiry into the payola scandal singled out Freed. Four years later, after a lengthy appeal, Freed died a bankrupt and broken man.

CHAPTER TWO

1. There was no overnight introduction of the 45. UK Record Companies introduced them as and when production allowed. UK Decca (London), for instance, actually manufactured 45s as early as 1950 for export only. Decca introduced the 45 onto the home market in 1954 – records being available on both 45 and 78 format until September 1960. EMI, on the other hand, began releasing 45s in the UK as early as 1952.

2. As well as London, Decca owned Vogue, Vocalion, Coral and Brunswick. Vocalion grew from Vogue, a label that for many years had dabbled in jazz, gospel and on occasion blues (they issued a Muddy Waters EP as folk blues). In the '60s, Vocalion went onto issue many memorable R&B sides such as 'She's Looking Good' by Rodger Collins (US Galaxy) and 'Mr. Soul' by Bobby Bland sound-alike Bud Harper (US Peacock). In the main though, Vocalion will be remembered for having the guts to issue many superb sides from Don Robey's Duke, Peacock and Back Beat stable. Included were superb 45s by artists such as Bobby Bland, O.V. Wright and Johnny Ace. Vogue/Vocalion also released four brilliant Bobby Bland albums: 'Here's The Man', 'Two Steps From The Blues', 'Ain't Nothing You Can Do' and 'Call On Me' and should be commended for doing so. Needless to say the sales of Vocalion releases were not particularly sensational.

CHAPTER THREE

1. Together with Davies and Korner, Blues Incorporated's early line up consisted of Art Wood on vocals (later replaced by Long John Baldry) and Jazz players such as Charlie Watts, later replaced by Ginger Baker, Dick Heckstall-Smith (tenor sax) and Jack Bruce (bass).

2. Groups in and around London and the home counties following in the wake of Korner and Davies (Stones, Yardbirds, Paramounts etc), were developing their own raw hybrid of Rhythm & Blues. Mostly influenced by the black music of Chicago they probably cut their teeth imitating black American records that were being issued in the UK on the London label.

3. Since the late 1950s in Manchester's Moss Side, West Indian immigrants had held illegal all-night drinking parties at 'shebeens', and many city-centre pubs and clubs broke licensing laws by serving well after 'Last Orders'. The Shanty Clare Club on Shudehill, by day a licensed drinking club and at night the haunt of working girls, held a number of 'Jazz' All-Nighters for a short time in 1961. The Shanty Clare's claim to fame was the performance to a reportedly packed house by Dizzy Gillespie, after he had appeared in the city. The Amber Moon on Balloon Street also held the occasional beat/pop all-night session, for example on Saturday October 12th 1962 when Brent Wade and the Wanderers were the featured act.

CHAPTER FOUR

1. Jack Abadi, together with associates Danny Betesh (later to form Kennedy Street Enterprises) and Johnny Swaki (later involved with the Manchester Cavern/Jigsaw and manager of the Place, Stoke) had all been involved in the club business from as early as 1957. Running a club in Macclesfield called The El Rio (famous for its 'Battle of the Groups' nights and early appearances by the Beatles and Ronettes). There were five Abadi brothers, for a fuller account see Chapter Nine.

2. The Stones' residency at the Crawdaddy was taken over by the Yardbirds in August 1963. Formerly the Metropolis Blues Quartet, with Keith Relf and ex-Rooster Eric Clapton (who by 1964 would link up with John Mayall) added to the line-up. They would go on to play the Marquee and the Twisted Wheel in June 1964 before embarking on a European tour with legendary Vee-Jay recording artist Sonny Boy Williamson.

3. The Spencer Davis Group came together at the Golden Lion pub in Birmingham in 1963, where they became resident band playing R&B and Soul – from Ray Charles to Betty Everett. The Spencer Davis Group consisted of bass player Muff Winwood, who at one time had been the leader of an eight piece jazz band, which had also featured his younger brother Stevie. Drummer Pete York, a fan of Count Basie and Duke Ellington; Spencer Davies, a former university lecturer who'd had his own spot in a local jazz band playing the Blues of Leadbelly and Broonzy on 12-string guitar and harmonica, and of course the hugely talented Stevie Winwood. Although still only fifteen, on the band's first date at the Golden Lion, the emotive vocals and keyboard prowess of Stevie, strongly influenced by the sound of Motown, quickly established him as the most focused upon member of the band. Within twelve months the

Spencer Davis Group would gain cult status at the Wheel with the Mods.

4. There are numerous clubs or premises which over the years have been singled out as being the place where the Mod movement really took off. Some have been mentioned earlier in this book, all had either pre-R&B roots in jazz or came along slightly after, notable examples being The Roundhouse, Ealing Jazz Club, Piccadilly Jazz Club, Barrelhouse Club, Studio 51, Crawdaddy, Ricky Tick, Ronnie Scott's and quite interestingly the 100 Club. The 100 Club has a long and distinguished musical history – originally owned by the Feldman family, it became Mack's 100 Club in 1955. At the start of the new millennium, under the direction of Ady Croasdell, the 100 Club has the longest-standing all-nighter in the history of Northern Soul. It is universally regarded as having the most adventurous music policy since the closure of the Wheel.

CHAPTER FIVE

1. Victor Brox, who would later play at the Wheel himself, had been in raptures about Bobby Bland since first hearing his records at Eagle's flat in Chorlton, a regular place for Eagle's close friends to hang out or crash on a Sunday morning. Whether Roger's mates from the Wheel, artists who had earlier played the All-Nighter like John Lee Hooker or Sonny Boy Williamson – just about everybody seemed to meet up there. On one such occasion, members of the Spencer Davis group heard a record that Don Robey had just sent over from the States, the Malibus' 'Strong Love' on Sure Shot. It had been tried and tested at the All-Nighters, was a big club favourite, and would become the Spencer Davis Group's next release, backed with 'This Hammer' on Fontana.

CHAPTER SIX

1. In actual fact it was Don 'Sugarcane' Harris.

2. The Abadi brothers were fervently opposed to any potential abuse of amphetamines at the Wheel, and fully co-operated on all occasions with corporation officials and the police authorities. Similarly any enquiries at the club regarding missing teenagers was given very serious and sympathetic regard. Again full co-operation was given to parents visiting the club. Parents and police were given full access and management assistance in searching the premises for missing youngsters.

CHAPTER ELEVEN

1. The Whitworth Street Twisted Wheel building still stands today, however the road layout has changed since the late sixties.

BIBLIOGRAPHY

BECKMAN, HUNT & KLINE Soul Harmony Singles 1960–1990 (Three-On-Three, 1998)

BENJAMINSON, PETER The Story Of Motown (Grove Press, 1979)

BOWMAN, ROB Soulsville USA (Books with Attitude, 1997)

BROVEN, JOHN Walking to New Orleans (Blues Unlimited, 1974)

CUMMINGS, TONY The Sound of Philadelphia (Methuen, 1975)

ESCORT, COLIN Clyde McPhatter-A Biographical Essay (Bear Family, 1987)

GARLAND, PHYL The Sound Of Soul (Henry Regnery Company, 1969)

GEORGE, NELSON Where Did Our Love Go? (Omnibus, 1985)

GILLETT, CHARLIE Sound Of The City: The Rise Of Rock And Roll
    (Souvenir Press, 1971)

GILLETT, CHARLIE Making Tracks: The Story Of Atlantic Records
    (Souvenir Press, 1986)

GREGORY, HUGH The Real Rhythm And Blues (Blandford, 1998)

GROIA, PHIL They All Sang on the Corner (Edmund, 1974)

GURALNICK, PETER Sweet Soul Music (Virgin, 1986)

HARALAMBOS, MICHAEL Right On! From Blues To Soul In Black America
    (Eddison Press, 1974)

HOARE, IAN Ed. The Soul Book (Methuen, 1976)

LAWSON, ALAN It Happened in Manchester (Multimedia)

LEE, C.P. Shake, Rattle & Rain (Popular Music Making In Manchester)
    (M.A. Thesis, 1996)

MELLY, GEORGE Revolt Into Style (Penguin, 1971)

MORSE, DAVID Motown (Studio Vista, 1971)

OAKLEY, GILES The Devil's Music (BBC, 1976)

PIDGEON, JOHN Rod Stewart And The Changing Faces (Panther, 1976)

PRUTER, ROBERT Chicago Soul (University of Illinois, 1992)

PRUTER, ROBERT Doo Wop-The Chicago Scene (University of Illinois, 1996)

RITSON, MIKE, & RUSSELL, STUART The In Crowd-Volume One (Bee Cool, 1999)

RYAN, JACK The Detroit Years (Whitlaker, 1982)

SALEM, JAMES M. The Late Great Johnny Ace (University of Illinois, 1999)

TREMLETT, GEORGE The Rod Stewart Story (Futura, 1976)

TREMLETT, GEORGE The 10cc Story (Futura, 1976)

WALLER, DON The Story of Motown (Shibner's, 1985)

WARD, BRIAN Just My Soul Responding (UCL Press, 1998)

WILLIAMS, OTIS & ROMANOWSKI, PATRICIA The Temptations (Putman, 1988)

WILLIAMS, RICHARD Out Of His Head: The Sound Of Phil Spector (Abacus, 1974)

MAGAZINES

Big Town Revue (USA '70s)
Billboard World of Soul (1968)
Bim Bam Boom (USA '70s)
Black Wax ('70s)
Blues Unlimited ('60s & '70s)
Blues World ('60s)
Chess Full of Goodies ('60s)
Collectors Soul (late '60s)
Home of the Blues/Blues & Soul ('60s & '70s)
Hot Buttered Soul ('70s)
Jazz Monthly ('60s)
Okeh Northern Soul ('70s)
R&B Scene ('60s)
Record Exchanger (USA '70s)
Remember Then (USA '70s)
Shout ('70s)
Soul ('60s)
Soul Bag (France '70s)
Soul Cargo ('70s)
Soul Music Monthly ('60s)
Soul Survivor (Canada '70s)
Soul To Inspect ('60s)
Souled Out ('70s)
The Rock & Roll Bulletin (USA '70s)
Time Barrier Express (USA '70s)
Yesterday's Memories (USA '70s)

TAPED INTERVIEWS

Ivor & Phil Abadi
Eddie Barnett
Spencer Davis
C.P. Lee
David Meikle
Zoot Money
Steve Pilkington
Brian Rae
Chris Rea
Phil Saxe
Brian Smith
Richard Watt
Pete York

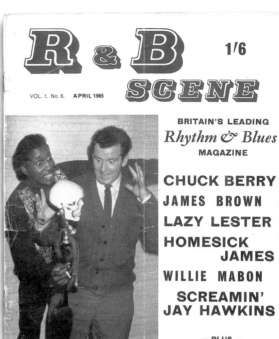

R & B SCENE

1/6

VOL. 1. No. 6. APRIL 1965

BRITAIN'S LEADING
Rhythm & Blues
MAGAZINE

CHUCK BERRY
JAMES BROWN
LAZY LESTER
HOMESICK
JAMES
WILLIE MABON
SCREAMIN'
JAY HAWKINS

— PLUS —
Record Reviews
Rhythm & Blues Quiz
Readers Letters
The Horror Scene
Say Man

SCREAMIN' JAY HAWKINS meets Brian Smith. The reason why we put a photo of our photographer on the cover may never be fully explained, but we do know the reason for the tremendous success of Jay's tour. SEE INSIDE

235

237